MIXED MESSAGES

MIXED MESSAGES

Mediating Native Belonging
in Asian Russia

Kathryn E. Graber

CORNELL UNIVERSITY PRESS   ITHACA AND LONDON

First published 2020 by Cornell University Press

Library of Congress Cataloging-in-Publication Data
Names: Graber, Kathryn E. (Kathryn Elizabeth), author.
Title: Mixed messages : mediating native belonging in Asian
    Russia / Kathryn E. Graber.
Description: Ithaca : Cornell University Press, 2020. | Includes bibliographical
    references and index.
Identifiers: LCCN 2019040729 (print) | LCCN 2019040730 (ebook) |
    ISBN 9781501750502 (hardcover) | ISBN 9781501750519 (paperback) |
    ISBN 9781501750533 (pdf) | ISBN 9781501750526 (epub)
Subjects: LCSH: Ethnic mass media—Russia (Federation)—Buriatiia. | Mass
    media and ethnic relations—Russia (Federation)—Buriatiia. | Language
    policy—Russia (Federation)—Buriatiia. | Buriat language—Political aspects. |
    Buriats—Ethnic identity. | Ethnology—Russia (Federation)—Buriatiia. |
    Buriatiia (Russia)—Ethnic relations.
Classification: LCC P94.5.M552 R8 2020 (print) | LCC P94.5.M552 (ebook) |
    DDC 302.23089/942—dc23
LC record available at https://lccn.loc.gov/2019040729
LC ebook record available at https://lccn.loc.gov/2019040730

For my parents,
Robert Bates Graber and Rosanna Ruth Stoltzfus Graber

Contents

Preface

The editor was sure I was a spy. It was clear within five minutes of my arrival at her office on a chilly spring morning. I had met with her there before, but this time she was cold and harsh. "There will not be any interview," she said gruffly, turning back to the work on her desk. I asked if there was a better time to stop by, but she waved her hand dismissively without raising her eyes from her work. I stood sheepishly for a few moments in her doorway, until she raised her head and stared at me. "Why are you still here?" she demanded. I mumbled some kind of apology, then turned away and wandered the halls of the office building looking for other acquaintances, not knowing what else to do. *Oh no*, I thought. *I've been frozen out.*

I had come to Buryatia, a Siberian border republic named for an ethnic minority of Russia, to study the role of minority-language media in society. This was in the 2000s, and I was a young graduate student—only in my twenties, and still new to ethnography. I knew I couldn't force rapport with people, but it isn't nice to be disliked in any case, and I was worried about access to the people I needed to participate in my research. The circle of journalists, linguists, and teachers involved in minority media production was small, and I couldn't afford to alienate anyone. One of my colleagues in that same circle, a linguist, later confirmed that the editor had decided I was a *shpionka*, a spy sent by the US government to learn about Russia's border regions, for unspecified but surely nefarious ends. Why else, the editor reasoned, would I have been learning the Buryat language?

This was exactly what Americans had warned me would happen. When I had told other Russianists about my plans to study media institutions, many of them had predicted I would never be allowed in. Most of Buryatia's minority media are produced inside media institutions funded and managed by the state, which do not have a reputation for welcoming foreigners. "What are you going to do?" asked one historian, laughing. "Show up and say 'I'd like to come in?' Hahaha!" Their skepticism was not unfounded. My research interests in language were not political per se, but media institutions in Russia were inherently political. And so was language. Any question I could ask about the Buryat language, from spelling to dialect differences, was intimately tied to political status, to state power, and to the past, present, and future of Buryat political autonomy. These are sensitive topics in Russia, and I, neither Russian nor Buryat, began my research as a total outsider. Why would anyone ever talk to me?

One answer is that not everyone is afraid of outsiders. The point of ethnography is to make humans intelligible to one another by explaining alternative possibilities and social worlds. Happily, many people are enthusiastic about sharing their culture with an outsider. The editor who was convinced I was a spy did not convince her colleagues of it. In fact, they told me later that she had always been "like that" (*takoi*)—that is, suspicious. They were quick to distance themselves from what they saw as a closed-minded and parochial response. Other editors—and reporters, linguists, activists, and many, many other people over fifteen years—generously opened their doors to me, both at work and at home, and shared their lives with me. One contact led to another contact. I was not an outsider for long.

There was also a more specific way in which my strangeness made me more approachable, not only to cosmopolitan linguists but to a wide variety of people I would not otherwise have met. Buryats are as diverse a group of people as any other, and in this book I wanted to include perspectives from across Buryat society. But at first I struggled to extend my social networks beyond well-educated elites. Then, in 2009, I gave two interviews in Buryat for local television. Strangers approached me for months afterward to tell me about the "big impression" (*bol'shoe vpechatlenie*) it had made to hear Buryat from a girl "of a European face" (*evropeiskogo litsa*). My pointed nose, creased eyelids, and freckles became my most salient features. Long, pointed European noses are the subject of racialized humor in Buryat, and Russians are often derogatorily called "big-nosed" (tomo khamartai or tomo nostoi). The first time I was referred to in this way, by my friend's mother, my friend had to explain the joke. "But you're very pretty," she quickly assured me. "Only a **little** big-nosed." Whatever its true extent, my nose's televised grandeur granted me new access to people throughout Buryatia. After those broadcasts, I could arrive in a village unannounced and be recognized on the street and invited into people's homes. Because recorded broadcasts have long afterlives, I still hear second- and thirdhand reports of my linguistic prowess. Such reports are exaggerated; my nose granted me latitude in people's estimation of my Buryat abilities, and my competence was persistently and generously overestimated. But the quality of my language wasn't the point. Speaking Buryat *at all* showed my sincere interest and investment in Buryat affairs writ large.

The way I was incorporated into Buryat communities shows how language, in all its mediated forms, connects seemingly unrelated aspects of social life. The editor who thought I was a spy was convinced that no American would learn Buryat unless pressed to do so by a foreign government. (I wasn't.) Audiences who appreciated my appearances on television took my learning Buryat as evidence of my deep interest in Buryatia. (It was.) While they reached different conclusions, they also agreed on some important points: that an outsider learning

Buryat was evidence of *something*; that there were people one could expect to know Buryat, or to not know it; and that knowledge of the language was somehow key to Buryat belonging. They did not articulate their views this way, but underlying their reactions to me were some powerful assumptions about what language can reflect and do.

This is why I wrote this book. In introductory courses in anthropology, we like to say that language is culture, or at least that language is a large part of culture. But how does language become a stand-in for culture, and for other forms of belonging? How do people in positions of power stand to benefit (or not) from making those connections? Why and how might institutions promote some ways of imagining language while denigrating others? This book goes to Russia, where state power has long permeated discussions of linguistic and cultural belonging, to answer these questions.

Acknowledgments

Over many years working on this book, I have accumulated an enormous debt of gratitude to people across two continents. First and foremost, I thank the people in Buryatia who opened their doors to me, especially the several families who hosted me and shared their lives, and the editors, journalists, and interviewees whose participation made this book possible. To protect their identity, their names do not appear here. But you know who you are, and I hope you see yourself reflected accurately in this book. <u>Hain daa</u>.

Colleagues in Buryatia's robust scholarly community always made me feel welcome in Ulan-Ude; among them I especially thank Zhargal Aiushievna Aiakova, Darima Dashievna Amogolonova, Irina Sergeevna Boldonova, Margarita Maksimovna Boronova, Polina Purbuevna Dashinimaeva, Galina Aleksandrovna Dyrkheeva, Tat'iana Dmitrievna Skrynnikova, and Babasan Dorzhievich Tsyrenov. I am grateful to the late Jargal Namtarov, a gifted linguist and my first Buryat language teacher, and Viktor Dashanimaev, photographer, ornithologist, and friend, whose early enthusiasm for this book spurred me on but who did not live to see its completion. Boris Zolkhoev kept bureaucratic angst to a minimum and made one of my trips to Aga possible. Andrei Bazarov kindly invited me on his Russian Academy of Sciences expedition to study Buddhist textual practices in the eastern steppe districts. To Nikolai Tsyrempilov I am grateful for more than I can say; he has always been a consummate colleague and dear friend. Special thanks are due also to my teacher of Buryat of many years, Tsymzhit Badmazhapovna Bazarova, for her unfailing patience with my endless questions. I wish to stress that although the words, experiences, and opinions of many people in Buryatia animate the pages of this book, no one in Buryatia is responsible for the analysis that I present, including as regards Buryats' political status. The conclusions I draw are mine alone.

This project began when I was at the University of Chicago and was lured away from geophysics to linguistics, linguistic anthropology, and Russia. I am grateful to Howard Aronson, Victor Friedman, Susan Gal, Kostas Kazazis, and Michael Silverstein for sparking my interest in marrying linguistic and anthropological approaches to studying the former Soviet Union, which in a roundabout way came together for me while reading about the history of the African National Congress one afternoon at the National Library of South Africa in Cape Town—for which I have John and Jean Comaroff to thank. Noel Taylor and Golosa,

Chicago's fabulous Russian folk choir, introduced me to the Semeiskii music that first brought me to Buryatia in 2001.

The core research in this book was undertaken while I was at the University of Michigan. I owe a great deal to Judith Irvine, Barbra Meek, and Sarah Thomason, and especially to Alaina Lemon. Undaunted by others' skepticism that I could do the research presented in this book, Alaina guided me away from easy answers, encouraged me to "propose the possible, then do the impossible!," and impressed on me the value of a solid pair of winter boots—all advice I still follow and find myself repeating to my own students. At Michigan (and beyond), this book benefited immensely as well from the feedback, criticism, and insights of Laura Brown, Nishaant Choksi, Elizabeth Falconi, Emanuela Grama, Zeynep Gürsel, Jennifer Hall, Brook Hefright, Emily Hein, Sarah Hillewaert, Matthew Hull, Jeremy Johnson, Webb Keane, Conrad Kottak, Sonja Luehrmann, Bruce Mannheim, Douglas Northrop, Susan Philips, Alex Reusing, Jessica Robbins, William G. Rosenberg, Perry Sherouse, and Susanne Unger, and from everything that ever happened in the linguistic anthropology lab.

For support during research and writing in Russia and the United States, I am grateful to several institutions. At different points, I was affiliated with the Institute of Mongolian, Buddhist, and Tibetan Studies (IMBiT) of the Siberian Branch of the Russian Academy of Sciences, and with Buryat State University. Field research was made possible by the Social Science Research Council (SSRC) with funds provided by the Andrew W. Mellon Foundation and by the US Department of State under the Program for Research and Training on Eastern Europe and the Independent States of the Former Soviet Union (Title VIII), by the US Department of Education Fulbright-Hays Program, by the Eurasian Regional Language Program of the American Councils for International Education, and by the National Science Foundation (NSF) under grant number 0819031. Initial analysis was supported by fellowships from the NSF and the SSRC Eurasia Program. At the University of Michigan, the Department of Anthropology, Rackham Graduate School, and the Center for Russian, East European, and Eurasian Studies generously funded my research. Additional field research was funded by a National Council for Eurasian and East European Research Indigenous Peoples of Russia Grant helmed by Justine Buck Quijada, who throughout this project has been a generous colleague, reader, and friend. Any opinions, findings, and conclusions or recommendations expressed in this book are those of the author and do not necessarily reflect the views of the NSF or any other research funder.

I have been fortunate to share my interest in Buryatia with an international circle of lively and generous colleagues, with whom I have often overlapped in the field and with whom I have traded many of the insights reflected in these pages: Anya Bernstein, Janis Chakars, Melissa Chakars, Tatiana Chudakova, Ted

Holland, Carolyn Kremers, Joseph Long, Katherine Metzo, Sayana Namsaraeva, Luis Ortiz Echevarría, Eleanor Peers, Brooke Swafford, Elizabeth Sweet, and Tristra Newyear Yeager. I am especially grateful to Jesse D. Murray for her friendship, guidance on archival research, and assistance in helping to maintain perspective during fieldwork.

Distilling this research into the present book's arguments took many years—and many discussions with students, policymakers, journalists, political scientists, historians, and other scholars outside of anthropology and Buryat studies, who were sometimes less immediately convinced of what a language-centered account, or a minority-centered account, could show about politics in Russia. I gratefully credit a Title VIII-supported fellowship at the Kennan Institute of the Woodrow Wilson International Center for Scholars, where the project's transformation into a book benefited from conversations with, in particular, Sarah Cameron, Karen Dawisha, Yedida Kanfer, William Pomeranz, and Blair Ruble.

I could not have asked for a better intellectual home in which to complete this book than Indiana University. IU's Russian and East European Institute funded transcription assistance through their Andrew W. Mellon Foundation Endowment, and the College Arts and Humanities Institute provided an invaluable semester of leave from teaching to complete the manuscript. For their collegiality, helpful feedback, and support of this book, I am grateful to my colleagues in the Department of Anthropology and Department of Central Eurasian Studies, particularly Gardner Bovingdon, Jamsheed Choksy, Ilana Gershon, György Kara, Sarah Phillips, Ron Sela, Nazif Shahrani, and Dan Suslak—and to those who have moved on in one way or another: Christopher Atwood, Richard Bauman, Jeanne Sept, Elliot Sperling, and Catherine Tucker.

In addition to the libraries at my home institutions, at different points I made use of archives and collections at Buryat State University, where I am grateful to Liudmila Leonidovna Kushnarëva; IMBiT, where I thank Marina Aiusheeva; the National Archives of the Republic of Buryatia, where I am especially grateful to Zinaida Fëdorovna Dambaeva; and the National Library of the Republic of Buryatia, where I thank Norzhima Garmaevna Lubsanova. The SSRC Eurasia Program supported a trip to Western Washington University in 2013 to consult Nicholas Poppe's collection of Buryat books with his own mark-ups and corrections; in Bellingham I thank Wayne Richter, Henry G. Schwarz, and Ed Vajda. The manuscript benefited from three talented research assistants: Ross Irons, who helped code television broadcasts and provided library assistance; Tolgonay Kubatova, who helped transcribe Russian-language recordings; and Jargal Badagarov, who helped transcribe Buryat-language recordings. I am profoundly indebted to Jargal for advising me over the years on various points of linguistic variation, social meanings, and Buryat-English translation.

Draft portions of this book benefited from astute comments from audiences at the University of Michigan, the University of Chicago, Indiana University, the University of Alaska Anchorage, Saint Mary's University in Halifax, the University of Virginia, and the Wilson Center. Charles Briggs, Alex Golub, Douglas Holmes, John Lucy, Robert Moore, Zhanara Nauruzbayeva, Bambi Schieffelin, Karl Swinehart, Suzanne Wertheim, and Kathryn Woolard gave insightful comments on conference papers that became sections of the book. Anna Babel improved my book proposal. My students at Indiana University have not been subjected to my drafts, but they have helped me work out problems of presentation, audience, and style—more than they realize, I hope. I asked a lot of last-minute questions of some trusted scholar-writer friends, whose quick answers and encouragement I deeply appreciated: Abigail Andrews, Sonia Das, Mary Doyno, Lauren Duquette-Rury, Rachel Haywood Ferreira, and María Alejandra Pérez.

A few patient souls read the entire manuscript and offered suggestions that improved it dramatically. From start to finish, this project has benefited from the keen editorial eyes, anthropological smarts, and indefatigable encouragement of Emily McKee and Mikaela Rogozen-Soltar. Our weekly writing meetings have carried this book from the stage of field notes and scraps of ideas through interminable drafts to something that I hope will do them proud. Alessandro Duranti and two anonymous reviewers for Cornell University Press provided thoughtful feedback that helped me reframe the introductory portion of the manuscript and develop some of the book's nascent arguments. Jim Lance has been a wonderful editor, consistently supporting my writing decisions and cheerfully believing in this project and in me.

Passages of chapters 2, 3, and 6 previously appeared in the following publications; I thank Elsevier, the American Anthropological Association, and Brill respectively for graciously allowing me to reuse and extend this material:

Graber, Kathryn. 2012. "Public Information: The Shifting Roles of Minority Language News Media in the Buryat Territories of Russia." *Language & Communication* 32(2):124–36.

Graber, Kathryn E. 2017. "The Kitchen, the Cat, and the Table: Domestic Affairs of a Siberian Language." *Journal of Linguistic Anthropology* 27(2):151–70.

Graber, Kathryn E. 2019. "'Syphilis Is Syphilis!': Purity and Genre in a Buryat-Russian News Story." In *Storytelling as Narrative Practice: Ethnographic Approaches to the Tales We Tell.* Studies in Pragmatics, vol. 19, edited by Elizabeth A. Falconi and Kathryn E. Graber, 226–52. Leiden: Brill.

Finally, I thank my greatest source of strength, my family, who have been tremendously patient with me, somehow trusting that this was all worthwhile, even as I missed our own family crises and events to be with other families on the other side of the world. I thank my parents for being who they are, for changing all the pronouns from "he" to "she" in *Little Raccoon and the Thing in the Pool* and making me believe I could do anything I set out to do. This book is dedicated to them. I thank my sister Karen, who, as I struggled to complete the manuscript with an infant, gave the best kinds of support: long phone calls and boxes of baby clothes, which meant I did not have to go shopping. I thank Richard F. Nance, my best friend and beloved wordsmith, without whose patience, love, and "just send it"s, this book might not exist. And I thank our son Jules, who joined this project late in its long life and who, running around the yard chasing fireflies and threatening to pull tomatoes off their vines while "mommy sit a chair a finish book," really has done more than anyone else to make me finish it.

Acronyms and Abbreviations

ASSR	Autonomous Soviet Socialist Republic
BGTRK	State Television and Radio Broadcasting Company "Buryatia"
BMASSR	Buryat-Mongolian Autonomous Soviet Socialist Republic
BNTs	Buryat Scientific Center (Buriatskii nauchnyi tsentr)
ChGTRK	State Television and Radio Broadcasting Company "Chita"
GTRK	State Television and Radio Broadcasting Company (Gosudarstvennaia televizionnaia i radioveshchatel'naia kompaniia)
IGTRK	State Television and Radio Broadcasting Company "Irkutsk"
NARB	National Archives of the Republic of Buryatia
NGI	National Humanities Institute
SO RAN	Siberian Branch of the Russian Academy of Sciences (Sibirskoe otdelenie Rossiiskoi akademii nauk)
USSR	Union of Soviet Socialist Republics (Soiuz Sovetskikh Sotsialisticheskikh Respublik, SSSR)
VSGAKI	East-Siberian State Academy of Culture and Arts (Vostochno-Sibirskaia gosudarstvennaia akademiia kul'tury i iskusstv)
B.	Buryat
E.	Ewenki
GEN	genitive
lit.	literally
NEG	negative
PST	past
R.	Russian
SLB	Standard Literary Buryat
2SG	second person singular

Note on Transliteration and Transcription

Transliteration of both Russian and Buryat examples in this book follows a modified version of the American Library Association—Library of Congress (ALA-LC) system for Cyrillic, except for terms that already have established English spellings (e.g., Buryat, Ulan-Ude, etc.), and for ease of pronunciation with recurring personal names (e.g., Sayana). The ALA-LC system was originally developed for Slavic languages, and the pronunciation of some characters in Mongolic languages differs, but not in ways that bear on the text. To transliterate the three "extra" letters of the Buryat alphabet, I follow the standard in Mongolian linguistics (Kara 1996, 557): Өө [ö] appears as *Öö*, Үү [ü] as *Üü*, and *hh* [h] as *Hh*. Spelling is based on the Cyrillic of standard orthography, except in those instances in which pronunciation deviates from standard spelling in a way that is socially meaningful for the example at hand.

Russian appears in *italics* and Buryat with <u>underlining</u>; when something is <u>*both italicized and underlined*</u>, it indicates that the form could be considered both Russian and Buryat in context. Periodic references to Mongolian are also <u>underlined</u>. In transcriptions, **boldface** indicates emphasis, and (.) and (..) mark pauses. I follow standard practice in linguistics in reserving single quotation marks for glosses and using double quotation marks elsewhere. Material quoted from audio recordings, print sources, or in situ notes is marked with double quotation marks; paraphrases and quotations that have been reconstructed based on scratch notes and memory do not appear in quotation marks. Most of the informal interactions described in this book were not digitally recorded, while nearly all of the interviews and focus groups were. Place names that do not already have common English-language versions are given in Buryat wherever possible, with one exception: when discussing dialects, I use Russian adjectives over Buryat (e.g., "Khorinskii dialect" rather than "Khori"), consistent with the way Buryat speakers most often identify dialects and dialectal forms. All translations are mine.

MIXED MESSAGES

"Look, she looks like a Buryat girl!" On the television screen, a young gymnast tore through the air like a boomerang, her black ponytail flying behind her. "Or maybe she's Korean." I was sitting on the living room floor of a family I lived with in Ulan-Ude, the capital of the Republic of Buryatia. Badma and Dorzhozhab, the aging matriarch and patriarch of this Buryat family, sat on the sofa and chatted about the news buzzing from their television set, which showed gymnasts training for an international competition. Their niece Chimita, a shy college student with long black hair, shifted between quietly doing her homework at a small desk nearby and plopping down on the floor next to me to watch TV and join in the conversation. When the gymnast stuck her landing and the camera zoomed in, a small American flag and the words "USA" were clear across her uniform. Badma jerked her head toward me. "Would you say she's American?" she asked.[1]

"Yes sure, why not?" I replied with a shrug, not immediately certain what Badma was asking. She was quiet a moment. Chimita squinted at the gymnast on the television screen. "Korean," she concluded confidently.

Badma turned to Dorzhozhab. "I want to just say 'I'm an American [amerikanka]' like that," she said to him in a sort of musing, wistful tone. "It's not possible here." Dorzhozhab knew Badma did not mean that she wanted to be American, but that she wished there were a term of citizenship in contemporary Russia that had scope over people of different backgrounds, ethnicities, and phenotypes. Dorzhozhab looked surprised and even a little offended. He was a retired doctor with a strong sense of propriety and patriotism. After a few vodka

1

toasts at a feast, he sang Soviet classics as often as Buryat folk songs, his deep baritone ringing out into a room with gravitas. "*Rossiianin* is possible," he offered, using the Russian term that refers to a citizen of Russia, rather than an ethnic Russian (*russkii*). "But everyone always says *russkii* and *buriat*," Badma countered, invoking the terms used to describe a person's ethnicity, or what is usually called in Russia her "nationality," as opposed to her citizenship. "They don't say *rossiiskii* [the adjectival form for a Russian citizen] or *rossiianin*." She sighed and turned back to the screen. "It's not the same."

Badma was right that it is far more common for Russian speakers to identify one another by nationality or race than by formal citizenship. When contemporary Russian speakers do use *rossiiskii* or *rossiianin*, it can be pejorative, to suggest that they are forced by social graces to use a euphemistic, politically correct term when what they would really like to say is a racist epithet. *Rossiianin* is used in this sarcastic way for labor migrants from Central Asia or the Caucasus, for instance, who are widely stigmatized. Journalists are careful to identify citizens of Russia as such, but that does not keep the snickering use of *rossiianin* out of the media. A popular Russian-nationalist internet meme labels images of *russkii* and *rossiianin* personages side by side, the former ethnic Russian well-groomed and white, often drawn from Slavic mythology or military history, and the latter "citizen of Russia" marked by some kind of non-Russian racial feature or dress and engaged in drinking, smoking, or thuggish behavior.[2]

Meaningful discussions of ethnonational politics happen in living rooms and internet forums at least as often as they do in courtrooms or legislative chambers. In Badma and Dorzhozhab's living room, in front of the television set, the family discussed everything from the meaning of *rossiianin* to the conditions of postsocialism to which Buddhist rituals they would attend for holidays. When Channel One, Russia's main state-owned television station and the source of most Russian citizens' news, showed images of New York City, Badma reminisced about a work trip she had taken there during the late Soviet period and the ease with which she had traveled to Yugoslavia. Sometimes family members knew a person being interviewed on the local evening news because it was an old friend, a relative, a former coworker, or someone Badma knew socially from the public bathhouse she visited once a week. So conversation would turn to who was married to whom, or to how so-and-so had recently traveled to Italy or Thailand. Members of their extended family, studying in Mongolia and St. Petersburg, kept in touch with each other via Skype and VKontakte, a Russian-language social media platform akin to Facebook, and relayed tidbits of news via telephone. They chatted in Russian and in Buryat, a Mongolic language that has become the focus of efforts to revitalize and maintain traditional Buryat culture. In these ways, media provided Badma's household with the means for understanding and negotiating their own belonging within the Russian Federation, as well as their belonging to families, clans, spiritual worlds, Soviet pasts and imagined futures, and Buryat- and Russian-speaking publics that are aligned with state borders unevenly at best.

The issues at stake in this living room scene are not unique to Buryatia. Some of the most central and impassioned struggles in contemporary Russia concern language, media, and the publics that they mark or create. From the Ukrainian border to the Russian Far East, language has taken on tremendous importance as a marker of ethnic affiliation, local and national pride, and a host of shifting social allegiances. Key to these struggles are vexing practical and theoretical questions about mass media: What languages should be used in newspapers, magazines, or radio and television broadcasts? Who should produce them? Among scholars, mass media have long been theorized as instrumental in fostering civil society and the public exchange necessary for democracy. In postsocialist contexts in particular, developing a "free press" has been treated as one of the primary means by which to restore a healthy public sphere independent of the state. In practice, however, a variety of existing cultural and institutional frameworks pattern the movement of discourses through mass media, calling into question the freedom of exchange. Rather than positing an idealized "free" space of unfettered, unstructured discursive movement, we might better begin by asking *how* discourse is patterned in and through different types of media. What kinds of publics can be created and sustained through media? How exactly do discourses move into, out of, and through the media to affect everyday social practices? Similar practical and theoretical conversations could be had across the Russian Federation's "ethnic republics," territories whose partial political autonomy is based on the principle of ethnonational self-determination.

Buryatia provides a particularly stark example of the anxieties—emanating from both centers of authority and local actors—that pervade these regions. Here, in what has alternately been considered a Mongolian homeland, a frontier of Russia, and a borderland between the vast Russian and Chinese states, the self-identification of Badma and her family as *rossiiskie* has high political stakes. The post-Soviet period and an increasingly cosmopolitan Asian context offer new possibilities for how and with whom to affiliate. Meanwhile, generations of speakers in the Buryat territories have been shifting from using mainly the Buryat language to using mainly or exclusively Russian, while experiencing rapid transformations in demography, economy, and lifestyle. Most ethnic Buryats in Russia are fully bilingual in Russian or are monolingual speakers of Russian, and Buryat use has contracted so much over the past few generations that some linguists consider the language functionally endangered (e.g., Grenoble and Whaley 2006). State-driven modernizing projects of the socialist period and uncertainty in the postsocialist period in particular have left many people with a sense of profound loss.

Feeling culturally and linguistically disconnected from their past and from each other, many Buryats now seek to reclaim a sense of ethnonational belonging. For residents of this embattled Siberian republic, language and media provide ways of performing and negotiating these affiliations on a daily basis across different scales of belonging. In particular, people traverse—and remake—the boundaries of identity by switching between Russian and Buryat and by making and engaging with local Russian and Buryat media.

This book is an ethnographic study of language politics and the media produced in and for the Republic of Buryatia and other Buryat territories. I focus on minority-language media—that is, media in which the bulk of the text or speech is in the principal minority language of the region, Buryat—to trace the circulation and uptake of ideas not just *in* Buryat but *about* Buryat, and about being Buryat. From herders in the 1920s to lexicographers in the 2000s, from reporters tracking down interviewees in syphilis clinics to grandmothers recording cellphone videos in their kitchens, I examine the heterogenous ways people have envisioned Buryat belonging through language and media.

Ethnonational attachments are not easily made, and simply producing media in a receding language is not enough to ensure its continued use. By examining ordinary, everyday interactions and engagements with media, this book shows how the people producing, reading, watching, listening to, learning from, enjoying, and sometimes hating these media become what I call a minority language public. Such a public, I argue, is not coterminous with an ethnonational construction of Buryatness, but it is a necessary component of such construction because it is within the minority language public that membership in the ethnonation is worked out. Who counts as a speaker of Buryat, for instance, is largely determined by the linguists, journalists, and commentators who publicly police the boundaries of the category on television and blogs, and who often send mixed messages. On a daily basis, people renegotiate their affective attachments to language, culture, and place via their social media networks and newspaper articles. I examine ethnonational politics as an everyday, mediated practice, so that we might see how Badma, or a student from a Buryat-speaking village, or a young woman working in a clothing shop each imagines her place in the world.

This is a history of imagined futures and of how people remake themselves in the context of cultural and linguistic change. It is also, however, a story about how individuals become caught up in, and constrained by, state projects. While the people populating this book's pages display humor, fortitude, and a great deal of agency in their interactions, identity is never a free-for-all. Badma and Dorzhozhab cannot choose the meaning of the term *buriat* any more than they can choose the meanings of the terms *russkii* and *rossiiskii*. Their own tools in everyday ethnonational politics, the Buryat language and Buryat media, are products of history. In the twentieth century, both were the targets of massive state-driven modernizing projects, as key means to controlling and institutionalizing ethnonational belonging in Asian Russia. The Soviet state poured resources into standardizing the Buryat language, creating norms of local media production, building a minority elite, and fixing what Buryat-language media could do and mean. Speakers of Buryat—variously defined—have been co-opted into an ongoing, ad hoc modernizing project within which central authorities and citizens alike have come to see developing and maintaining a strong literary standard as a linchpin of ethnonational legitimacy. These efforts have only partially succeeded, however. The specific resources available to people for expressing Buryatness today have been shaped by projects of modernization, urbanization, and standardization that were never completed, and that ironically resulted in the very rupture and loss so many are trying to counteract.

Linguistic Anthropology in Siberia

Asian Russia occupies an odd and largely unrecognized place on the world stage. Russia's vast East, comprising the territories roughly from the Urals to the Pacific (figure 1a), appears infrequently in world news, and when it does, it is most often as an unpopulated expanse rich for extracting some kind of resource, be it lumber, coal, oil, or diamonds. Russian speakers typically divide it into Western Siberia (Omsk, Tomsk, Novosibirsk, and the Altai), Eastern Siberia (Baikal and the Lena basin), the Russian Far North (north of the Arctic Circle), and the Far East (the Amur basin and the Pacific coast). Speakers of English, however, tend to use one word for the whole landmass, full of frosty romance and imagined desolation: Siberia.

Siberia as a field awaits careful attention in the social sciences, including linguistic anthropology. Although it covers nearly one-tenth of the Earth's landmass and hosts remarkable cultural and linguistic diversity, political conditions and stereotypes have conspired to prevent the sustained research the region deserves (King 2006). In historical treatments, Siberia has often been either considered incidental to Moscow's and St. Petersburg's power or neglected entirely. The many people inhabiting this space—including diverse Mongolic, Turkic, and Tungusic-speaking people, political exiles and convicts, and recent migrants from other parts of the former Soviet Union—have most often been studied for what they show about how European Russians have conceived of *themselves*. This emphasis in scholarship has revealed much about how ethnic Russians have used Asian

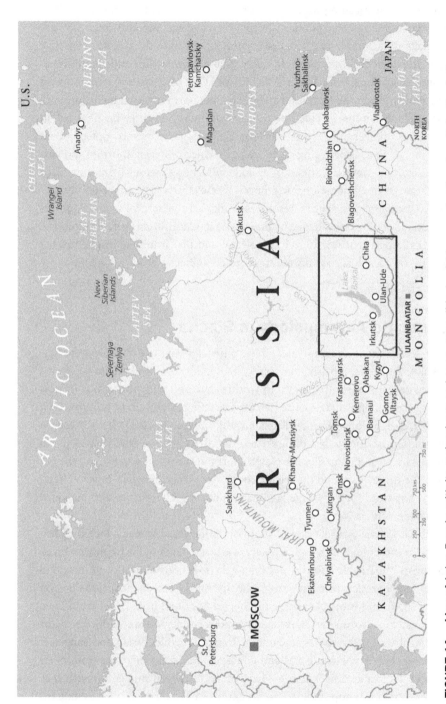

FIGURE 1A. Map of Asian Russia, with its major rivers and seas, geopolitical neighbors, and regional capitals. Box indicates the area of detail shown in figure 1b. (Map by author; base layer by Peter Hermes Furian/Shutterstock.com.)

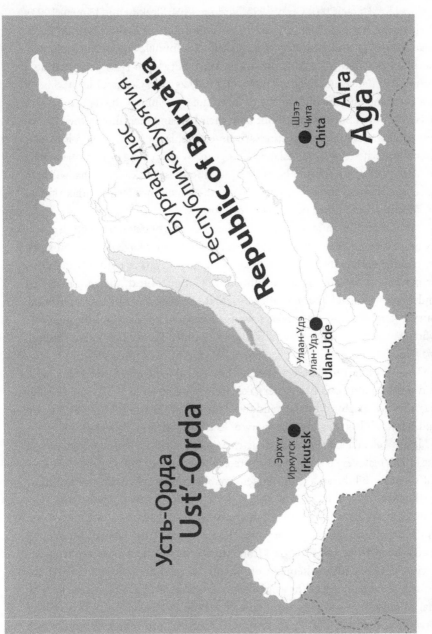

Республика Бурятия
Буряад Улас
Republic of Buryatia

Шэтэ
Чита
Chita ●

Ара
Aga

Улаан-Үдэ
Улан-Удэ
Ulan-Ude ●

Усть-Орда
Ust'-Orda

Эрхүү
Иркутск
Irkutsk ●

FIGURE 1B. Detail of the Buryat territories of Russia. (Map by author and Emma Percival; base layer by OpenStreetMap and contributors.)

populations, especially native or indigenous Siberians, as a quintessential Other, against whom western Russians can figure themselves as civilizers, builders, and saviors (e.g., Geraci 2001; Grant 1993; Slezkine 1994; Slezkine and Diment 1993). Such studies have productively shown the importance of looking beyond European Russia for understanding Russian self-conceptions, but focusing too narrowly on the view from Moscow (or St. Petersburg) also risks perpetuating a notion that native Siberians are important only as foils. Geographically, Siberia is a heartland and the bulk of the country, not a periphery. Russia is mostly in Asia. And when Buryats talk about both their past and their future, they invoke linguistic and cultural connections, commodities, labor markets, and information flows that are as much Asian as European. By conceiving of Buryatia as part of Asia as well as Europe, this book shifts attention eastward, a move that will help us see the Siberian and Far Eastern territories on their own terms, rather than as an addendum to Europe or a satellite of Moscow.

Thinking of Buryatia within these different scales of belonging will also help us move beyond the center-periphery discussions that have dominated studies of large nation-states. Rather than seeing the Buryats as naturally marginal or peripheral, we can ask for whom, and in what context, they are marginal and begin to unpack the semiotic work that has been done to marginalize the Buryat language and its speakers within Russia—and, likewise, the semiotic work that is being done now in trying to re-index Buryat belonging through mass media.

The Buryat territories are nestled around Baikal—the world's deepest, oldest, and most voluminous freshwater lake, variously known as the "pearl of Siberia," the "Galapagos of Russia," and the "blue eye of the world." In both Russian and Buryat, it has long been known not as a lake but as an inland sea (R. *more*, B. dalai). Lake Baikal is part of an active geological rift system, at which two of the earth's plates are pulling apart at a rate of three to four millimeters per year—sufficient to roil the area with frequent tremors and occasionally a catastrophic earthquake (Radziminovich et al. 2012). Someday, perhaps 650 million years from now, the Eurasian continent might break apart here to form a new ocean. In the meantime, the Buryat territories lie strung along the Russian-Mongolian border, about three and a half days from Moscow by train and three days from the Pacific. They include the Republic of Buryatia, a semiautonomous ethnic republic with its own president (downgraded to "head" in 2012, with a status closer to that of governor) and state legislature (the People's Khural);[3] and two smaller territories, Aga and Ust'-Orda, that were formerly also semiautonomous but were merged with the surrounding Russian-dominated regions by administrative restructuring and federal recentralization in 2008 (figure 1b). In this book, I use "Buryatia" to refer to the historically contiguous Buryat territories in general, and "Republic of Buryatia," "Aga," and "Ust'-Orda" to refer to the bounded political and administrative units.

Buryats provide a compelling example of how ethnic minorities may be incorporated into multinational states, and especially of how this is done linguistically. As many other ethnographers and historians of Siberia's ethnic minorities have argued, Soviet nation building in Siberia encouraged very explicit associations between language, nation, and territory.[4] Soviet authorities defined a group's right to self-governance and semiautonomy in terms of cultural and linguistic distinctiveness, while simultaneously encouraging the use of Russian as the language "first among equals." These practices continue to have an impact on interethnic relations, language contact, and language change in the region. In particular, Soviet-era commitments to providing state support for the languages of officially recognized "nations" and "nation-like peoples" continue to inform language politics. Siberians *expect* the state to fund Buryat-language media and to support language revitalization efforts, both materially and rhetorically. Yet institutional support paradoxically does not appear to be staunching Buryat language loss.

There are 326,500 self-reported speakers of Buryat today, concentrated in Russia, northern Mongolia, and the Shénékhén region of Inner Mongolia in the People's Republic of China.[5] In the last all-Russian census, conducted in 2010, 218,557 people within the Russian Federation reported controlling Buryat. Several thousand of these respondents reported their ethnicity as something other than Buryat, but most said they were Buryat, and most lived in the Republic of Buryatia and the neighboring Buryat territories.[6] This number makes Buryat one of the major indigenous languages of North Asia (second only to Sakha/ Yakut), despite over four centuries of Russian-Buryat contact in which Russian has decidedly been the code of general political and economic power. But from generation to generation, speakers in Buryatia have been shifting from Buryat to Russian, with an especially precipitous decline in the 2000s. Because the Buryat language has been so strongly tied to a sense of Buryat belonging, loss of the language has come to index, or point to, a broader loss of cultural continuity. Thus language has become a touchstone in debates over Buryat cultural loss and a central domain for reclamation.

These conditions—explicit state ideologies linking language and culture, a well-documented language shift away from a minoritized language, and active debate over language loss—make native Siberia a fruitful place to study concerns central to linguistic anthropology. Anthropologists of language have increasingly described the social life of language in terms of "language ideologies," or cultural systems of ideas about "social and linguistic relationships, together with their loading of moral and political interests" (Irvine 1989, 255).[7] Language ideologies are subtler, more pervasive, and arguably better internalized than the "ideology" of a political party, so they are harder to excavate analytically, but they help explain how people unconsciously naturalize political stances into their understanding of the world. Consider, for instance, the common belief among speakers of American English that German and Russian are "ugly" or "harsh" languages, while French is the "language of love." Does this belief have to do with the intrinsic aesthetics of vowels and consonants, or is it also (or mostly, or even just flat-out entirely) about the political history of US relations with the nation-states with which these languages have been associated? To what extent can speakers even separate the two? Language ideologies are *ideological* both in the sense that they imply moral and political positions and in the sense that they appear totally natural to the people employing them, like "commonsense notions" (Rumsey 1990, 346). This is not to say that ideologies are uniformly shared within a given social group; Americans harbor a variety of sentiments about German, after all.[8] But they will appear obvious nonetheless.

One of the strongest language ideologies operative in Buryatia links your "native language" to your ethnicity and race, which affects how people determine who counts as a speaker of Buryat. In the discipline of linguistics, a "native speaker" is generally someone who acquired active knowledge at a young age, say before five years old. But socially, determining who counts as a speaker depends at least as much on the ideological interplay of linguistic expertise and social circumstance as on ability to meet a linguist's criteria of grammatical production (French 2003; Hill 2001; Hill and Hill 1986). When people in Buryatia refer to knowledge (*znanie*) of Buryat, they generally mean the ability to produce Buryat, not only passively understand it; and people identify themselves or others as "carriers" (*nositeli*) of the language only if they actively use it. The term "speaker" in English reflects this by emphasizing active, productive use. Yet Buryat is owned by—and ascribed to—many people who do not know or speak it. As census figures make clear, many Buryats report their "native language" (*rodnoi iazyk*) as Buryat despite having no active or passive competence. Thus in the 2010 census, 82 percent of the Republic of Buryatia's Buryat population reported their "native language" as Buryat, despite only 43 percent reporting knowledge (Rosstat 2012–13, 212, 290). Similarly, some of the people in this book identify their native language as Buryat but do not claim to speak a word. Others do not hesitate to tell someone whom they take to be Buryat that she *should* speak her "own native language." They are following a Soviet practice that made *rodnoi iazyk* equivalent to what English speakers call "national language," "heritage language," or "ancestral language."[9] For my purposes, "native speakers" may include anyone who self-reports linguistic competence *or* who demonstrates linguistic competence by judgment of fellow speakers. Throughout this book, we will see that self-identification as a speaker and active linguistic competence do not necessarily match up. Even more importantly, how a person self-identifies and how *other people* identify her, and what they expect of her, do not necessarily match up.

How such competence is socially ascribed and brokered is in part the subject of this book. Language ideologies provide the media makers and audiences described here with naturalized frameworks for making sense of sociolinguistic complexity, ascribing knowledge and claiming authority, and rationalizing their own social positions vis-à-vis others. Because they are naturalized, assumptions like those linking language, race, and ethnicity, and about who counts as a speaker, are rarely stated as such. Rather, they crop up in metalanguage, or how people evaluate and comment on the way they and others speak. We can access them ethnographically, especially by looking at how language has been caught up in Russian and Soviet projects of belonging.

Projects of Belonging

Where do ideologies come from? The answer is always partly historical. Russian and Soviet authorities have tended to treat native Siberians fundamentally as "backward" and as dangerously, though also sometimes tantalizingly, Asian. So they have employed many strategies, from hygiene campaigns to radiofication, to modernize Siberians and incorporate them into a European civilizing project. In a sense, this book is about the central legacies of contact, and of a set of projects that are today remembered variously as a triumphant civilizing mission, ideological quest for utopia, systematic oppression of minorities, or gross corruption of what was supposed to be the "natural" progression of Buryat cultural development. But history here is no mere "background" to the present day. To think of racial categories, projections, or the terms that Badma laments as merely the holdovers or effluvia of times past would be to misapprehend the extent to which people's sense of self—or selves—has been fundamentally altered by history. History sets the conditions of possibility.

The civilizing mission of "Europe" has involved extending European visions of ideal national and linguistic development into Russia's Asian territories. Harnessing language to ethnonational categories has been central to this project, along with the institutionalization and standardization projects that so often appear inevitable in nation building. Imperial and Soviet initiatives to rule and develop diverse Asian Russian lands included describing, cataloguing, reforming, and standardizing their languages. During the Soviet period, central authorities estimated the likelihood that a group of people would coalesce into a nation (*natsiia*) based in part on its adherence to a single, unified language (Hirsch 2005). And leaders measured their success in fostering regional national development by how well they had indigenized Soviet institutions, such as by how well they were training new indigenous cadres to be teachers or journalists, working in a common language. The presence of a strong literary standard for each Soviet minority came to index larger successes in forging ethnonational units.

Institutionalizing indigenous media has also been an important political tool beyond fostering linguistic or national development per se. Minority media are both modernizing tools and political tools of voice, providing many ways to perform political participation. Media such as newspapers, radio, and VKontakte are part of the texture of daily life, making them easily accessible ways for individual readers and viewers to demonstrate their affiliations. Subscribing to a Buryat-language newspaper or giving an interview on Buryat-language television, for example, shows membership and participation in a public of Buryat speakers. On the production side, minority media have been a dominant way to maintain an integrated, native Buryat elite. Moreover, developing minority media is a way for the state (or private companies or nonprofits, albeit less often) to demonstrate support for minority communities while simultaneously making them legible to the majority, within genres and platforms that are understandable to mainstream society. In the Buryat territories, legislation guarantees the production of Buryat-language media by supporting print and broadcast media institutions and by requiring official signage, government documents, and product packaging to appear in Buryat as well as Russian. Although these promises are not consistently fulfilled with financing or enforcement, they do go some way to inserting Buryat into public life, and the Buryat media that are produced may be held up as evidence that Buryat ethnonational concerns are supported, whether by the state or by society at large.

Perhaps most subtly, media institutions provide opportunities to institutionalize predominant ways of speaking a minority language or belonging to a minority public. At some historical junctures, this has been an intentional, carefully crafted process. Script reformers in the 1930s, for instance, tried to open Buryat to intermixing with other Soviet languages by transitioning newspaper printing to the Latin script. In the 1970s, journalists exhorted one another to keep semispeakers of Buryat (partial speakers, not believed to control enough of the language) off the air so that they would not embarrass themselves. More often, however, journalists and other media makers correct, standardize, and reform speech without explicitly announcing their policy or engaging in public debates about who speaks Buryat better or worse. Instead, they quietly go about their work in the background, leaving their labor, ideas, and decision making—in short, their role in shaping conceptions of Buryat belonging—implicit. But their decisions are hugely consequential. Just as schools regulate proper speech and comportment for children, for adults who counts as a "real" speaker of Buryat and who counts as a "real Buryat" are matters largely determined by who is presented on the radio as an authoritative speaker, or how speech is cleaned up by newspaper journalists. In this sense, media institutions in many ways act like other institutions, such as schools, courts, universities, and governmental bureaucracies. They create authoritative accounts, standardize practices, and exclude performances that they deem inadmissible. They distribute and diffuse responsibility, such that it is the institution itself that appears agentive, and such that the goals of individual actors working within them become conflated with the goals of "the media." Thus, examining the production and uses of minority-language media can show us how knowledge, competence, power, and belonging are construed and brokered through institutional practices, and with what effects.

One of the reasons institutions so effectively inculcate ideologies is that they appear to be monolithic—even when their constituent members actually hold diverse opinions, and even when their actions develop on a reactive or ad hoc basis. Take the projects of minority-language standardization and the institutionalization of minority media in Siberia. It is tempting to see these as elements of a unified Soviet campaign of projecting "a" new state ideology into distant peripheries. Both had roots, however, in a much longer history of encounter between Russians and their eastern subjects. Sometimes the agents of Siberia's modernizing projects have been central state authorities envisioning a Soviet future, while at other times, they have been local activists or Russian Orthodox missionaries. During the twentieth century, for instance, the Soviet state embarked on a major effort to standardize Buryat on the basis of a single dialect and create a unified script for use across Siberian languages. It had been, however, Orthodox missionaries working in the nineteenth century who first set out to write Buryat in a Cyrillic script and reform the language to be more conducive to Russification (Graber and Murray 2015). Such continuities make it easy to conflate Russian imperial, Soviet, and once again Russian projects and to think of the Buryats as struggling out from under a continuous, four-hundred-year colonial encounter. And indeed, many of the Buryats animating the pages of this book think of the past in exactly those terms, as "before" and "after" an unspecified moment of cultural contact with Russians and the West.

Yet history shows a much messier development. Visions of the multinational state, and with them approaches to minority languages and minority media, have changed over time. What has evolved is an ad hoc response to shifting goals. Today neither the ongoing project of standardizing Buryat nor the ongoing project of institutionalizing Buryat media is experienced predominantly as a matter of Soviet or Russian authorities projecting state ideology into the Buryat territories. Quite the opposite. Local Buryat activists, media producers, and their audiences now see both projects primarily as antidotes to increasing Russification, or to the potentially negative effects of globalization. Activists have taken up minority-language radio, television, and internet initiatives as tools of language revitalization—though this has only recently become a goal of producing minority-language media in Russia.

This should make us rethink what standards and institutions do. They control and regiment behavior, but they also provide the resources by which individuals negotiate their own position within complex social fields. Even when contested, they provide crucial reference points in social fields that are otherwise difficult to traverse. Sometimes this is overt: censuses and surveys, for instance, provide statistical data that can prove useful for identity politics by showing, in an authoritative way, that a language or people is "at risk" and in need of resources (Urla 1993; cf. Muehlmann 2012). More subtly, by objectifying the otherwise messy, ephemeral activities of day-to-day human existence into, for instance, "a" language, or "a" way of life, standards and institutions help us make sense of our experience and delineate *what* might have been lost. Thus institutions of education and media, as the long-time arbiters of linguistic and cultural authority, have also become the sites of the most sustained, concerted efforts to reclaim Buryat in the twenty-first century.

Many people who argue for the reinstatement of Buryat in public discourse, or for tougher language legislation, or who lament the loss of Buryat are not necessarily interested in learning or using Buryat themselves. Rather, they are invested in the indexical meanings of Buryat—or how Buryat points to nonlinguistic aspects of the person who uses it, such as her ethnic, national, gender, or familial identities and affiliations. Efforts to counter language loss, shift, and endangerment are usually discussed in terms of "revitalization," but the metaphor of breathing new life into an ill body, in need of resuscitation, does not quite capture the mood of contemporary Buryat cultural politics. It is not that Buryat culture and language are languishing or moribund, but that they are seen as rightfully the property or substance of Buryatness, and as things that have been unfairly or unnaturally *taken away*—whether by one's parents and grandparents, by Russians, by Soviet authorities of the past, or by structural changes beyond anyone's control. Wherever blame is placed, Buryat traditional culture and language figure in contemporary cultural politics as rightful heritage to be reclaimed.

The stakes of this reclamation are both emotional and geopolitical. In the twenty-first century, Buryats must imagine themselves as *different* through new means, rather than through the Soviet doctrine of national self-determination or geopolitical borders drawn on a map. Buryat autonomy within Russia has always been partial and contingent, subject to a kind of "graduated sovereignty" within the larger nation-state (Ong 2000), but the terms of autonomy have changed.[10] As political sovereignty has been chipped away and territorial sovereignty increasingly threatened, assertions of cultural sovereignty—such as language preservation campaigns, religious revitalization, and other efforts to maintain or develop cultural alterity—have become more important in Buryat cultural politics.[11] The state has taken less and less interest in defining individuals as Buryat, removing nationality designations (e.g., *russkii*, "Buryat," or "Chuvash") from internal passports and dismantling affirmative action. The burden, as well as the opportunity, of working out who counts as Buryat and whether and how it should matter is shifting instead into less state-directed domains, such as discussions in living rooms around the television and in the very active Russian- and Buryat-language blogospheres.

Mixed Media Methods

The field research at the core of this book was conducted over five periods, totaling twenty months, between 2005 and 2012.[12] I collected ethnographic, sociolinguistic, and archival data on Buryat-Russian language use and on the development, production, and consumption of local media across a range of platforms, including print, radio, television, and "new"/digital media. During all five research periods, I was based in Ulan-Ude, where I lived with host families, in private apartments, and briefly in the dormitory of Buryat State University. From this base, I conducted field research at different times in the three principal Buryat territories: the Republic of Buryatia, Ust'-Orda, and Aga.[13]

More than one-third of the republic's one million residents are officially registered as residents of Ulan-Ude (Burstat 2010). In size, population density, and industry, Ulan-Ude is roughly comparable to Wichita, Kansas. However, so many people disregard the cumbersome registration system and live in Ulan-Ude "illegally" (*bez registratsii*, lit. without registration) that the city's population is probably much higher than the official number suggests. Complicating the picture is the fluidity with which many residents—ethnic Buryats in particular—move seasonally between the city and the countryside through extended kinship networks. The city empties out in the brief Siberian summer, when children typically spend their school holidays with relatives in the villages, and adults enjoy long vacations at dachas, relatives' homes, or tourist camps on the shores of Lake Baikal. It is possible to visit Ulan-Ude in the summer and stroll only the bustling, clean-swept streets of the central commercial district, sampling the sparkling fruits of Ulan-Ude's emerging service and retail (not to mention credit) economies. "Ulan-Udentsy," however, live in very different material circumstances, from swanky new high-rise apartments to humble wooden buildings without indoor plumbing, and from the city center to the impoverished surrounds of a shuttered glass factory (figures 2a, 2b, and 2c).

FIGURE 2A. Mixed traditional and contemporary wooden houses in Ulan-Ude. (Photo by author, 2011.)

FIGURE 2B. New apartments in Ulan-Ude. (Photo by author, 2011.)

FIGURE 2C. A Soviet "Khrushchev-style" apartment complex in Ulan-Ude. (Photo by author, 2007.)

FIGURE 2D. A village homestead in Amgalanta, eastern Buryatia. (Photo by author, 2009.)

Research for this book was sited across these different urban neighborhoods, as well as in villages (figure 2d), because the networks of media workers, language elites, and audiences I describe extended across them. Many (though not all) of the journalists I describe in this book belonged to the intelligentsia and emergent middle class, their membership conspicuous in their centrally located apartments, *biznes lanches*, and memberships in American-style gyms. But most of the city's residents, including most members of the journalists' audiences, could not take advantage of fancy coffee or chic vacations to Thailand, and were benefiting only peripherally, if at all, from the republic's supposed economic progress over the first decade of the twenty-first century.

During most of my field research, I was a student of Buryat, and my role as a foreigner studying Buryat defined my social position in the field. In 2005, I began studying the standard literary language with tutors at Buryat State University through what is now the National Humanities Institute (NGI, then the Buryat Philological Department, or *burfilfak*), which became one of my institutional homes during subsequent research. I also attended less formal classes through the Regional Union of Young Scholars, where Buryat was taught mainly for heritage speakers with emphasis on intergenerational communication (for people who wanted to be able to speak Buryat with their grandmothers, for example), workplace use of Buryat, and general language revitalization. Studying minority-language media requires attending to the practices of intellectuals and cultural producers, who often play a central role (Cormack 1998, 49; Jaffe 1999). Because of my own educational background and my ongoing education in Buryat, I had particularly good access to language elites: teachers, professors, linguists, performers, journalists, language activists, writers, and other cultural workers.

This book draws on a mixed-methods approach to achieve two goals. First, to show how historical legacies matter in the present, I draw heavily on archival materials and integrate them with contemporary ethnography. Archival records from media institutions in Moscow, Ulan-Ude, and Aginskoe provide evidence of past linguistic decisions in materials such as biographical documents, official policy statements, and—especially—Soviet-era editorial meeting notes from the Communist Party organizations of the editorial collectives.[14] Within the Party documents of <u>Buriaad ünèn</u> (R. *Buriat-Mongol'skaia pravda*, 'The Buryat truth,' a local analogue of the Soviet-wide *Pravda*) and the current State Television and Radio Broadcasting Company "Buryatia" (BGTRK)'s predecessor, the Buryat Autonomous Soviet Socialist Republic's Television and Radio Broadcasting Committee, members of the editorial collectives discussed language policies, sanctioned one another for perceived errors, and otherwise debated linguistic decisions and practices.[15] These materials show how linguistic practices and ideologies in and of media have changed over time (or not), as well as how current negotiations of linguistic and cultural authority draw on that past.

Second, I eschew the analytical trichotomy of newsroom-based production studies, decontextualized media analyses, and audience/reception studies to focus instead on how these sites of linguistic action are interconnected and mutually informing. To establish the relationships between media language and everyday linguistic activity—that is, how what a news anchor says might affect a viewer's own language use, and vice versa—I conducted both production and audience studies, in addition to formal analyses of the language of media texts and transcripts. Thus I can show how contemporary media are used, approached, and discussed both inside and outside of newsrooms and broadcasting studios. Primary data include media samples, transcripts of speech events, and ethnographic descriptions of the contexts of their production and consumption, collected through participant observation, structured and semistructured interviewing, and focus groups.[16]

Keeping up on locally produced media was one of my most important daily methods. I reviewed locally produced media throughout my fieldwork—collecting newspapers, magazines, and other print media and recording and analyzing many television and radio programs. Trips to different newspaper kiosks around Ulan-Ude were part of my daily routine, and I came to know several kiosk workers. I also compiled and systematically reviewed two collections of media: (1) all available media produced in the Buryat territories during February 2009, offering a comprehensive snapshot of Buryat regional media; and (2) a historical corpus of Buryat- and Russian-language newspapers from 1929 to 2009, showing change over time in literary standards.[17]

In the production study portion of this research, I interviewed journalists and conducted workplace observation (and sometimes participant observation) at sixteen different media institutions, shadowing reporters when possible and following the editing process. I also surveyed journalists working in bilingual newspaper, radio, and television offices to produce a demographic snapshot of Buryat-language media workers and compare the experiences of workers specializing in Buryat versus Russian media production. Additionally, I interviewed correspondents and retired journalists who had previously worked at these institutions and at an additional four district and republic newspapers, bringing the total sample of local institutions represented in the production study to twenty.

The audience study consisted primarily of informal interviewing and participant observation within households: observing the media practices of friends and acquaintances, watching television with them, asking them about newspaper articles, looking through their stacks and newspaper clipping files, and generally discussing the news and other programming. I documented the circulation of newspapers, cassette tapes, text messaging, and other media through rural communities, as well as rural access to mobile phone service, internet service, and television and radio broadcasts. Ultimately, I observed media practices and conducted informal interviews in approximately sixty households. These households were not selected systematically, and because I relied heavily on invitations through personal networks, the sample was biased toward Buryat and Buryat-speaking families. The sample also included many more women than men, approximately 65 percent women to 35 percent men. The gender skewing was partly a result of my easier access to women in domestic contexts, but it also reflected the Russian Federation's gender imbalance.[18] However, because I was able to conduct research in multiple districts, across rural and urban communities, and through multiple unrelated contacts, the sample was ultimately diverse in terms of other household demographic factors, such as educational level, income level, and size.

To document more systematically the kinds of audience responses I was hearing, I also conducted a series of audience focus groups in Ulan-Ude. Participants read newspaper articles, listened to radio clips, and watched television clips, then discussed the language use of the writers and speakers, along with general issues in Buryat language and media. Both the household media observation and the focus groups revealed systematic, differential language comprehension across media platforms and genres.

The product of these mixed methods is a holistic linguistic ethnography of media, elucidating the total process of textual production, circulation, consumption, and reproduction. Ethnographic description provides the context within which judgments are made as to who and what count as authoritative speakers and authoritative statements. By taking a linguistic ethnographic approach to media, this book thus addresses the mutually dependent relationship between linguistic and cultural belonging.

Overview of Chapters

I begin this book by examining how Buryats have been figured as "Siberian Moderns." Part I explores the notions of modernity and progress into which Buryats have been (often quite willingly) co-opted, as well as the unintended consequences of modernization efforts. Chapter 1 examines conceptions of autonomy, indigeneity, and other dimensions of native belonging in the multinational Russian state. This chapter explains why many Buryats have *not* taken up discourses of indigenous rights, even though doing so would likely benefit them in concrete financial and political ways. Instead, Buryat cultural leaders pursue ethnonational visibility within the multicultural "Friendship of the Peoples," as encapsulated in the native-language media described in chapter 2. Native-language media have been a special site of social action in Asian Russia, first as a way to indigenize state-driven modernizing projects and build a Soviet Buryat public, and later as a way to reclaim local and regional power through a minority elite and further linguistic and cultural revitalization projects. This chapter examines the role of such media in evoking a minority language public, both between and alongside media circulating at other local, national, and international scales. Chapter 3 examines the legacies of the twentieth century's massive modernization efforts by turning to the terms in which contemporary Buryats predominantly understand the history of their culture, language, and land: rupture and loss. I examine a series of temporal and spatiocultural disjunctures informing these feelings, chief among them language shift. The four-century shift from Buryat to Russian is an especially salient instance of cultural change; while it is far from the only example of Russification, it is one that affects everyday life and to which people refer often as evidence of a broader, more thoroughgoing rupture. Thus discussions of language stand in for debates over the past and ideal future of Buryat belonging, and disagreement over what counts as *speaking* "real Buryat" implies disagreement over what it means to *be* a "real Buryat."

Part II, "Mediated Standards," narrows our focus to a particularly complex disjuncture between sources of authenticity and validity: that between the literary standard, encapsulated in news media, and a wide variety of informal ways of speaking offstage and off screen. Chapter 4 examines Buryat language standardization as an example of what I call truncated standardization, a problem that characterizes many minority languages in postcolonial contexts. While the standardization of any language is always an ongoing process, indigenous languages like Buryat are more likely to be surrounded by a different lingua franca—in this case, Russian—that can be used between speakers of different dialects, reducing the immediate need for a standardized indigenous language. Media makers and other language elites persist in trying for standardization, however, because they see creating and maintaining a strong literary standard as such a crucial component of the Buryat modernizing project. Consequently, contemporary audiences who control colloquial forms of Buryat have a hard time understanding Buryat-language media, particularly news media, which further encourages them to default to Russian-language sources. Chapter 5 examines the native language elite, namely media personnel, who are supposed to uphold this (truncated) standard. Ethnographic examples from workplaces and homes reveal that native-language journalists work within value systems that are sometimes at odds with one another. On one hand, they strive toward the professionalism and hyperinstitutionalization of journalism within the majority society, as all journalists do. On the other hand, their role as *native-language* journalists grants a narrower elite status within the minority that draws on rural "prestige" and *non*institutionalization.

While Part II focuses on the language ideologies pursued within media production and on the people who embody them, Part III, "Participation and Performance," turns to media consumers and consumption, including reactions to media, uptake, and participation in media by noninstitutionalized media makers. Chapter 6 examines the shame and anxiety that many would-be Buryat speakers feel in either not controlling Buryat at all or in not controlling the literary standard—that is, not speaking "well." Individuals racialized as Buryat expect one another to be invested in the continuation of Buryat language and culture and to demonstrate their ethnonational belonging through the performance of good speech. Yet very few Buryat speakers can produce what they feel counts as "good Buryat," which affects their tendency to count themselves as belonging to the minority language public. As revealed in interviews for television and radio, media contexts heighten people's sense of potential disaster, because they are generally framed as a space for Buryat language and culture to be presented as such, cordoned off from the much more syncretic and fluid linguistic and cultural practices of daily life. The performance anxiety engendered by language shift, uneven control of the standard, and racialized expectations, brought to a head in media interviews, paradoxically motivates silence and furthers language loss. There are, however, efforts to counter this, such as attempts to revitalize and re-index Buryat through digital media, as examined in chapter 7. This final chapter looks at the political ramifications of native-language media by examining the types of political participation and public making that are made possible—or precluded—by media circulation in the digital age. I examine emerging patterns of media participation in digital contexts, particularly the increasing participation of nonlinguists in linguistic metacommentary and the Buryat diaspora's growing presence on internet-based discussion boards and social media. While these possibilities may seem to democratize engagement and expand the Buryat public to include members beyond the region, they also offer new opportunities to police language use and reterritorialize Buryat belonging within the geographic boundaries of Buryatia.

Throughout the chapters to come, we see the effects of "mixed messages" produced and circulated in this region of Asian Russia. Minority-language media are always "mixed" to some degree, and media producers as well as consumers are orienting toward an idealized standard that, in practice, is not anywhere to be found. Additionally, the same practices that are correct, prestigious, and progressive at one scale of belonging are denigrated as backward and retrograde at another. Across these scales, contemporary native Siberians encounter impossible expectations, leveled by both themselves and others: that they are supposed to be native, wild, exotic, and Asian but also somehow European and quintessentially modern. Most importantly, minority media institutions are supposed to be indigenous—and, as illustrated throughout the book, genuinely do represent key means for negotiating Buryat belonging—but the forms they take are also assimilatory and hyperinstitutional. Navigating these tensions is a challenge not only for Buryats in Asian Russia, but for other ethnic minorities grappling with the trappings of twentieth-century modernity and reorienting to new global publics in the twenty-first century as well.

Part I
SIBERIAN MODERNS

NATIVE AUTONOMY IN A MULTINATIONAL STATE

One snowy afternoon in a friend's apartment in Ulan-Ude, I met a remarkable octogenarian whose wealth of knowledge about local Buryat culture was surpassed only by his presentational style. We whiled away several hours over steaming cups of milky tea as he spun tales of distant kin, endless steppes, and Buddhist lamas of yore who could, he claimed, cross all of Lake Baikal metaphysically, in meditation. My friends and I sat rapt, in the thrall of an accomplished storyteller. He spoke about the Buryat past in an admixture of fact and fiction, science and magic, historically verifiable event and legend.

One story he told that day concerned the *shou* symbol in figure 3b, often used as a talisman for longevity. This symbol has long been popular in China and Mongolia and has also become popular in Buryatia, where cultural and linguistic connections with Mongolia are being enthusiastically revitalized. Chinggis Khan, the elder said, had taken the symbol of the imperial Chinese army, cut it in half, and put it on the soles of his warriors' boots, so that they might walk on the Chinese army with every step. Now, he continued, most people don't know this, but that is why it is such a powerful symbol of the Mongols.[1]

Around the same time in 2009, renovations to several government buildings and Ulan-Ude's main square (figure 3a) were underway. The Square of the Soviets is the site of the world's largest head of Lenin, which some local residents were beginning to find an unwelcome piece of kitsch. Chunks of old asphalt were hauled away, and the city hired a team of Chinese workers to install a new tiled surface that was supposed to be reminiscent of ethnic Buryat patterns.

FIGURE 3A. The newly tiled Square of the Soviets in Ulan-Ude. (Photo by author, 2009.)

I frequented one of the government buildings under renovation, and one afternoon, I happened upon some shiny new tiles with the same *shou* symbol.

A passing man in a suit, who I later learned worked in one of the republic's ministries, paused where I stood. "A Mongolian symbol!" he explained, nodding enthusiastically and pointing to the floor.

"Yes, I recently heard a story about this," I said, and I briefly recounted the Buryat elder's tale about Chinggis Khan's boots.

"Ha ha, yes!" the ministry worker cried, breaking into a wide grin and chortling, so that the security guard looked up. "Chinggis Khan," he said to the security guard. "You know, his mother was a Buryat." He leaned in toward me, his eyes sparkling. "We Buryats were no forest tribe [*plemia*]!"

This characterization might not make sense to western Russians, most of whom view Buryats as simply another impoverished post-Soviet ethnic minority. But Buryats once dominated the Baikal region. The distinction of not being a "forest tribe" privileges this period of Buryat sociopolitical history, starting in the early thirteenth century, when Buryat tribes allied with other Mongols under the banner of Chinggis Khan and his sons to conquer much of Eurasia.[2]

FIGURE 3B. *Shou* symbol. (Vector art by bc21/Shutterstock.com.)

When Russian authorities first learned about Buryats in 1609, it was because some forest-dwelling Ket and Samoyedic peoples living along tributaries of the Yenisei River informed would-be Russian protectors that they already paid tribute to the powerful nearby Buryats (Forsyth 1992, 87).[3] This tension led to a brief battle in 1628 or 1629 on the Angara River—the first documented direct contact between Russians and Buryats (Abaeva and Zhukovskaia 2004, 39; Forsyth 1992, 89; Montgomery 2005, 62). Indeed, early political conflicts between the Russian Empire and Buryats hinged on the right to exact tribute from surrounding forest-dwelling peoples.[4] Pride in being the conqueror rather than kin of forest tribes hints at one of the main reasons that most Buryats have *not* claimed indigenous status in the post-Soviet era, even though it might be politically and economically advantageous.

Insisting on Buryats' historical status as conquerors is a way of resisting dominant narratives that figure them as the recipients of Russia's largesse and of emphasizing cultural resilience and continuity in the face of dramatic change. Over the centuries, Russian missionaries, tsarist administrators, Bolshevik agitators, and Soviet scholars and revolutionaries have all set out to reform Buryat cultural practices, and although they did so in different ways, the leitmotif of their efforts was that Buryats were in need of modernization. So to claim that Buryats were "no forest tribe" is more than an idle observation about Buryat history; it is also a rejection of the notion that Buryats needed Russia's civilizing aid.

The narrative of modernity inscribed within the Soviet state was not exactly unique to it—it had its roots in the European Enlightenment. But the Soviet state acted on this narrative of modernity with totalizing force in Asian Russia. This and the next two chapters examine what it means to be "Siberian Moderns" by exploring the notions of modernity and progress into which Buryats have been co-opted, as well as the legacies of the twentieth century's massive modernization efforts. This chapter examines conceptions of native autonomy in the multinational state of Russia. Each section examines a dimension of contemporary Buryat identity: as products of the civilizing mission of European Russia in Asia, as semiautonomous subjects of a newly ethnic-nationalist Russia, and as pacifistic multiculturalists. Together these factors explain why most Buryats have not taken up discourses of indigeneity and indigenous rights. Instead, Buryat efforts at maintaining ethnonational belonging continue to draw on the existing hyperinstitutional model, pursuing political autonomy and symbolic visibility for a minority public within the framework of institutionalized ethnonational multiculturalism.

Discourses of Indigeneity (or Not)

Elsewhere in the world, key goals of minority-language media have been language maintenance and revitalization (e.g., Cormack and Hourigan 2007), which in turn have been understood as issues of indigenous rights (e.g., Dinwoodie 1998; Harnel 1997; Hornberger and King 1998; Niezen 2000; Weaver 2001). Buryat speakers have not, however, generally taken up (or benefited from) the romantic rhetoric of indigenous language endangerment and death often marshaled in defense of minority-language speakers elsewhere (cf. Errington 2003; Moore 2006). Indigenous rights are not the primary framework in which Buryat leaders and activists have asserted their language rights—or their rights to political autonomy.

Indigeneity is a vexing concept in Siberia. While there is no doubt that imperial Russia colonized Buryatia, it has been difficult to locate Siberian nationalities within postcolonial discourse because it is neither clear that the Soviet project constituted a form of imperialism nor that there is anything "post" about it. This creates something of a rift in scholarship. In the post-Soviet period in Buryatia, for instance, local mainstream historians have tended to emphasize consensus and interethnic mixing in their interpretation of Russian colonization, continuing to focus on class as the basis of conflict (e.g., Zateev 2002), while foreign historians (e.g., Forsyth 1992; Montgomery 2005; Schorkowitz 2001a, 2001b) and Buryat nationalist historians (e.g., Chimitdorzhiev 2001a, 2001b) have tended to focus on interethnic conflict and cultural assimilation and have described Russian acquisition of territories around Lake Baikal as a bloody conquest. Some Buryat historians, most notably Vladimir Khamutaev, argue that Buryatia is still a colony of the Russian state. Even if we grant that the Buryats are in a colonial or postcolonial relationship with the Russian state, the criteria of indigenous recognition as they have been established within Russian law leave out many groups, including Buryats, who would qualify as "indigenous" elsewhere. Thus indigeneity remains a secondary way for peoples who might otherwise be called "indigenous" to claim rights and resources within Russia. Instead, current claims to land and mineral rights, as well as to financial resources supporting native-language education and mass media, are based on an idiosyncratic set of principles and categories established during the tsarist and Soviet periods.

Three aspects of the model of ethnonational autonomy inherited from early Soviet nationalities policy are important to understanding the current structural position of native Siberians in Russia. First, although words like *ètnicheskii* (ethnic) and *korennyi* (indigenous) are used, the most salient category of identity, affiliation, or allegiance based on cultural and linguistic criteria is nationality, or *natsional'nost'*. In the Soviet period, *natsional'nost'* was a basic demographic category deployed in many areas of daily life. It appeared on people's internal passports, census forms, and everyday bureaucratic paperwork like housing and school registrations. *Natsional'nost'* disappeared from Russia's internal passports in 1997, a change that "faced considerable resistance from non-Russian elites" who saw it as necessary to affirming national status and maintaining titular nationalities' hold over key government posts (Arel 2001, iii). It remains so ubiquitous that when I conducted research in Buryatia in 2005–12, it was a piece of information that people would often offer about themselves, unsolicited. It is also important that *natsional'nost'* is self-reported, meaning that at the level of the individual, officially claiming membership in an ethnic minority requires only self-identification with a particular *natsional'nost'*. It is not, however, viewed as flexible by most residents of Russia; the controversy over whether it should be retained in passports concerned, as Dominique Arel (2001) has pointed out, whether it should be revealed, not whether it exists as a primordial category acquired at birth (see also Gorenburg 1999).

Second, the main purpose of identifying indigenous Siberian peoples in the Soviet period was to whisk them away on a grand Marxist-Leninist modernizing adventure. Numerous scholars of indigeneity elsewhere in the world (e.g., Golub 2007; Muehlebach 2001; Nadasdy 2002; Povinelli 1998, 2002) have emphasized how the legalistic demands of colonial or Western powers have significantly shaped the identities of the indigenous groups that they have claimed to "discover"—and vice versa. In the fledgling Soviet Union, native groups were elicited in terms of V. I. Lenin's principle of national self-determination, according to which each "nation" was supposed to be granted the latitude and resources necessary to determine its own path within the new Soviet Union, thus minimizing the chance of separatism in a large and heterogenous collection of territories. Lenin and early Soviet ethnographers drew on Marx and the work of Friedrich Engels (and, by extension, Lewis Henry Morgan) to conceive of the peoples of Siberia as existing at different temporal stages of sociocultural evolution, as evidenced mainly by class stratification: some living at an "early" stage with little differentiation, others beginning to coalesce and stratify economically, and still others drawing closer to achieving nationhood. While the initial identification of ethnic minorities was imagined as a process of discovery, classifying them as peoples (*narody*), nationalities (*natsional'nosti*), or nations (*natsii*) and formulating policy to help them "develop" was also an explicit attempt to incorporate outlying native populations into the Soviet telos (Grant 1993, 1995; Martin 2001; Slezkine 1996; Suny 1993, 1998).

More obliquely, Lenin's idea of the "nation" to be achieved was rooted in a powerful ideology of the ideal nation-state, generally credited to Johann Gottfried Herder, in which the bounds of the nation correspond with those of a discrete people (*Volk*), a discrete language, and a discrete culture. According to this view, the ideal political unit consists of a linguistically and culturally homogenous territory that is supposed to reflect an existing, perhaps *rightfully* existing nation. As most famously pursued and encapsulated in France with its *lingua franca*, a common language fosters a sense of belonging in multiple ways: by enabling communication but also by symbolizing, metonymically, more thoroughgoing similarity and fellow-feeling (Grillo 1989, 22–42; Woolard 1998a, 16–17; see also Silverstein 2010). Early Soviet nationalities policy promoted Herderian nation-state ideals on similar premises: nationhood would be the natural endpoint of Siberian peoples eventually anyway, and the job of Soviet modernization would be to help that process along. The best strategies for doing so would be delimiting ethnic territories, establishing standardized national languages, and investing in native cadres and institutions. Over the ensuing decades, Lenin's ideal of national self-determination from the 1920s gave way to a different goal, of interethnic mixing such that separate nations (and languages) would meld into a single, pan-Soviet people (and language). Nonetheless, the notion that there were discrete peoples at definable stages on parallel trajectories of sociocultural evolution continued to hold sway.

These distinctions still matter a great deal, and many people within Buryatia—including scholars—talk about development of nation and culture in terms of prescriptive stages, from the more "primitive" to the more "civilized."

A third legacy of Soviet nationalities policy that is crucial to understanding contemporary minority politics in Siberia is that the principle of ethnic autonomy has been written onto the landscape as territorial autonomy. Siberian peoples that were believed to be further developed on the cultural evolutionary timescale and closer to being full-fledged nations, like the Buryats, were granted Autonomous Soviet Socialist Republics and oblasts (roughly equivalent to states or provinces), most of which became ethnic republics of Russia in the early 1990s. (One, the Jewish Autonomous Oblast in the Far East, has remained an autonomous oblast.) Native peoples believed to be less developed, especially those living with lower population density in rural areas and the far north, were granted autonomous okrugs (territories or enclaves). This has led to the peculiar status of Russia's "ethnic" republics and territories, including the Republic of Buryatia and the formerly autonomous okrugs of Aga and Ust'-Orda. Although this principle of governance is now being partially dismantled, its legacies are strong and help explain why the position of Buryats in twenty-first-century Russia feels qualitatively different from the position of ethnic minorities in other parts of the world.

Embedded in the Marxist-Leninist timescale of sociocultural evolution is the notion that some proto-ethnonational groups of people are more advanced than others—not as a product of race or biology, but more advanced nonetheless, by virtue of material, historical experience. While on this scale all Siberian peoples were in some sense considered "backward," some were considered more backward than others. Buryats had been exacting tribute in furs from surrounding tribes; some of them practiced sedentary agriculture; and, like the Mongols to the south, they showed enough class differentiation to be termed "feudal" by early Soviet ethnographers. For these and other reasons, they ultimately became the titular minority of their own republic, a far cry in Soviet evolutionary terms from small communities of reindeer herders.[5] This is the source of pride in *not* being members of a forest- or tundra-dwelling "tribe," and it is a powerful reason Buryats have hesitated to align themselves with other Siberian ethnic minorities.

Members of some post-Soviet Siberian nationalities have successfully claimed indigenous status to productive ends. In the early 1990s, groups like the Sakha (Yakuts) were proactive in reaching beyond the Russian state to tap nongovernmental organizations (NGOs) and international organs like the United Nations for the resources—both material and discursive—to win rights to land, subsurface minerals, and cultural projects. They were instrumental in the Russian Association of Indigenous Peoples of the North (RAIPON), until it was disbanded by the Russian government, and they have actively directed Russian policy on the intergovernmental Arctic Council, comprising eight nations of the circumpolar North. Through the proactive use of international pressure, the Sakha Republic (Yakutia) has managed to retain control over diamond mines and oil fields, while elsewhere in the Russian Federation similar resources have been nationalized.[6]

Some Siberian native peoples have been able to advance such claims from within the Russian Federation. A notable case is the Soyots of the Sayan Mountains, located between Tuva and Buryatia. The Soyots were identified in ethnographic surveys in the nineteenth century but were heavily Buryatized and considered "extinct" in the early twentieth century. Then, in 2002, the Russian state recognized their claim to a separate ethnic identity, based on a reconstruction of the Soyot language and historical and archaeological data establishing that a distinct cultural group had inhabited the Sayan Mountains before the arrival of Mongols from the south. The local politicians spearheading the movement for Soyot recognition argued their case to control subsurface mineral rights in the Sayan Mountains, appealing to the international discourse of indigenous rights over sacred land and traditional land use.[7]

The officially titled "indigenous small-numbered peoples of the North, Siberia, and the Far East" who have most successfully claimed oil and mineral rights within the framework of indigenous rights are legally recognized groups who number under fifty thousand and meet specific criteria, such as living in their "historical territory," preserving traditional lifeways, and recognizing themselves as a separate ethnicity.[8] The number alone precludes membership by groups like the Sakha and the Buryats, who bore the status of powerful, well-developed titular nationalities during the Soviet period. Such groups could nonetheless call themselves "indigenous," as the Sakha sometimes have done, by pointing to their history of colonization, structurally inferior political status, and long, continuous occupation of the same territory. Yet, although the benefits of this status are not lost on many Buryats, for some it is also degrading to place themselves within the same sociocultural category as the Chukchi—the brunt of many racist jokes in the former Soviet Union. They point to the Buryats' glorious Mongol past, as heroic warriors of the thirteenth century. "We Buryats," after all, "were no forest tribe!" Unfortunately, tracing your own history to Chinggis Khan (and his boots) entails an acknowledgment that your ancestors were not only warriors but conquerors, precluding claims to territorial "firstness."

Thus, despite international paradigms of indigeneity that might treat Buryats and Ewenks (for example) within the same framework, Buryats tend not to identify with Ewenks on the basis of shared minority status. Moreover, the historical emphasis on territorial autonomy and titular nationalities has generated a territorial view of linguistic rights that can exclude solidarity across regions. Ewenki is a case in point. Ewenki is a Tungusic language with approximately 4,800 speakers in the Russian Federation (Rosstat 2012–13), among 15,800 total speakers dispersed across a vast area of Russia, Mongolia, and China (Eberhard, Simons, and Fennig 2019). The language once enjoyed official status in the Ewenk Autonomous Okrug (E. Ėvedy Avtomody Okrug, R. Ėvenkiiskii avtonomnyi okrug), but the okrug lost its autonomy when it was merged with Krasnoyarsk Krai in 2007 according to a 2005 referendum, as part of the same process by which the Ust'-Orda and Aga Autonomous Okrugs were dissolved. Within Buryatia, Ewenki is mainly spoken in the northern districts, around Baunt. Ewenki is not a language of state, but it receives state support in Buryatia in the form of a small language and cultural studies department at Buryat State University, occasional book publishing, and a weekly television program on BGTRK on Ewenk culture.[9] One Buryat journalist I interviewed, who was otherwise quite liberal in her political views, summarized her position against even this minimal support: "Of course, it's nice for everyone to have materials in their own language [rodnom iazyke, po-svoemu]. The Ewenks have their own okrug [svoi okrug], where they can have their own newspapers and radio." Similar arguments are made for Armenian, Ukrainian, Azeri, and other languages that are widely spoken in Ulan-Ude but have "national" status elsewhere in the former Soviet Union.

Paradoxically, the subset of Buryats who do actively want to claim indigenous status is not the subset of Buryats who most neatly fit the criteria for indigenous citizenship. For instance, Katya, a twenty-something Buryat woman, gushed to me one evening about the importance of preserving her family's traditions by going to the Buddhist datsan (temple). She had grown up in the city and had already traveled extensively; her Russian, English, and Chinese were all far better than her Buryat. As Katya talked about how someone needed to stay in the village to preserve the language and culture, I listened to the click-click-clacking of her stiletto-heeled boots making their treacherous way across the hard-packed snow and ice, and I could not help but wonder how long her conviction would last. She did not control the local cultural knowledge or authoritative mytho-historical genre of our octogenarian. Young urbanites like Katya are the best acquainted with the paradigm of indigenous citizenship and the most likely to imagine their position as members of a global community of indigenous peoples, but they are also the least likely to fit its criteria of membership.

Jessica Cattelino (2010) has described a similar double bind among the Florida Seminole in the United States, who have grown wealthy through casinos and therefore cannot be recognized as indigenous by a state and society that expect their indigenous population to be needy and dependent. Certainly this expectation is at play to some extent in Russia, too: some ethnic Russians and Buryats speak derisively of how the Sakha, supposedly dripping with diamonds and sending their children to expensive foreign universities, get special dispensation from the state. But Cattelino's observations also point sideways to the negative possibilities of claiming an indigenous self-image when that self-image includes neediness, dependence, or degradation. In this light, even if a group has access to the cultural, linguistic, historical, and legal resources to claim indigenous status, it is not clear that its members would want to.

In sum, Soviet categories of indigenous peoples, based on relative development along the Marxist-Leninist evolutionary scale, have left an indelible mark on self-perception in the post-Soviet era. Largely because of this legacy, there have been striking differences in how Siberian ethnic minorities have self-identified in the post-Soviet period. Peoples judged to be the most developed and "nation-like" of the Soviet period, like the Buryats, have not uniformly claimed indigenous citizenship. By contrast, the "small-numbered peoples" have been grouped together in Russian state policy since the nineteenth century, and this gives them—ironically—a framework of solidarity within which to appeal to bodies like the UN and work through RAIPON and the Arctic Council. Buryats likewise appeal to a Soviet-era category when they argue that Buryats are, as a nation, bigger, wiser, and more developed than the Nenets or the Chukchi. But this is less successful. A category that once seemed to offer so much has fallen out of ideological favor.

Enacting Eur-Asia

Another factor in Buryats' collective reluctance to adopt discourses of indigeneity has to do with their status as European Asians. Regionally, the Buryats find themselves in the complicated position of being a border people who have often been viewed as a bridge between Europe and Asia, more like cultural brokers than indigenes.

Straddling Europe and Asia, the Russian state has long struggled with how to best characterize itself vis-à-vis "the East" and "the West." In Eurasian political imaginaries, the Mongolic, Turkic, and Tungusic peoples populating the eastern parts of Russia have doubly served as exotic, Oriental Others and as evidence that Russia embodies the ethnic (and, in many accounts, racial) heritage of both European and Asian pasts.

Contemporary Asian Russians continue to play this dual role. Russia's leaders have been struggling to economically develop what is known in Russia as the "Far East": that is, the regions east of Baikal, including the Pacific coast, Amur Oblast, and the vast Sakha Republic. Buryatia's government and businesses have increasingly invested their economic hopes in tourism centered on Lake Baikal's unique ecology, fishing and hunting, national parks, and shamanic and Buddhist practices that appear exotic to the wealthier residents of Russia's western regions. Tour companies have developed special packages showcasing the songs, dances, foods, and rituals of local Buryats, as well as other picturesque ethnic minorities of the area. This exoticism extends to the sex trade. On websites, pornography businesses market Buryatia's "Asian women" to western Russian men, and prostitution is a minor industry in the hotels of Ulan-Ude and the rural summer resorts around Lake Baikal.

Cultural politics and the rapidly growing ethno-tourism industry thus call on Buryats to remain somehow Asiatic. But Buryats also face expectations to participate in cultural institutions that are understood to be quintessentially European, from classic ethnolinguistic nation-state configurations and newspaper journalism to a love of bread and potatoes. Here "Europe" and "Asia" are not only places but concepts. If Asia is the inscrutable Other in need of salvation, Europe is a civilizing mission.

In everyday interactions, Buryats enact multiple scales of belonging in relation to both Russia (and Europe) and Mongolia (and Asia), moving between what we might call the national and continental scales of belonging. Despite extensive Russification, ethnic Buryats generally consider themselves a separate "nationality" (*natsional'nost'*) and "people" (*narod*), distinct from ethnic Russians. At the same time, they are distinguished from their Mongolic co-affiliates in Mongolia and China by their political and cultural position in Russia, which often places them within Europe rather than Asia.

It might not be immediately clear how "Europe" could be invoked this far into Asian Russia at all. But ethnic Buryats have long been figured as a point of access for western Russians and other Europeans to Mongolia and China: a "bridge" between Russia and its Orient. Ill-fated English Protestant missionaries of the nineteenth century, for instance, saw converting Buryats in the Novoselenginsk region south of what is now Ulan-Ude as a step toward their ultimate goal of missionizing in China (Bawden 1985). Russian Orthodox missionaries established a foothold in Irkutsk and attempted to Russify and convert Buryats as part of a larger effort to civilize the eastern frontier (Graber and Murray 2015; Murray 2012). Later, Soviet authorities capitalized on this history by using Russian-speaking Buryats as a political and cultural diplomatic bridge to Mongolia and Tibet (Andreyev 2003; Rupen 1964).[10] By the same token, many Buryats have capitalized on their geographic position to profit from brokering political and cultural capital across Eurasia. Just as Buryatia's growing tourism industry benefits from marketing Asia to European Russians, its universities are emerging as a premier destination for the children of China's burgeoning middle class.

During the Soviet period, the socialist Mongolian People's Republic (MPR) to the south was a satellite state of the USSR, often spoken of in patronizing terms as Russia's younger brother. Today Buryats within the Russian Federation tend to approach Mongolia with ambivalence, envious of their independence and preservation of religious, cultural, and linguistic traditions but wary of the Mongolian state's tenuous economy and unsure of whether they, as Russian Buryats, are "real Mongols." Mongolia has seen an unprecedented, if precarious, economic boom providing coal, copper, gold, and other mineral resources to feed China's rapidly expanding energy and construction needs. Because most Mongolians have not yet reaped these rewards, however, residents of Buryatia still know the country as their poorer, wilder "brother" to the south.[11]

Yet more than economic possibilities, perhaps, Buryatia's position vis-à-vis Mongolia and China offers discursive possibilities: the Russian-Mongolian and Russian-Chinese borders provide terms in which Buryats can experience and discuss their belonging to a pan-Mongolic community transcending borders, to an indigenous Buryat public within the Russian Federation's Buryat territories, to an emerging Asian economy, or to a decidedly "European" culture within Asian Russia. In everyday interactions, Buryats draw on cultural features that would otherwise seem minor or mundane to illustrate that they are truly European. When my Buryat friend Tuyana returned from living in Ulaanbaatar, the capital of Mongolia, she echoed what I had heard so often before: that she had felt herself to be Asian until she spent time in Mongolia, whereupon she realized that "we're Europeans" (*my evropeitsy*). She explained this epiphany not in terms of language choice or religious practices but in terms of food choices, household cleaning products, and the social mores prevalent in night clubs. Such epiphanies were fairly common among Buryats who studied abroad in Mongolia and China. Another friend reported the same after a trip to Japan, where she desperately missed bread and potatoes and began to experience her Europeanness in their terms.

Bread and potatoes are central to the Russian diet but are practically anathema to the traditional, pastoral-nomadic Mongolian diet of meat and milk products, so they are locally taken to be a strong indicator of Russian cultural influence— not only in the sense that Russians introduced Mongolic peoples to these foods, but also in the sense that at various stages of colonization, Russians (and Soviets) encouraged the sedentarization that made growing grain and potatoes possible. Linguists and language teachers are quick to point out that the Buryat words for 'bread' (khilèèmèn, from R. *khleb*) and 'potatoes' (khartaab, from R. *kartoshka*) are Russian borrowings, albeit old ones.[12] Thus the physical taste or longing for these starchy foods has become a very salient metonym for successful Buryat assimilation into Russianness—expanded, in these accounts, to Europeanness-at-large.

Conversations can also involve more subtle movement between scales. Two women, Èrzhena and Badma, and I sat at a kitchen table, drinking milky tea and brandy for several hours. They mostly spoke Buryat with one another. As proud members of the same Buryat community and tracing ancestry to the same region, they referred often to their own territorial kin as "we" or *nashi* (ours). They also referred to a pan-Buryat scale of belonging. Badma described something mean-spirited that a coworker had recently done, turning a close associate away without helping him, which they agreed was possible only because this coworker was an ethnic Russian. Or maybe a Jew, she mused—she was not certain about the woman's ethnicity or nationality, only that a Buryat would not have done that. *We*, they both agreed, would not have done that—meaning, in this case, Buryats. Through most of their conversation, these two women spoke of belonging at a local scale, within which they differentiated between themselves as territorial kin or as Buryats and the non-Buryat "others," mostly but not exclusively ethnic Russians, who surrounded them in daily life.

Then Ėrzhena narrated a recent event, by way of illustrating how the Chinese labor migrants increasingly inhabiting Ulan-Ude do not observe proper public behavior. She had been in a government office, standing in a line that included some Chinese men. One of them spat on the floor. Ėrzhena mimed spitting ("PUTUI!"), colorfully expressing the indignation that she had felt at the time. "We don't do that here!" she cried, reporting what she had said to the man and switching from the Buryat that she had been using almost exclusively into Russian. "'Maybe you do that in China, but not here,' I said." She threw her head back dramatically, eyebrows raised high. "'In **Russia**,' I said, 'we don't spit on the floor!'"

Ėrzhena soon switched back into Buryat, but not before commenting in Russian that Chinese migrants were degrading life in the city. Badma opined, also in Russian, that Chinese migrants were not accustomed to life in a European city. Their code choice here was consistent with the content of their comments, in that they were policing Russian public behavior, or what "we" do and do not do in Russia. And they deftly used this codeswitch to move from the national scale, opposing Buryat nationals to other nationalities, to the continental scale, stressing the need to be vigilant in monitoring public space as "European" in contrast to geographically Asian surrounds. Thus within a single interaction, a person might identify as a member both of the Buryat "we" and the Russian-citizen "we," either by invoking the territorial boundaries ("in Russia," for example) or by switching from the language that marks one public to the language that marks another.

A single speaker may move between scales, and sometimes between languages, to shift personal allegiances and to make judgments about others and about oneself that may seem contradictory. The word "Siberia" in Russian, for instance—*Sibir'*—has many of the same connotations of desolation and marginality that it carries in English. In small Buryat-Russian villages such as Tarbagatai, residents call an outlying district of the village *Sibir'*. To live "in Siberia" (*v Sibiri*) is to live way out on or beyond the periphery, even "in the sticks" (*v glushi*). Tarbagatai has a Buryat name (meaning 'with marmots') and is inhabited by Semeiskie, Sibiriaks, and Buryats—all Siberians. But calling an outlying district "Siberia" suggests that its residents orient themselves as European Russians do, albeit in a tongue-in-cheek way.[13] Tracing the use of semiotic resources across scales like this gives important clues as to how people imagine themselves and their place in the world.

In some ways, Ėrzhena and Badma's movement across scales invites a recapitulation of recursive Us/Them dichotomies, in which the scope of "Us" grows and shrinks (Irvine and Gal 2000). Their interaction shows something more specific, however, about *when* they will choose an "Us" and "Them" of a particular scale. They seemed to want to emphasize their Buryatness within a discourse about workplace morality, but their Europeanness within a discourse about public propriety, when it came to enforcing a behavioral border with China. In other words, speakers inscribe cultural practices and the physical spaces to which they are linked as "European" or "Asian" differently within different discourses: of Buryat indigeneity, of the imagined economic futures of Russia and East Asia, and of lamentations over increasing Chinese immigration into Buryatia.

What is it about these different discourses that prompts people to identify in apparently contradictory ways? Broadly speaking, Buryats are more likely to identify politically/governmentally and economically as European, and as morally, religiously, and spiritually Asian. It is remarkable, given the political and economic crises in Europe, not to mention the worsening of diplomatic relations between the Russian state and European powers, that Buryats continue to invoke their position within "Europe" at all—and all the more remarkable that they claim to be European in precisely those domains in which Europe is supposed to have failed (except perhaps in the domain of bread). Yet the concept of an orderly, well-starched "Europe" remains a bulwark against perceived entropy, an aspiration for future publics in what is otherwise Asian Russia and a powerful deterrent to spitting indoors.

Degrees of Autonomy

Whether Buryats discursively assert themselves as "European-not-Asian" or as "Asian-not-European" may be politically significant for the future of the state. There is some anxiety in Russia that the federation will dissolve along ethnonational lines, despite a strong countervailing trend toward Russian ethnic nationalism. Central authorities consider it necessary to constantly reaffirm the incorporation of semiautonomous border republics like the Republic of Buryatia into Russia, as evidenced by the propaganda employed in the 2011 celebration of the 350th anniversary of the "voluntary entry of Buryatia into the composition of Russia" (*350 let dobrovol'nogo vkhozhdeniia Buriatii v sostav Rossii*). This slogan significantly recasts the story of a violent military conquest and moves the date of creation of a discrete territorial unit called "Buryatia" earlier by about 250 years. These facts were not lost on the well-educated members of Buryatia's cultural elite, who grumbled and sarcastically emphasized the word "voluntary" (*dobrovol'nogo*) every time they repeated the slogan. Perhaps this lack of local enthusiasm is why the campaign's slogans had to be repeated on every building, billboard, supermarket plastic bag, and other available surface that year, and why federal authorities poured funds into conferences, construction projects, events, and public health initiatives in exchange for using some version of the campaign's slogans and imagery, even when it made no sense (figures 4a and 4b).

This lavish campaign revealed a deep anxiety on the part of federal authorities that was perplexing, both to me and to the Buryats with whom I spoke that year, because it seemed so unnecessary. Most Buryats have internalized a

FIGURE 4A.   A poster on a building in Ulan-Ude celebrates Russian-Buryat friendship with the slogan "350 years—Together through time!" (Photo by author, 2011.)

FIGURE 4B. A public service announcement in Ulan-Ude reminds citizens to brush their teeth while also celebrating Russian-Buryat friendship with the slogan "350 years—Together through time!" (Photo by author, 2011.)

pacifistic (if not passive) acceptance of their position vis-à-vis ethnic Russians. But the authorities sending cash were correct to think that residents' ongoing identification with multiculturalism, and specifically Russian-Buryat brotherhood, is a key centripetal force in regional minority politics. Specifically, it has helped ameliorate opposition to the steps Moscow has taken to lessen ethnonational autonomy.

The dissolution of the Aga and Ust'-Orda Buryat Autonomous Okrugs signaled the possible end of a long and interesting experiment in native governance. The initial division of the Soviet Union included within the Russian Soviet Federative Socialist Republic (RSFSR) a Buryat-Mongolian Autonomous Soviet Socialist Republic (BMASSR) uniting most of the Buryat lands north of the Mongolian border.[14] In 1937, the borders of the BMASSR were redrawn to divide Buryat territories into three separate political units: the Buryat-Mongolian ASSR (now the Republic of Buryatia), Ust'-Ordynskii Buryat-Mongolian National Okrug (now the Ust'-Orda Administrative Okrug within Irkutsk Oblast), and Agynskii Buryat-Mongolian National Okrug (now the Aga Administrative Okrug within Zabaikal'skii Krai).[15] Buryat territory was thus carved up into a republic and two enclaves, and Ust'-Orda and Aga became islands within Russian-dominated oblasts. Buryats then essentially had three capital cities: Ulan-Ude in the BMASSR, Ust'-Ordynskii in Ust'-Orda, and Aginskoe in Aga. From 1993 to 2008, the okrugs were federal subjects—direct subjects of the Russian Federation, autonomous from the surrounding administrative units of Irkutsk Oblast and Chita Oblast, respectively. Although Aginskoe and Ust'-Ordynskii each currently contains only about fifteen thousand residents, they were both administrative centers housing their own okrug governments with locally elected officials and a "Head" (*Glava*) who belonged to the Kremlin's State Council (R. Gosudarstvennyi sovet), reporting directly to Russia's president.[16]

Since the mid-2000s, federal policies in the Russian Federation have increasingly favored administrative centralization at the expense of territories whose autonomy was previously based on the principle of ethnonational self-determination. This has meant the dissolution of several autonomous ethnic okrugs, including Aga and Ust'-Orda, and an official decoupling of indigenous citizenship from territory.[17]

In every case, Putin and his powerful ruling political party, United Russia (Edinaia Rossiia), have put considerable effort into making the mergers appear as democratic as possible. Many mergers have been discussed and abandoned, at least temporarily, including a plan to merge the Republic of Buryatia with surrounding Russian-dominated territories. Those that have been pushed through have been voted on, at least nominally, as referendums in the affected territories.

In Aga and Ust'-Orda, the referendums passed for complicated reasons. Aga, on the eastern steppes, was a hard sell. Linguistic and cultural preservation has long been a point of pride there, and the region is renowned as a sort of "ark" (R. *kovchëg*) where songs, dances, stories, marriage customs, clan affiliations, and Buddhist traditions forgotten elsewhere have been preserved. In Aga, merger advocates emphasized economic benefits and the goodwill that voting to merge would generate in Moscow. In Ust'-Orda, economic considerations were also a factor, but pro-merger officials additionally argued that the Ust'-Orda Buryats' extreme language shift and cultural Russification proved that the autonomous okrug model had not worked to maintain distinctive lifeways. When protesters pointed to the success of Aga (which was still intact at that point), the retorts bore a common refrain: that it had been incumbent on the Buryats of Ust'-Orda to maintain their own language and culture in the face of Russian settlement. Ultimately the referendums gained support through these arguments and a combination of economic incentives, building projects, public support from the popular and trusted former head of Aga, and a desire not to rock the proverbial political boat. A few small but passionate protests notwithstanding, the mergers of Aga and Ust'-Orda were characterized on the whole by a remarkable lack of public opposition.[18]

This is not to say that Buryats are uniformly pacifistic assimilationists. Buryatia has had its share of nationalist activists, including serious advocates for greater political control—including fully independent status—based on the principle of ethnonational autonomy. To take one example, in 2010 the republic's legislature, the People's Khural, initially rejected a suggested measure to rename the president something other than "president," despite the support of the Russian Duma and the president of the Republic of Buryatia himself, Viacheslav Vladimirovich Nagovitsyn. (The measure was adopted the following year.) More radical opposition to centralized authority was voiced in 1988–90, a period of intense Buryat nationalism. Among the most vocal and important organizations of Buryat nationalism during this time were the People's Front for the Assistance of Perestroika (Narodnyi front sodeistviia perestroike), Gésér (named for Buryatia's national epic hero), and the Buryat-Mongol People's Party (B. Buriaad-Mongol Aradai Nam, R. Buriat-Mongol'skaia narodnaia partiia). The main goals of this party, led by Mikhail Ochirov, were Buryat language revitalization, a reunification of Buryatia based on its pre-1937 borders, decentralization in favor of local government, and the establishment of a demilitarized zone in the Baikal region. In the fall of 1991, they championed seceding from the Russian Federation and joining Mongolia; an offshoot, the Movement for National Unity led by Arkadii Tsybikov, went further and suggested unifying the Buryat territories of Russia, the Buryat territories of China, Tuva, Kalmykia, and Mongolia into a single state (Muzaev 1999; see also Khamutaev 2005). These more radical national aspirations did not find wide support, even in republic-level politics, as Buryatia's people apparently saw their economic and political future in Russia.

The main active descendants of this period's political turmoil have been the Congress of the Buryat People (Kongress buriatskogo naroda, or KBN) and the All-Buryat Association for the Development of Culture (Vseburiatskaia assotsiatsiia razvitiia kul'tury, or VARK). Both KBN and VARK remained important centers of Buryat nationalism, political foment, and language revitalization initiatives in the 2000s. During my fieldwork, they had a reputation for embodying the aging "old guard" of Buryat nationalism. However, a major meeting in 2011 thrust KBN and VARK back into the forefront of a reenergized movement for Buryat cultural and linguistic rights, including more access to Buryat-language media. The basic principles of Buryat nationalism at the beginning of the twenty-first century have been remarkably continuous with those animating Buryat nationalism at the beginning of the twentieth century, focusing on language issues as part and parcel of restoring ancestral rights to ethnic territory, lessening Russification and Europeanization, and restoring cultural unity with Mongolia and the larger Buddhist world (Amogolonova 2008).

Some initiatives of the reenergized movement for Buryat cultural development have succeeded. Efforts to establish an all-Buryat-language radio station, which began in the 1990s and which often appeared politically and financially impossible to many of the language activists arguing for it, did eventually bear fruit. Since September 1, 2016, Buriaad FM has been broadcasting on air at 90.8 FM and streaming online at buryad.fm. This "Buriaad aradai radio" (radio of the Buryat people, using the Buryat term for people that most closely corresponds to Russian *narod*) aims to be accessible to speakers of multiple Buryat dialects across a wide territory and the diaspora. Its goal could have made it appear politically threatening as a pan-Mongolic endeavor, and indeed one of the reasons cited for the difficulty in procuring a broadcasting frequency was Ulan-Ude's position near a federal border and military installations. The station's focus on cultural events, music, and human interest stories, however, made it appear sufficiently politically safe, and its founders won a broadcasting frequency and government funding with support from the Buddhist Traditional Sangha of Russia and both regional and federal government entities. On the opening of the station, a representative of the government of Buryatia, Irina Smoliak, underscored that Buriaad FM's goal would be the "preservation and development of language" (*sokhranenie i razvitie iazyka*) and observed that the station would never become—and could not become—"commercial" (*kommercheskim*). It needed to be supported, she emphasized, by the state. The success of Buriaad FM exemplifies a rule that activists know well: ambitious initiatives for Buryat cultural revitalization are achievable but only if they are safely, visibly, and explicitly emplaced within existing political structures.

There are several reasons that most Buryats have not supported efforts for greater political autonomy, either during the breakup of the Soviet Union or now. Clearest, perhaps, is the fact that the Republic of Buryatia—the only Buryat territory in which independence has been seriously discussed—could not survive economically as an independent nation-state. Compared with other regions of Russia and with the federation as a whole, the Republic of Buryatia is markedly rural and poor. According to the 2010 census, the Russian Federation's population is 72 percent urban and 28 percent rural, while the Republic of Buryatia is 58.4 percent urban and 41.6 percent rural (Rosstat 2011). The rural economy is based on small-scale animal husbandry, especially cows and sheep, and secondarily on crops that can withstand the region's harsh continental climate, like wheat.[19]

Ulan-Ude was also an industrial powerhouse in the late Soviet period, but this ended with perestroika (restructuring) in the late 1980s, when the USSR attempted to stimulate the economy but instead lost control of it, shuttering many factories. Rapid privatization in the early 1990s made matters worse and was followed by a devastating ruble crash in 1998. Reminders of this period can still be seen everywhere, from the dilapidated heating plants belching diesel and coal smoke to the fields of broken glass and crumbled concrete surrounding the closed glass factory. In some households, workers and managers who lost their jobs during perestroika in the late 1980s and in the economic chaos of 1991 never found new employment, relying instead on meager state pensions and kinship networks to scrape by. Neighborhoods grew up on the outskirts of the city around factories that are now closed, leaving some—like Steklozavod, where I lived in 2007—desperately poor. Among the industries that survive are vast manufacturing complexes that produce train cars, helicopters, pasta, and packaged meat for Russian and international markets. Until 1991, the airplane factory's focus on military aircraft and radio technology meant that the entire city of Ulan-Ude was closed to foreigners, which seems to have produced a disproportionate sense of isolation during the Soviet period and a disproportionate sense of freedom afterward. There are also various mining operations for minerals and precious metals, which operate in an uneasy tension with new projects to capitalize on the region's natural beauty through tourism.

A strong reason for residents not to argue for greater political autonomy since perestroika has been exhaustion. Daily decision making in contemporary Buryatia has been suffused with a historically specific desire to live a "normal" and quiet, peaceful life in the face of chronic crisis. By 2007, Russia's death rate far exceeded the birth rate, and the country was in the throes of what the state termed a "demographic crisis" (*demograficheskii krizis*), spurring initiatives to improve maternity leave, increase support to "many-childrened families," and promote traditional marital and family values (Rivkin-Fish 2010).[20] The federal government named 2008 the "Year of the Family," and much of my research took place among billboards and advertisements imploring men and women to stay together, have children, and live healthily. Just as these initiatives were getting underway, the world financial crisis of 2008–9 hit Russia hard, resulting in a steep fall for the Russian ruble and substantial "optimization" (*optimizatsiia*) and "rationalization" (*ratsionalizatsiia*)—that is, layoffs—in many sectors of the economy.[21] In Buryatia, strong kinship networks provide a sense of security: there is always access to milk, potatoes, and basic sustenance from village relatives. Moreover, people remembered far worse crises. Thus in terms of simple survival, the financial crisis, though technically deeper in Russia than in the United States, did not appear threatening or paradigm-shifting in the way it did to US commentators and was more often a source of mirth. As both Buryats and Russians liked to joke to me, "Why worry? There's always a cow in the village!" However, the concatenation of financial and demographic crises produced some job anxiety and a subtle but noticeable reemphasis on traditional gender norms. Because it is illegal in Russia to lay off a woman during her three-year maternity leave, some women hoped to get pregnant to protect their jobs.

Most importantly for media workers, the financial crisis exacerbated the global crisis in journalism. With the rise of the "citizen journalist" and audiences increasingly turning to noninstitutional sources for information exchange via digital media, news media institutions that operate on market-driven advertising- and subscription-based models (i.e., most global news organizations) have suffered sharp reductions in revenue. Most Buryat-language journalists were relatively protected from this development as state-subsidized employees. Even so, media institutions and the people who work (or worked) in them felt the pain of the joint crises. All of the offices in which I conducted research in 2008–9 experienced some kind of staff "reduction" (*sokrashchenie*, short for *sokrashchenie kadrov*). Most of my conversations with media workers ranged at some point over financial coping strategies such as limiting print runs, reducing printing and production costs, or reducing staff, and job security was a primary concern for many of my interlocutors.

Residents of Buryatia have, however, become inured to a state of almost constant crisis—what Olga Shevchenko terms Russia's state of "chronic crisis" (2009, 3). Shevchenko refers to the late 1990s, but her observations about the rhetorical "stability of the crisis metaphor" and its resulting ennui held true a decade later as well (2009, 35; cf. Ries 1997). For many of my interlocutors, the word conjured stress and "abnormal" circumstances, but it also formed the only background against which everyday life could be experienced. "*Krizis, krizis,* there's always a *krizis,*" one Buryat woman of about fifty sighed, throwing up her hands. Others took crisis humor a step further. Rocking along on the Trans-Siberian Railroad between Moscow and Novosibirsk, a jovial woman handed me a round white pin, on which was printed in big red letters: "KRIZIS 2008–2009."

Exhaustion with crisis leads many residents of Buryatia (and of Russia more generally) to place huge importance on living not only "normally" (*normal'no*), but also in peace—or, as my friends and research participants often put it, to "*zhit' spo-koino*" (live peacefully). Many people, Buryats and Russians alike, appeared willing to suffer various injustices in exchange for peace, regularity, security, and being left alone. This was, for example, one of the primary reasons cited by people who were strongly but quietly opposed to the referendum to merge Aga with the surrounding Chita Oblast who nonetheless voted *for* it (Graber and Long 2009). I heard similar opinions expressed, usually quietly, among journalists. When a decision made in Moscow was going to result in one local media institution losing some support for its minority-language activities, I asked one of its senior employees whether there had been any consultation. I probably seemed indignant. Where exactly had the decision been made? What reasons did they offer? He put forward his opinion very plainly. "It is better," he said seriously and forcefully, his voice lowered, "to be quiet and calm and not draw attention. Then we are left alone."

Regional Multiculturalism

The desire to "live peacefully" is closely related to another subtle but powerful reason that Buryats have been slow to press for more political autonomy or claim indigenous status: pride in regional multiculturalism. Many residents of Buryatia believe their region to be more tolerant and pacifistic than other parts of Russia, particularly than other ethnic republics, such as Chechnya and Tatarstan. Interethnic peace is displayed in countless ways around the republic, not only in imagery motivated by the Russian state's goals (e.g., figures 4a and 4b) but also in locally produced performances. Public performances on holidays and at other civic events in Buryatia routinely include songs and dances not only from Buryat and Russian folk ensembles, but also from Cossack, Ewenk, Semeiskii, and Azerbaijani ensembles. Each ethnicity of the republic is represented by its own performers, carefully crafting and reproducing a highly formatted culture that is at once inclusive, secular, and compartmentalized. Such management of ethnic and linguistic diversity is indebted to the format of multinational cultural programming used in the early Soviet era (and currently pursued in China).[22] But its use in the current era also reflects a multinational-turned-multicultural live-and-let-live ethos peculiar to Buryatia.

In both onstage performances and in everyday "offstage" conversations, speakers invoke the *druzhba narodov*, or Friendship of the Peoples, a popular slogan of the Soviet period promoting interethnic brotherly love between all peoples (*narody*) of the Soviet Union. This is the idea illustrated historically in figure 5 and more recently in figures 4a and 4b, with a stereotyped Russian and a stereotyped Buryat, identifiable by their stylized national dress and facial features, shaking hands or linking arms. In the lead-up to the merger referendums in both Aga and

FIGURE 5. A Russian peasant and Buryat herder, easily identifiable to Buryat readers by their facial features and dress, shake hands on the cover of an instructional booklet published by the Buryat Cooperative Union, 1924 (OPP IMBiT: MI-557).

Ust'-Orda, United Russia capitalized on the same imagery, mounting billboards depicting Buryats and Russians in traditional dress holding hands, with the slogans "Together, We're Stronger!" and "Together Is Better" (Graber and Long 2009). The Friendship of the Peoples principle presumes that there are distinct, discrete peoples to be in friendship, and indeed, Buryatia's cultural politics presume that there is an identifiable Buryat people for whom the republic exists. In addition to invoking a distinctive ethnonational identity, however, residents of Buryatia strongly identify their region as a site of peace, pacifism, and successful multiculturalism.

The Friendship of the Peoples was widely used across Soviet space, but it took on special importance in Buryatia, where it remains a point of local pride and a powerful deterrent to physical violence, if not latent racism.[23] There are several reasons for Buryatia's exceptionalism on this count. By the time the Baikal territories were incorporated into the Russian Empire in the seventeenth century, they were already multiethnic, multilingual, and multiconfessional spaces. Thereafter there were two clearly dominant ethnic groups in the region, Russians and Buryats, which made a partnership easy to capitalize on rhetorically. The friendship was also well institutionalized through mass media and the educational system, which Buryats took advantage of with more than average fervor. While all native Siberians experienced Russification and Sovietization to some extent, these assimilatory practices were notably more successful (or crippling, depending on how you look at it) among Buryats, who were often held up as a darling "model minority" by central authorities. As Melissa Chakars (2014) has argued, Buryats were not merely the victims of Soviet modernization; they received advantages and benefits for participating in Soviet projects and making conciliatory gestures to the state. Writing about the late Soviet period, Chakars observes the importance Buryats placed on practicality, living "peacefully," and working within the system—where they did very well, capitalizing on educational opportunities in particular more than most Soviet nationalities and serving as an "outpost of Soviet culture" in Asia (Damdin Zhalsabon, quoted in Chakars 2014, 14). Finally, most of my Buryat interlocutors cite the Buryats' mass conversion to Buddhism over the eighteenth and nineteenth centuries as a reason to live peacefully alongside Russians. The idea that Buddhism is inherently pacifistic is historically wildly inaccurate (Jerryson and Juergensmeyer 2010), but the fact that people take their Buddhist identity to entail pacifism does motivate tolerance.

In the current century, the Russian-Buryat "friendship" is part and parcel of Buryatia's identity, appearing everywhere from fashion and grocery advertisements to public service announcements about the Year of the Family (figures 6a and 6b). Some companies are known locally as predominantly Russian or Buryat, with preferential hiring practices within the nationality. For instance, among Buryatia's greatest capitalist success stories in the 2000s were two rival chains of grocery and housewares stores, MegaTitan and Absoliut. They were widely known for the wealth and panache of their (respectively) Russian and Buryat owners, and whether fairly or not, many people believed that they hired preferentially within families. My Russian acquaintances in particular often complained about what they saw as nepotism within Absoliut, as well as in other Buryat-run businesses and government offices. Other businesses seek to capitalize instead on a middle path. One of the Republic of Buryatia's largest and most successful companies, the Nikolaevskii agricultural holding and supermarket chain, advertises its "clean, homegrown" meats with an interracial family—the Russian father, Buryat mother, and multiracial children strongly suggesting to viewers in the area that this is a local family and a local business.

In this self-identification, residents of Buryatia often contrast themselves with (what they see as) stereotypically violent Chechens, parochial Chukchi, or chauvinistic Russians. They contrast the Republic of Buryatia with other parts of Russia where racially motivated hate crimes—directed most violently and egregiously toward Central Asians, Africans, people of the Caucasus, and Asians—have become a part of daily life. Like most stereotypes, the assumption that western Russian capitals are hostile environments for Asians contains

FIGURE 6A. An advertisement for a men's fashion store in Ulan-Ude depicts interracial harmony. (Photo by author, 2008.)

a grain of truth. Buryats living outside the Buryat territories, such as in sizable and multigenerational diasporas in Moscow and St. Petersburg, face significant xenophobia. Racial hate crimes have been perpetrated against Buryats based both on ignorant assumptions that they are foreigners, most often Chinese, and on generalized Slavic supremacism. A spate of murders on the streets of Moscow in

FIGURE 6B.   A billboard for the Year of the Family in Buryatia depicts a racially and ethnically diverse society. (Photo by author, 2008.)

2007 that appeared racially motivated drew anguished attention in the Buryat territories, and when most of the killings were not prosecuted as hate crimes, many Buryats deduced that Russian law enforcement and the judiciary would not protect them from Russian nationalist violence (Vostok Teleinform 2009).

Buryats living in Ulan-Ude often cite the xenophobia rampant in other parts of Russia as a reason to live in Buryatia or to move back "home." People I knew in Ulan-Ude in the late 2000s and early 2010s increasingly cited examples of friends or family members who were fleeing xenophobia in the urban capitals of western Russia, or even in neighboring Irkutsk Oblast. Whether anti-Asian sentiment was actually on the rise or not, the perception that the Republic of Buryatia was a safer, more peaceful, and Asian-friendly territory became motivation enough.

Reconfiguring Buryatia as a safe homeland in the face of rising ethnic-Russian nationalism might risk privileging Buryat nationalism within Buryatia. That is indeed a fear of some non-Buryats living in Buryatia, who already complain of the stranglehold ethnic Buryats have over government and certain industries. But the mitigating ideals of multicultural tolerance and pacifism are part of Buryat self-understanding, even if they are not always achieved. This was evident in the reaction of Arsalan, a Buryat friend, to a photograph that I had taken in Baikal'sk, an industrial town and ski area right outside the boundary of the Republic of Buryatia (figure 7). *Rossiia dlia russkikh!* (Russia for the [ethnic] Russians!), the graffiti on a shed proclaimed. As Arsalan and I flipped through my recent photographs, he noticed this image and pointed to it as an example

FIGURE 7. Graffiti in Baikal'sk proclaims "Russia for the (ethnic) Russians!" *(Rossiia dlia russkikh!).* (Photo by author, 2009.)

of the ignorant Russian nationalism that exists right outside the borders of the territory. Arsalan is something of a Buryat nationalist himself, so I half-teasingly asked whether he would prefer that it say *Rossiia dlia buriat* (Russia for the Buryats). Of course not, he said, offended by the suggestion. Either statement is anathema to a regional identity that elevates visions of multicultural statehood over ethnic political autonomy. The graffiti also pushes against a tacit agreement operative in the Baikal region that Buryats will not demand more political autonomy as long as ethnic Russians refrain from being overtly nationalistic on Buryat territory.

Contemporary Buryats' continuing advocacy of the Friendship of the Peoples is part of what holds the Baikal region together—and part of what keeps it firmly emplaced within the borders of Russia. As Asian economies continue to grow and young people increasingly seek commercial and educational opportunities in Mongolia and China rather than Moscow and St. Petersburg, there are centrifugal economic forces pushing these border republics away from Russia's zone of cultural and political influence. Thus the rhetorical importance of the "friendship" has reemerged over the last few years within the context of Moscow's "regathering of the lands."

These stakes are subtly reflected in the geopolitical terms that people choose to denote the Buryat territories. During fieldwork, I experimented with using the terms "ethnic Buryatia" and "Buryat-Mongolia," both of which were favored by some local scholars and activists, informally asking many of my friends and research participants what they thought of these alternative terms. Their varied responses demonstrate the profound ambivalence with which many Buryats think of the position of the Buryat territories in Russia—and vis-à-vis neighboring states.

The term "Buryat-Mongolia" in particular sparked much discussion about the relationship of the contemporary Buryat territories to Russia and Mongolia. Some progressives and Buryat nationalists championed this term, citing precedent in the popular work of nationalist historians (e.g., Chimitdorzhiev 2004), because it evokes pre-1937 borders of the republic that more closely correspond to Buryat ethnic territories. Although the republic had been created as the Buryat-Mongolian ASSR, the word "Mongolian" was removed from "Buryat-Mongolian" in 1958 as tensions between the Soviet Union and China ramped up (which is also why the language and people are called "Buryat," rather than "Buryat-Mongolian," today). Reintroducing the term, they argued, would be a provocative way of reclaiming Buryats' historical, cultural, and linguistic connections to Mongolia.

Others, however, particularly older Buryat leaders, were very uncomfortable with it. This became clear in a conversation one afternoon at a café with a senior newspaper editor, Chingis, and his colleague Nima. Speaking in Russian, I explained that I had been having difficulty deciding how to represent Buryatia in my work. Chingis was in a position of great authority in Buryatia, and his opinion was important to me. What do you think of that term, I asked, "Buryat-Mongolia"? Chingis shifted uncomfortably in his seat and looked to Nima, who averted his eyes and pretended to study his napkin. "I . . . ," he started and stopped, then took a deep breath and began to speak slowly and emphatically. "I am a great advocate [*storonnik*] of the Friendship of the Peoples," he said, and proceeded to extol the virtues of cooperating with ethnic Russians.

While Chingis's statement can be cynically read as kowtowing to Russian political dominance or as a rote reperformance of Soviet propaganda, these interpretations elide the sincere faith that many Buryats invest in the Friendship of the Peoples. Chingis implied that reidentifying Buryatia as Buryat-Mongolia would be not only a serious political statement but also tantamount to abandoning a cherished principle of interethnic tolerance and cooperation.[24]

These shared social values are reaffirmed on a daily basis through Buryatia's multiculturalism and a Baikal regional identity that is capacious enough to include Ewenks, Soyots, Cossacks, Sibiriaks (non-native people who identify as "Siberian" and are often the descendants of early traders and exiles), and even diasporic Ukrainians, Poles, Armenians, and Azerbaijanis.[25] In addition to pacifism and interethnic tolerance, the regional identity is anchored in shared details of local Siberian life, such as surviving harsh winters, laughing at Muscovites and Petersburgers who believe that bears walk the streets, and loving Lake Baikal. There are also some regional linguistic quirks in Russian like using *no* to mean 'yes' or 'yeah'—what is locally called the *sibirskii da* (Siberian yes)—and some isolated Buryat and Ewenki words that have been borrowed into Russian, especially place names.

At the same time, there are some important indications that living in the region is not quite sufficient to claim the regional affiliation, and furthermore that this regional affiliation is partially ethnicized or racialized. To claim ethnic outsiders as "our own" (R. *nashi*) in Buryatia, local residents often extend to them traits strongly correlated with Buryatness. Throughout my fieldwork, friends and acquaintances used the fact that I was learning Buryat as evidence not only that I was *nasha buriatka* (R. 'our Buryat girl,' with a kind of affectionate but humorous honorary membership status in the ethnonation), but also that I belonged in the *region*. One of my ethnically Russian friends commented that I was like one of the Decembrists, a reference to the Bestuzhev family and other members of a failed coup against the Russian state in 1825, who were exiled to what is now Buryatia and became accomplished ethnographers. "You're a real girl of the Zabaikal [*devushka Zabaikal'ia*]," he joked. Additionally, there was a keen desire on the part of a great many of my acquaintances and research participants to insist that I must have Buryat ancestry far back. At the very least, I should find myself a good Buryat husband so that I could have Buryat babies.[26]

More public evidence can be found in how the Republic of Buryatia's former and current presidents, neither of whom is ethnically Buryat, have been celebrated as—or made into—a "native son" of the region. Among the more controversial and symbolically important language protections is a clause in the republic's constitution requiring that the president of the Republic of Buryatia control Buryat.[27] With the first, elected president of the republic, Leonid Vasil'evich Potapov, this was not an issue. Potapov is an ethnic Russian who grew up in a mostly Buryat village in Buryatia's northern Baunt District. He reportedly spoke a northern dialect of Buryat natively and, while he did not speak Buryat at length in official settings, he frequently intoned holiday greetings and the symbolic openings of speeches in Buryat—which, according to Buryat language teachers and other native speakers, he did quite well. Many people considered Potapov a member of the old guard and disagreed with his politics, but no one questioned his regional affiliation. Occasionally, I heard someone remark that it seemed perverse to have a Russian president of a Buryat republic, but just as quickly, someone else would retort that he had grown up in Baunt, that he had grown up among Buryats, or that he spoke Buryat better than most Buryats—all biographical details that served to root him in a way that was simultaneously multiethnic and Buryatized and thus perfect for the region's self-image.

In 2007, however, a new president, Viacheslav Vladimirovich Nagovitsyn, was appointed by Putin according to a controversial policy that the heads of all federal subjects—including the presidents of semiautonomous republics—would be appointed by the federal executive branch. Electoral rights were restored to the regions in 2012 in the wake of protests, but not before the policy had sowed lasting resentment. Nagovitsyn, in contrast with his predecessor Potapov, had no personal connection with Buryatia when he was appointed president and had had no exposure to the Buryat language.

After some disagreement over the constitutionality of appointing a non-speaker of Buryat in light of the clause, and additional disagreement over the fairness of the clause itself, Nagovitsyn assumed the presidency and assured the people of Buryatia that he had begun taking language lessons to satisfy the constitutional requirement. Yet many Buryats, including people who do not speak Buryat themselves, were dissatisfied with the results. During fieldwork, I often asked what would be enough to say that he "controlled" (*vladeet*) the Buryat language: a second sentence? A whole speech? Speaking on television with a cattle breeder in the countryside? Even people who usually had strong opinions about language did not really answer my question but shrugged, or sighed, or changed the subject. One teacher replied that since he would always have an accent and it would never be "native" (R. *rodnoi*), he should go to some extra effort to learn Buryat *do kontsa* (R. to completion), a common way of expressing fluency. I pointed out that it seemed like I need speak only a few words of Buryat to be considered an excellent speaker; I had not learned Buryat *do kontsa* but was often praised as though I had, and I felt that my knowledge of Buryat was routinely overstated. She seemed to consider this. "Well," she said at last, "there should be desire. The most important thing is that there's desire [*dolzhno byt' zhelanie. Samoe glavnoe—èto zhelanie*]." In an important sense, Nagovitsyn's knowledge of Buryat was beside the point. The problem was that he had been appointed from outside and evinced little excitement about his new post. It did not matter to the political process whether Buryatia's residents liked him or not, so they appeared indifferent to his linguistic efforts for good reason. What induced sighs was not that he did not control Buryat, but that he did not seem to try, and that no one beyond Buryatia seemed to care about this symbolic principle of post-Soviet governance.

To legitimize his presidency, some of Nagovitsyn's champions began emphasizing that by nationality (*natsional'nost'*), he was not Russian but Udmurt and was born in the Udmurt ASSR. He too had grown up around ethnic Russians and understood well the Friendship of the Peoples, they said. As if that were not enough, he had gone to university and spent his career before Buryatia in Tomsk—the message being that he was not a Moscow functionary being sent from the center to the periphery but rather was moving from one periphery to another. Other people, possibly sensing that this analogy was rather oblique and potentially offensive because it treated peripheries as somehow the same, took a different tack and argued that the Finno-Ugric peoples to which Udmurts belong ultimately share a common ancestor with Buryats and other Mongols (an idea discredited by evidence from historical linguistics and population genetics). Weirder suggestions have been that Nagovitsyn has Buryat ancestors about whom he does not know, or that he shares a shamanic connection to Buryatia that drew him there.

All of these cases suggest that while a regional identity based on shared lifestyle and social values carries great weight, some Buryat nativization still needs to be performed in order for the regional affiliation to be fully legitimate. This illustrates how ethnonational and regional affiliations have become so intertwined that one has become part and parcel of the other: to be multicultural and respect the Friendship of the Peoples is part of being Buryat, and having some connection to Buryatness—whether by blood, spirit, or desire—is part of living in the Baikal region. Nagovitsyn's struggle to be seen as a locally legitimated leader also reveals the extent to which learning and using Buryat has become metonymic of a broader personal commitment to Buryatia, to the region, and to the principle of native governance within a multicultural ethos.

A Double Bind

In their unique regional position on the geographical and metaphorical border between Europe and Asia, Buryats have historically been under pressure to play both the exotic Asian foils to European Russia and the trustworthy, culturally intelligible diplomats that the Russian state has needed along its Mongolian and Chinese borders. The Eurasian border provides terms in which Buryats like Érzhena, Badma, and potato-loving exchange students can experience, interpret, and discuss their cultural and linguistic assimilation, as well as articulate a place (or ideal future place) for Buryat ethnicity and the Buryat language within the world. Elliptically, it also gives Chingis and Nima a reason to adhere to the supposed "brotherhood" between Russians and Buryats. In part because of their long-standing external and self-identification as a "bridge" between Europe and Asia, Buryats have readily translated the Soviet era's Friendship of the Peoples and multinationalism into a multi*cultural* ethos in the post-Soviet era, even as they hesitate to translate the rhetoric of national self-determination into the rhetoric of indigenous citizenship.

This chapter outlines several reasons why Buryats have not, on the whole, embraced discourses of indigeneity and indigenous rights circulating globally and within Russia, even though claiming indigenous status would probably benefit them in some concrete financial and political ways. This is one way local groups remain fragmented and isolated at larger scales of belonging. At pains to distinguish themselves from one another, native peoples living along Russia's southern, Pacific, and Arctic borders do not always recognize the similarity of their structural position within the federation.

And they have something else important in common. Teleological visions of sociocultural development have left native Siberians with a set of impossible combinations. They are supposed to be internal "Others," yet loyal to the national Russian (if not Russian-nationalist) cause. They are supposed to be native, wild, exotic, and Asian but also somehow European and modern—by predominantly European criteria.[28] These paradoxes exemplify the difficulty that modern Siberian subjects confront in reconciling historical images of benighted, forest- and tundra-dwelling natives with rapidly changing conceptions of state belonging. In Russia, centuries of administrative practices basing ethnonational belonging and rights on national "homelands" have left vivid traces. Ethnonational borders—cultural, linguistic, geographic, and spiritual—that are no longer officially recognized still play a meaningful role in daily life, and they have argu-ably taken on even greater social salience as Russia's class divisions have widened. Meanwhile, however, the state works to decouple indigenous citizenship from territory and encourages a form of federalism that will have no place for eth-nic nationalities as such. As the liberal principles underlying the multicultural nation-state flounder in Europe and the United States, and while social science has largely moved on to consider transnationalism and postnationalism, native Siberians have been left to grapple with the legacies of a European model that no longer provides any grand telos for their future.

This leaves contemporary native Siberians in a double bind. In post-Soviet Siberia, the right to what was once called national self-determination increasingly appears to require that ethnic minorities demonstrate cultural distinctiveness, language preservation, and traditional land use practices, on a native territory. Achieving all of these things, as in Aga, is no guarantee; they are necessary but not sufficient. All of these criteria, however, have been seriously undermined by imperial and Soviet projects of the nineteenth and twentieth centuries. In the case of Buryatia, pastoral nomadism was systematically dismantled to create settled populations who would run collective farms and work in new industrial centers. A new "Soviet culture" was carefully forged, with new social mores and a strong emphasis on the Friendship of the Peoples, that subordinated ethnic nationalism to an ideal of the cooperation and commingling of multifarious ethnic groups into a new Soviet people. Over the past several generations, Russification, includ-ing language shift from Buryat-Russian bilingualism to Russian monolingualism, has been extreme. The Buryat public that was carefully crafted by Soviet efforts, particularly through native-language media, was very different from what might be politically and emotionally advantageous now. How such media have created and sustained a minority language public, to shifting purposes, is the subject of the next chapter.

MEDIA AND THE MAKING OF A BURYAT PUBLIC

In daily life, people experience media as a mashed-up mélange of languages, styles, and sources. A given household in Buryatia may contain copies of the federal *Rossiiskaia gazeta* (Russian newspaper) and the Oka District's newspaper Akha, in Russian and Buryat, alongside handwritten Buryat-language prayers and a cellphone running Facebook in English and Russian. Internationally circulating fashion magazines like *Vogue* and *Cosmopolitan* shimmer in the windows of Ulan-Ude's newspaper kiosks with impossibly high price tags, above the rows of chewing gum and Buddhist horoscopes people are more likely to buy. Elderly pensioners spend afternoons watching Brazilian soap operas dubbed into Russian, then flip the channel to catch the evening news in Buryat. At the periphery of global cultural flows and at the center of Buryat cultural flows, the Buryat territories have a media landscape composed by overlapping scales of circulation: there are print, radio, television, and digital media produced for global markets; Russian/federal markets; regional markets at the Siberian and republic levels; and local markets at the district, city, and village levels—as well as media produced for hyperlocal purposes, such as schools and factories. How, in this flux of competing information and potential affiliations, do native-language media single out a Buryat public?

The previous chapter lays out the development of a particular conception of native autonomy in the multinational Soviet, then Russian, state. This chapter examines how native-language media have come to play a central role in that conception. Tacking between the twentieth and twenty-first centuries, it uses the making of a Buryat public to elucidate how media create and sustain minority language publics more generally. Publics, I argue, are not givens already existing in the world but are crafted projects of political legitimation, recruiting particular kinds of political subjects. Buryat media evoke a minority language public that has taken on an outsized role in cultural politics, in ways that should make us rethink minority media.

Like the preceding chapter, this chapter focuses on mid-level, regional scales of belonging between the hyperlocal and the federation. I intend this in part as a corrective to studies of media and globalization, because in our increasing analytical focus on the "local" and the "global," we risk losing the regional. In a multinational state like the Russian Federation, it is at this middle, regional level where most ethnonational politics play out. Media produced by and for the Republic of Buryatia, Aga, and Ust'-Orda most clearly articulate (both explicitly and, more often, implicitly) the position of Buryats and Buryatia within national and global imaginaries. This is also the scale at which most native-language media are produced.

What are native-language media? "Media" is a capacious term. Most broadly, it might refer to any form of mediated communication, including instant messaging on social media, telephone-mediated conversations, road signs, or the cooking instructions printed on packages of pasta. Most often, however, when people use this term, they are referring to media that have been institutionalized within newspaper offices and broadcasting networks, and that are produced for large groups of potential strangers. This is what people call "**the media**" in English, or *SMI* (pronounced *smee*, for *sredstva massovoi informatsii*, lit. the means of mass information) in Russian. Authorities and media producers in Russia call minority-language media "native"-language mass media (*SMI na rodnom iazyke*), with the implication that Russian is the federation's lingua franca and that secondary media will be produced at a regional scale in the "native" (i.e., heritage) languages of titular and other nationalities. The term thus assumes that the audience for media in Buryat—and the public evoked by it—will be circumscribed within a larger, mainstream public that is Russian-speaking by default.

The term "public" has a more motley history in Russia, so bears some discussion. The notion of publics, as inherited from Jürgen Habermas's ([1962] 1989) study of how the "public sphere" developed out of communicative practices in England and France in the seventeenth—and eighteenth—centuries, has a robust history of discussion in media studies. It also has a number of drawbacks for analyzing post-Soviet minority media. It assumes, for one thing, homogeneity in the language of communication. In Habermas's study and much of the work that followed it, members of the "public sphere" already speak a single, shared denotational code (French, for instance, or English). And within that code, they can more or less already understand one another. Habermas also emphasized face-to-face interaction, as opposed to the mass-mediated language more central to contemporary conceptions of public discourse (Gal and Woolard [2001] 2014).

Another, less often discussed problem with the notion of the "public sphere" derives from the way it has been used in studies of Soviet and post-Soviet media. In this field, critics of state socialist and postsocialist societies have deployed Habermas's focus on interclass conversation and diversity of opinions to argue that the "public sphere" never properly functioned in state socialist societies. This is a pillar of the argument that state socialist societies lacked, but desperately needed, civil society (e.g., Garnham 1992). In the post-Soviet period, this conviction has encouraged scholars on both sides of the Cold War's old curtains and walls to retrospectively interpret many cultural developments of the late Soviet period as incendiary, liberating attempts to build civil society. Cafes and literary circles, for example, have been analyzed as emergent forms of political protest on the basis of Habermas's conception of the public sphere—despite the fact that participants "explicitly distanced themselves from dissident discourses or political protests" (Yurchak 2006, 145, critiquing Zdravomyslova 1996). Media scholars have argued that Marxist-Leninist theories of state and media indeed oppose a radical democratic view of the public sphere—because, according to what James Curran calls "old-style marxism," "the liberal concept of the public sphere is a chimera, disguising the reality of bourgeois domination" (1991, 36; see also Splichal 1994).[1] Discursive space, in other words, will always be controlled by the dominant class, and to think otherwise is to have already accepted its terms. Mass media, in this case, cannot develop an organic, interclass conversation; they must rather be taken over by the proletariat and used for explicitly political ends, as a weapon to awaken the masses. According to this view, the "public sphere" widely discussed in Euro-American liberal theory and media studies was never a *goal* of Soviet media, so searching for it is anachronistic at best. At worst, it risks recapitulating dichotomies of the Cold War that are better treated as objects of analysis than as means.

Despite these limitations of the "public sphere," the concept of the *public* has great utility for analyzing the sense of "groupness" generated by mass media. A public, in my analysis, is a collection of people oriented, however temporarily, around a mutually perceived, shared social fact. In particular, the concept of the public as I employ it here foregrounds (1) processes of circulation; (2) evocation by someone to some particular purpose, such as political legitimation;

(3) self-awareness of participation; and (4) ephemerality. Publics share these four key points, examined in turn in the sections to follow.

Circulating a New Voice

First, publics are constituted by mediatized (Agha 2011) textual circulations. This immediately shifts focus from thinking of media as "arenas," "forums," or other kinds of demarcated spaces to thinking of them as conduits or channels of circulation. One of the most influential explorations of this idea has been Benedict Anderson's (1991) argument that the historical emergence of print capitalism enabled strangers to be interlinked into the "imagined community" of the nation. Novels, printed on a large scale in vernacular languages for popular audiences, enabled readers in locations distant from one another to realize that they spoke the same language, both literally and figuratively. In part this is a technological argument. As Friedrich Kittler (1999) has stressed, media technologies extend parts of the human body to grant a sense of *immediacy*, bringing something distant immediately to hand (see also Fisher 2016; Kunreuther 2014). But Anderson's argument is also about the subtle psychology of sharing and fellow-feeling that underlies ethnonational attachments. He suggests, for instance, that novelistic discourse encouraged readers to feel that they inhabited similar times and social worlds.

Linguistic anthropologists have similarly shown how language and speech communities are mediated by the circulation of discourse. Debra Spitulnik (1996), for instance, describes how people who listen to Radio Zambia reinforce their sense of community by sharing a bit of circulating discourse. On the radio, "Hello Kitwe?" is a way for the broadcaster to try to establish a connection with a correspondent, which is frequently interrupted. Listeners then use this as they go about their daily lives, such as to get someone's attention or suggest that a connection has been lost. Both addressees and onlookers laugh, showing that they too listen to Radio Zambia.

Notably, these accounts suggest that the ways textual circulations mediate communities, while potentially politically consequential, are neither state-driven nor planned. No one is intentionally steering (or even trying to steer) the process; communities are emerging organically. But this process is often intentional. In the 1920s, for example, Bolshevik activists attempted to force exactly the kind of fellow-feeling Anderson and Spitulnik describe, by creating a shared cache of new slogans, terms, and canonical literature for their fledgling society. Newspapers throughout the Soviet Union organized new cadres of "worker correspondents" and "village correspondents" who were supposed to forge a new "voice" between the ideological slogans of Bolshevism and their everyday vernaculars, infusing newspapers with proletarian authenticity and the "language of the people" (Gorham 2003, 126).

Tasked with forging and circulating this new voice, mass media institutions were central to Soviet modernity. They rationalized and delimited information flows, created a professional class of journalists and other media workers, and aligned systems of government, production, and communication. Encouraging literacy and developing a secular literary standard with a rational, standardized writing system were part and parcel of this modernization. In Buryatia in the 1920s and 1930s, Bolshevik activists argued over the standardization of Buryat and established "red yurts" to teach literacy. Newspapers depicted Buryats reading alongside productive industrial endeavors like driving tractors and running factories (figure 8), strongly implying that these were related components of building a Soviet future. Reading was visually linked to plowed fields, mechanized agriculture, industrial smokestacks, gender equality, and sedentism—all hallmarks of Soviet modernity at a time when most Buryats were seminomadic pastoralists who associated reading instead with Buddhist lamas.

Within the larger project of building Soviet institutions and circulating a new Soviet voice, *native-language* media served their own political functions. Bringing the titular minority languages of Russia's ethnic republics visibly into public life was another key project of the Soviet state, first as a means of

FIGURE 8. An artist imagines an ideal Soviet socialist future in Buriat-Mongolun ünén 67(354), September 24, 1929 (National Archives of the Republic of Buryatia).

indigenizing Bolshevism and performatively enacting the principle of national self-determination, and later as an (unevenly successful) way of placating ethno-national concerns while pursuing Russification. Throughout the Soviet period, native-language media were key modernizing tools, even as notions of the relationship between modernity, media, and the minority public changed.

In the prerevolutionary era, there had been some limited attempts to create Buryat-language newspapers and newspapers containing material (thought to be) relevant to local Buryat communities. From 1895 to 1897, Petr Badmaev, best known as a doctor of Tibetan Buddhist medicine to royalty in St. Petersburg and proponent of Russian expansion, ran a bilingual publication for the Russian-Mongolian border's burgeoning tea trade.[2] This publication was shut down by tsarist authorities in the Baikal region who feared it contained political criticism (Kim and Baldanov 1994). Although national activists' writings contain references to the desirability of founding a Buryat-language newspaper (e.g., Amagaev and Alamzhi-Mérgén 1910), minority-language newspapers were established only at the discretion of the imperial censor's office in St. Petersburg, which remained hostile to Buryat efforts. Thus native-language media were first institutionalized as such only in the early Soviet period.

There had been no efforts so thoroughgoing, so self-consciously institutional, or so squarely targeting a broader Buryat public as in the 1920s. It became a priority of the young Soviet state in this period to build cadres of newspaper workers fast and professionalize them into new ideals of Soviet journalism. This was not peculiar to the Buryat territories. But the project took on special importance in non-Russian territories like Buryatia, because professionalizing specifically *Buryat* journalists was also part of the broader movement of *korenizatsiia*, or "indigenization." Media development through *korenizatsiia* was a stunning example of some of the reasons a majority state might build media institutions for its ethnic minorities: to integrate them into the majority culture, to assimilate them into mainstream values, and, arguably, to preempt more radical media from arising on its own (Riggins 1992). Often analyzed as ethnic particularism (Slezkine 1996) or affirmative action (Martin 2001), *korenizatsiia* followed Leninist and early Stalinist nationality policy, which explicitly emphasized local language development, suppression of "Great Russian chauvinism," and the principle of national self-determination. As the state worked quickly to train new cadres in Soviet political ideology and basic journalism, they put special emphasis on those minority populations they believed were farthest along the Marxist-Leninist trajectory of sociocultural development and would become full-fledged nations, including the Buryats.

In the 1920s, "Buryatization" (*oburiachivanie*) of state apparatuses like the newspapers primarily aimed to incorporate ethnic Buryats into the workforce.

The Ministry of Culture aggressively recruited young Buryats, especially women, to work alongside the ethnic Russians and Jews who had been running Buryatia's newspapers and to attend meetings, ideological training sessions, and professionalization seminars in distant Moscow.[3] *Korenizatsiia* effectively changed the face of Buryat-language journalism by shifting emphasis for qualification from linguistic ability in Buryat, which had previously been fulfilled by Russian and Jewish writers as well as Buryat, to ethnic and gender identity.[4] It also made ensuring local, ethnic representation in media institutions a fundamental responsibility of the state, which would have repercussions long after the Soviet state disappeared.

Over time, the state's goals in producing native-language media significantly changed. Initially, revolutionaries' main goals were to inform residents of the Bolshevik revolution (news of which was slow to reach the Buryat territories) and enlist them into collectives, workers' unions, and communal apartments, which was necessarily done in Buryat to reach a predominantly Buryat-monolingual population. By stages, however, the state's goals in producing Buryat-language media morphed into consolidating Buryats speaking a variety of dialects around a common language, building cadres of native Soviet journalists, performing support for an ethnic minority, and incorporating the minority language public into a broader *Soviet* public whose lingua franca was Russian.[5] By the time the Soviet Union broke up, distributing referential content was not the main purpose of Buryat-language media.

In part, the change in goals reflected language shift—which is to say that the goals of producing native-language mass media changed because such media were so successful at incorporating non-Russian peoples into the Soviet enterprise. As more of the population in the Buryat territories has become bilingual or monolingual in Russian, the percentage of people getting their information from Buryat-language media has necessarily shrunk relative to the percentage getting their information from Russian-language media, and the composition of the Buryat-language media audience has profoundly changed. As language shift in the Buryat territories has progressed, media in Buryat have taken on an increasingly symbolic (rather than informational or referential) social role, with content becoming more culturally circumscribed. Over the past century, the primary purpose of producing minority-language media has evolved from integrating non-Russian-speaking minority populations into the state to preserving those very aspects of ethnonational distinctiveness—language, performing arts, traditional kinship, religion—that were obscured by integration.

Native-language media have thus become a special site of social action in Asian Russia, albeit not for the same reasons as elsewhere. Mass media are often seen as a modernizing force because they provide a way to exercise one's "voice," usually conceived of as an expression of an individual citizen's discrete, coherent self in a democratic public forum. But how particular media come to embody "voice" is historically contingent. Laura Kunreuther (2014), for example, has shown how radio in postdemocratic Nepal became the site in which individuals could perform their new citizenship. Soviet media similarly forged new ways for readers, viewers, listeners, and interviewees to perform Soviet citizenship—not as individual actors within democracy but as active participants in Soviet projects of modernization. Some aspects of that use and engagement with Soviet media—such as using it to perform support for a Buryat minority public, to visually and audibly represent a commitment to the Friendship of the Peoples, or to demonstrate one's own participation in that public—remain central to native-language media today. But whereas native-language media once performed a primarily referential-informational function, the social significance of Buryat-language media today lies in its ability to symbolize the continuing relevance of a Buryat public.

Symbols of Support

The shifting goals and functions of Buryat media illustrate a second key point about publics: they are forms of political legitimation (Gal and Woolard [2001] 2014). The notion of "publics" can be more useful than "communities" in analyzing the role of media in ethnonational politics, because it focuses our attention on how the feeling of groupness is evoked *by someone* and *to some particular purpose*. Some of the main goals of Buryat media makers, for instance, have been to legitimate the Buryat nation by publicly displaying standardized, Buryat-language text and recruiting new members of the Buryat-speaking public. Attending to publics, rather than or in addition to language and speech communities, allows us as analysts to capture this calling-forth aspect of media technologies. A media technology performs what Brian Larkin (2008, 43) has called a "double function:" it functions technically, yes, but it also has an "ideological mode of address," by which it recruits or calls forth individuals as particular kinds of subjects (see also Cody 2013).

Current language legislation is underpinned by an assumption that the simple act of putting Buryat print and speech into view will call forth Buryat subjects who belong comfortably to both a culturally defined Buryatia and a geopolitically defined Russia. With the enduring importance of the Friendship of the Peoples, the ideal—if not the practice—of providing equal footing to Russian and Buryat language publics is deeply engrained within Buryat cultural politics, and this is one of the main motivations behind continuing to support native-language media in the post-Soviet era. In principle, Buryat is granted extensive support within the republic by the constitution, which guarantees all peoples of the republic "the right to preservation of [their] native language [and] creation of the conditions for its study and development,"[6] and by provisions in the law "On the Languages of the Peoples of the Republic of Buryatia," enacted in 1992, and its federal analogue from 1991, "On the Languages of the Peoples of the Russian Federation."[7] According to the 1992 law, all official documents, street names and other place names, and package labels of products manufactured in Buryatia are supposed to appear in Buryat as well as Russian.

Signage, a type of "small media," is one of the main ways that an average resident of Buryatia sees Buryat on a regular basis. Buryat has a limited but symbolically significant presence on the bilingual signs of government buildings in Ulan-Ude, such as the city administration's cultural division, the central city library, and the Buryat State Children's Library (figures 9a and 9b). The portions translated into Buryat are nearly always limited to the buildings' names; other information, such as hours and event announcements, are generally in Russian, making it the "matrix language" of these scenes. In Buryat-dominant villages, schools, religious buildings, and Houses of Culture are often labeled only in

FIGURE 9A.   Ulan-Ude's Kalashnikov Central City Library displays bilingual signs in Russian and Buryat. (Photo by author, 2009.)

FIGURE 9B.   The Abiduev Children's Library in Ulan-Ude displays a bilingual sign in Russian and Buryat. (Photo by author, 2009.)

Buryat (e.g., <u>soëloi baishan</u>), and occasionally villages erect their own highway signs in Buryat, although official street and highway signs are only in Russian. Buryat enjoys much less exposure on bilingual signage than, say, Irish in the Republic of Ireland, but it is at least visible in these limited ways.

Similarly, government websites do have some content in Buryat (as well as English), and official announcements are made in Buryat as well as Russian. Indeed, one of the major functions of the state-funded Buryat-language newspaper is to provide a forum in which the government can publish such announcements. Despite these efforts, however, the language laws have not been fulfilled; Buryat does not function fully in the spheres of government, manufacturing, service, and trade (see also Dyrkheeva 2002).[8]

Buryat-language mass media thus remain the most visible symbol of state support for Buryat today. Perhaps that visibility is why newspapers and radio and television broadcasting in Buryat have continued to be supported while other parts of the language law have been ignored. The legislation has proved especially important for protecting Buryat-language news media, embedded as it is primarily in state media institutions. While nation-building efforts elsewhere in the world have focused on entertainment genres of media, such as television serials in Egypt (Abu-Lughod 2004) or soap operas in Kazakhstan (Mandel 2002), the main media of Buryat national development have been news. Without strong ideological investment in this domain of media production, news media would almost certainly have lost out by now to the inefficiency argument: Why produce information in two languages for a bilingual audience who could understand it as well or better in Russian? There is some evidence that native-language programming, despite appearing redundant, is able to *create* demand rather than simply respond to it. Commercial efforts to produce Buryat-language media suggest that there is enough of an audience to make it financially viable—even perhaps labor-intensive news programming. For several years Arig Us, a privately managed television channel, has produced a popular Buryat-language cultural program called Müngén sérgé (Silver hitching post). At least one foreign evangelical Christian organization, the Far East Broadcasting Company, has attempted to found a Buryat-language radio station.[9] During my research Tivikom, a popular private television company in Ulan-Ude, tried to establish a Buryat-language news program. According to interviewees, Tivikom went so far as to audition anchors and recruit seasoned Buryat-language journalists before the project folded for reasons that remained unclear. The difficulty apparently faced in getting these interesting new projects off the ground is a reminder of how remarkable Buryatia's many long-running mass media are—not only in beginning at all but also in surviving the many political and economic upheavals that have occurred in Buryatia and in Russia at large. These media institutions give the impression of rare continuity over time, even while their relationships to their reading, listening, and viewing publics have changed.

Metapragmatic Work

By examining media institutions not as monolithic units but as peopled collectivities, embedded in social networks, we can explore a third characteristic of publics: publics are self-aware. They are constituted through mutual perception, consciousness, or, as Michael Warner (2002) has argued, *attention*. Just as Habermas underscored the importance of the members of the public's mutual awareness of participation, Warner observes that "the notion of a public enables a reflexivity in the circulation of texts among strangers who become, by virtue of their reflexively circulating discourse, a social entity" (Warner 2002, 11–12).[10] In other words, it is not only that there are shared communicative practices, as in language and speech communities, but further, that there is some shared attention to the fact of sharing them.[11] We can see this self-awareness in Spitulnik's example, when audiences of Radio Zambia say "Hello Kitwe?" to one another.

The speaker, addressees, and onlookers in such an interaction already share a bit of circulating discourse, as well as knowledge of its origin and its pragmatic uses. Through their interaction using that bit of shared culture, they become aware that they have it in common.

Given this reflexive and self-fulfilling nature of publics as co-imagined and co-constructed social entities, it can be difficult to operationalize publics without conflating them with readers, listeners, viewers, or audiences. How does one identify reflexivity or self-awareness from afar? Warner (2002, 12) underscores the impossibility of ever making the "metapragmatic work" of the daily making and remaking of publics fully explicit. Yet ethnography does allow us to see how people conceive of themselves. And the linguistic projects of states, from censuses to standardization efforts to literacy campaigns, routinely include a great deal of metalinguistic commentary and judgments as to the composition and nature of an existing or ideal public. How linguists, pedagogues, political theorists, and "average" people alike imagine the publics that they are creating and to which they belong can be excavated from discourses about mass media, particularly those about minority-language and multilingual media.

Consider, for instance, how people in Buryatia treat Buriaad ünén. Among the twenty-nine republic-level newspapers available for subscription in the Republic of Buryatia in 2009, Buriaad ünén was the central Buryat-language daily and the most important newspaper "for families that haven't yet forgotten the Buryat language," as one of my focus group participants put it. Buriaad ünén's circulation rate had been growing in the years leading up to my research, from 23,000 in 1999 to 30,100 in 2008, even while other newspapers' circulation rates dropped and Buryat language use overall declined.[12] This is probably because some people report subscribing to Buriaad ünén even though they cannot read it, as a sign of supporting the Buryat public it has come to represent.

Moreover, journalists and their audiences talk to each other; elites are not just producing for silent audiences, but engaging in a constant debate over what "counts" as Buryat and what should be represented in print or on air. Media institutions like BGTRK and Buriaad Ünén are intertwined with a number of other institutional sites of metapragmatic work. This is both a product of educational, media, scientific, and governmental institutions' mutual integration in the Soviet period and a more general effect of the way language ideologies move through networks of elites. Definitions of what counts as "a" minority language or of good, proper, or worthwhile minority language use often owe much to those brokers—nationalists, politicians, writers, editors, language activists, and so on—who move knowledge and ideas from scientific journals into the domain of mass consumption. They decide, for example, what counts as the proper form of Mayan to be revitalized (French 2003) or what forms of Spanish-Aymara mixing (if any) are acceptable on the radio (Swinehart 2012).[13] In her study of Corsican language politics, Alexandra Jaffe (1999) found that some of the most influential brokers of this type were well-educated language pedagogues trained in classroom teaching, which is true in the Buryat case as well. Among the most influential sites of language work in Buryatia are the Buryat Scientific Center (BNTs), located within the Siberian branch of the Russian Academy of Sciences (SO RAN), and the National Humanities Institute (NGI), housed within Buryat State University. BNTs trains graduate students and supports dedicated researchers, among them many sociolinguists, folklorists, lexicographers, and literature specialists who direct the course of Buryat linguistics. NGI trains undergraduate and graduate students in linguistics, language pedagogy, journalism, and Buryat culture, folklore, and literature; its faculty also engages actively in linguistic research and hosts academic conferences.

Scholars in these institutions, along with those in linguistics programs at other local universities, reflexively circulate ideas about the boundaries of Buryat, about what of the language should be preserved, and about who is sufficiently expert to decide. While they have been integral to the development of Buryat descriptive linguistics, their importance lies not only in their *descriptive* but also in their *prescriptive* role, as they invest students with the (institutionally approved) linguistic expertise necessary to take up language and culture work in the wider Buryat language public. NGI and its predecessor in Irkutsk in particular have trained many of Buryatia's current native-language journalists, and NGI will no doubt be the main source for new native-language journalists in the years to come. Other important institutional sites of metapragmatic work include the republic's Ministry of Education, which produces pedagogical materials including books, posters, and innovative interactive CDs; the Buryat national boarding school (*internat*) in Ulan-Ude, which is supposed to provide full Buryat-language immersion; and the National Library of the Republic of Buryatia, which frequently hosts native-language events involving poets, symposia, and memorial services, in addition to Russian-language events like chess championships. Buryat language education and Buryat-medium education within primary schools have long been the target of public debate and angst, and several sociolinguistic studies have detailed the problems of language maintenance in this sphere (e.g., Bazheeva 2002; Dareeva 2007; Dyrkheeva 2002).

Buryatia's native-language media institutions are intimately connected to these other sites of metapragmatic work, both in terms of extended social networks and in how journalists circulate, physically, between their offices and diffused places of daily reportage. To take just one historical example, Buryat-language broadcasting for children in the 1970s depended heavily—almost exclusively—on interviews with children at the Buryat national boarding school, which offered a rare immersion environment (NARB f. 914, op. 1, d. 22, p. 6). When change is felt in one such institution, it thus directly affects other interlinked institutions and loci of language preservation and development, heightening the sense that a larger Buryat-speaking community is changing en masse.

Overlapping Scales

The sense of stability that Buryatia's interlinked language institutions provide is illusory, in that all publics are transitory. This fourth key point about publics is a product of the first: if publics are constituted by textual circulations, they cannot outlive the stories, songs, news reports, jokes, and so on that evoke them, even if the social facts at their centers endure. By the same token, new publics constantly emerge, not necessarily to the exclusion of existing ones. Any individual may belong to multiple, overlapping publics that come and go as the social facts at their centers become more or less salient.

This can be seen in the way that people encounter media of overlapping scales in their daily lives. Mass media are always scaled by virtue of circulating within particular geographic territories and targeting particular audiences. In commercial media development, these scales are discussed in terms of "markets"—that is, the total population who might reasonably be expected to actively consume or at least passively be exposed to your magazine or radio broadcast. Buryat-language media are consumed within multiple media markets, from the immediate city market within which advertisements for Ulan-Ude's businesses are distributed to an international market of dubbed films and pirated music. Buryatia's position along Russia's southern border grants access to some transnational Asian media. World-band and satellite radios pick up stations from Mongolia and China, and cable packages in Ulan-Ude include CCTV, the national television network of neighboring China, which broadcasts news and cultural programming from Inner Mongolia. At newspaper kiosks and kitchen tables, people read major Russian publications produced at the federal or what is called in Russia the "central" (*tsentral'naia*) level, such as *Argumenty i fakty* (Arguments and facts), *Izvestiia* (News), and *Rossiiskaia gazeta*. They watch federal-level programming on Channel One and Rossiia, which together produce the overwhelming majority of the situational comedies, historical dramas, and national news that people consume and discuss on a daily basis. These two channels' main news programs are broadcast in the evenings as *Vremia* (Time) and *VESTI* (NEWS)—by far the most watched and most influential news programs in the Russian Federation.[14]

Most of the more locally relevant news and content is produced for the regional markets of republics, krais, and oblasts (Russian administrative units roughly equivalent to states or provinces). A few federal newspapers run local versions, much like the Russian versions of *Cosmopolitan* and *Vogue*. The popular weekly *MK v Buriatii* (*Moskovskii komsomolets* in Buryatia), known for its back-page soft pornography (labeled "sex-shop" very classily in two scripts, as "SEX-ШОП"), is printed in Irkutsk for distribution in Buryatia. Most regional media, however, is produced locally. The regional television affiliates of national networks produce their own local news programs, such as *VESTI-Buriatiia* (NEWS-Buryatia) and *VESTI-Sibir'* (NEWS-Siberia), covering west and east Siberian cities like Novosibirsk, Omsk, Irkutsk, and occasionally Ulan-Ude.[15] Republic-, oblast-, and krai-level affiliates send in candidate materials for these intermediate-level shows. In Buryatia, *VESTI-Sibir'* runs only during the day, not during the prime news hour, but it serves to keep residents of Buryatia informed about and connected to cities that might otherwise seem quite distant. In this way, national news programming draws on and reproduces a Siberian regional identity.

Finally, there are mass media for districts (R. *raion*, B. <u>aimag</u>), cities, and villages. Newspapers are more common local media in Russia than radio and television, largely because print media are easier, faster, and cheaper to produce on a small scale—though commercial television stations like Ulan-Ude's popular Arig Us also produce substantial advertising and content that is relevant and meaningful only to residents of Ulan-Ude. District-level newspapers and city and village newspapers embody localism. It is fully possible for a well-connected resident of Buryatia's mountainous southwestern district of Akha, for example, to open the eponymous newspaper and recognize every single person pictured and quoted within. (The young woman who demonstrated this for me expressed surprise when I expressed surprise.) And at the smallest, most local scale, some institutions have continued the Soviet tradition of having amateur newspapers—and sometimes radio and television—within factories, collective farms, universities, and schools. In their scale, hyperlocal media like this are akin to personal networks on social media, or to the "small media" of signage and personal letters, but they often mimic the structures and standards of larger media institutions.

The political alignment of the Buryat territories is reflected in the structure of some of its central media institutions. Three regional television affiliates, including the State Television and Radio Broadcasting Companies Buryatia (BGTRK), Chita (ChGTRK), and Irkutsk (IGTRK), are ultimately part of the powerful, overarching federal State Television and Radio Broadcasting Company (GTRK), which broadcasts on the dominant Channel One. A small affiliate of ChGTRK in Aginskoe broadcasts local programming for Aga. Here the media structure mirrors the administrative reality that the former okrug is nested within Zabaikal'skii Krai, which is in turn nested within Russia—all in a vertical alignment, with no lateral relationship to the Republic of Buryatia or Ust'-Orda. By the same token, the Republic of Buryatia demonstrates its subjectivity and semiautonomy within Russia by having a semi-independent media system and reporting straight to Moscow.

Native-language publishing and broadcasting are undertaken mainly at the levels of the republic and district, making them a subset of regional media. State news organizations and some private media companies provide publications, broadcasts, and limited web services in Buryat. Buriaad ünén and Tolon (Ray of light) are the most substantial Buryat-language news publications currently being produced. Buriaad ünén traces its origins to an early Bolshevik newspaper, Shéné baidal (A new life), founded in December 1921 in Chita for Buryats of the short-lived Far Eastern Republic. Soon after, it became the flagship Buryat-language newspaper of what was then called the Buryat-Mongolian Autonomous Soviet Socialist Republic (BMASSR) and has survived, against the odds, to the present day, with remarkable institutional consistency. Currently, it is printed onsite in Ulan-Ude by the Republic of Buryatia's state publishing house, also called Buriaad Ünén, which also publishes cultural journals, books, pedagogical materials, and various newspaper inserts and supplements covering special topics such as business and sports—not all in Buryat, but with Buryat language and culture as their focus. The press and this paper are state-run and state-funded, and the newspaper serves as an organ of the government, not a particular party as was the case in the Soviet era.[16] Tolon, a large-format weekly based in Aginskoe, is a postperestroika endeavor to link the otherwise disconnected Buryat territories of the Republic of Buryatia, Aga, and Ust'-Orda by means of an "all-Buryat" newspaper (Graber 2016). In radio and television, the three stations running the bulk of Buryat-language news and cultural programming are BGTRK, ChG-TRK's Aga affiliate, and Arig Us.[17]

How much Buryat-language media does all of this add up to? Among the media circulating within the Republic of Buryatia during the period covered in this book, Buriaad ünén, Tolon, and several district newspapers were printed in part or in full in Buryat; VESTI-Buriatiia aired Buryat-language news daily on television and radio broadcasts (about twenty minutes each, repeated two or three times per day); and weekly cultural programs on television and radio (on BGTRK television, BGTRK radio, and Arig Us) amounted to another two to three hours of Buryat-language programming per week. Several websites hosted Buryat-language articles, music, and chat threads, but because these were largely noninstitutional activist projects, online content was diffuse and sporadically updated. By contrast, in the 1950s, both of the republic's major newspapers, *Buriat-Mongol'skii komsomolets* for teens (the Komsomol being the youth division of the All-Union Communist Party) and Buriaad ünén's predecessor *Buriat-Mongol'skaia pravda* for adults, ran duplicated (*dublirovannye*) versions in Russian and Buryat every day. At the time of my field research, there had never been a radio or television station dedicated solely to Buryat-language material. Some journalists thought, however, that they had come close to launching a Buryat-language television station in the heady days of Buryat nationalism in the late 1980s and early 1990s, and activists and journalists persisted in trying to establish a radio station. This resulted in Buriaad FM.

Despite their limitations, these media play a central symbolic role in Buryat belonging. Linguistic choices often presuppose one scale of belonging or another, and this is nowhere clearer than in the simple act of buying a Russian- or Buryat-language newspaper at one of Ulan-Ude's ubiquitous kiosks. Just as using native Russian is a primary way of indexing one's citizenship within the Russian Federation, using Buryat, consuming Buryat-language media, and producing material in Buryat or supporting its production are main ways of indexing membership in a minority language public, as well as stewardship of that public's future. Moreover, within the newspaper's pages, readers and writers work out indexical connections between language use and a speaker's background, commitments, and social position. Readers have their pictures taken, give interviews, and write letters to the editor. In all of these ways, minority-language media provide a very public forum for demonstrating participation within a minority language public.

Media and the Minority Language Public

These four key points of publics—that they are constituted by mediatized textual circulations, politically legitimating, self-aware, transitory and scaled—make them a powerful analytical tool for examining the role of mass media in minority politics. In a minority language public, too, members are reflexively aware of belonging to that public.[18] They are temporarily called on to attend to what they have in common—namely, the minority language—which may or may not correspond to an understanding of perduring nationhood. These points in particular distinguish a minority language public from an ethno-linguo-national group and explain why the public is not necessarily coterminous with the ethnonation; while you need not identify yourself as Buryat to be identified by others as Buryat, you must actively participate in the Buryat language public to belong to it, even if only by turning on your television. At the same time, you are being actively recruited, not only as the member of a "community" but as a particular kind of subject, for a project of political legitimation.

What kind of publics are evoked, created, and sustained through media that is specifically "minority"? The concept of minority media implies that there is some kind of majority or mainstream media to which it is opposed, or to which it runs parallel. Minority-*language* media thus efficiently evoke what Warner calls "counterpublics," "parallel publics," and "subpublics." After all, why produce information in two languages for a bilingual audience who could understand it as well or better in the majority language? If media production were exclusively a matter of information transfer, producing Buryat-language media would make no sense. But this misses the point. In multilingual contexts, discourses about media routinely involve debate over how material resources are allocated to media in different languages, and by extension to their various publics (e.g., Spitulnik 1998). Few practices make more explicit the relative valuation of different codes in the local linguistic "marketplace" (Bourdieu [1982] 1991), within which the very concept of a "minority language" or "linguistic minority" likewise implies exclusion from a dominant mainstream national language (Heller 2007).[19] Minority-language media perform an important symbolic function even for individuals who do not control the language but who nonetheless identify with it and feel represented by it, and who care passionately about its existence.

Minority-language media produce locality by presupposing a public that is circumscribed within a larger society—the mainstream public to which majority-language media are oriented. Usually this scalar production is reflected in content. Picking up a Hindi-language newspaper on Devon Avenue in Chicago, you may reasonably expect to find something other than a simple translation of *USA Today*. When you pick up a copy of <u>Buriaad ünén</u>, the Buryat-language masthead similarly indicates that you may expect to find local television listings; advertisements for local home internet service, beef, and potatoes; and schedules of services at Buddhist datsans and shamanic rituals, but not necessarily trenchant analysis of world events.

Form and content are not, however, always consonant in this respect. During the Soviet period, *dublirovannye* publications in Buryat reproduced Russian-language content, including coverage of Soviet politics and international events. Initially this was done to reach Buryat-speaking audiences who did not yet know Russian, but as audiences grew more bilingual, presenting Union-scale news in Buryat continued to demonstrate Soviet authorities' commitment to making Sovietness a Buryat phenomenon—or, perhaps more to the point, to making Buryatness a *Soviet* phenomenon (Graber 2012). In this sense Buryat media—like the media of other titular minorities including Tatars, Yakuts, and Georgians—echoed early Bolshevik calls to make cultural production "national in form, socialist in content" and was part of the Soviet project that Francine Hirsch (2005) has called "double assimilation": to assimilate non-Russian peoples into both a nation and a multinational, pan-Soviet society.

Although the Soviet practice of directly duplicating media in *dublirovannye* publications has mostly ended, most of the media produced in titular minority languages parallel media in Russian. A state radio station like BGTRK, for example, will have a Russian-language division and a native-language division that may share material and stories. To save time and resources, a single television crew will go out to record the same story on a given morning in Ulan-Ude, sharing material and ideas, although not usually interviewees. Buryat-language media are rarely exclusively in Buryat, instead combining a Buryat-language frame and Buryat-language material with words, phrases, and sometimes whole stories from Russian. This mixed format is true even of the Buryat-framed publications from Buryatia's flagship native-language media institution, Buriaad Ünén. Moreover, the workplaces within which Buryat-language media are produced and the homes, streets, and other environments in which they are consumed are also largely Russian-speaking. In these respects, Buryat-language media are always already Russian-language as well.

These assimilatory aspects of Soviet and Russian minority media caution against seeing "indigenous media" as naturally oppositional or empowering. Scholarly work on ethnic minority and minority-language media, largely based on West European and Anglophone-majority cases, has tended to focus on such media's potential to politically and culturally empower the minority communities producing them. It has also focused on ways to overcome or at least mitigate the possibility that minority media will unwittingly reproduce power structures and assimilate audiences into mainstream values (e.g., Browne 1996; Ginsburg 1995; Riggins 1992). How can indigenous media be kept indigenous? How can the public evoked by minority media remain distinct? But these have not been goals of Buryat media. Native-language media and the institutions that produce them have been developed in Siberia not within the discourses of indigenous sovereignty or empowerment that we find elsewhere in the world but, rather, as part of the multinational state at the federation's scale and as part of multiculturalism at the regional scale. Both in Russian and in Buryat, the overwhelming majority of post-Soviet Buryat media has been produced either directly by the state or with state funding, and it has represented Buryat national politics in almost exclusively nonsubversive ways (Dagbaev 1995, 1999, 2004; see also Peers 2009). Indeed, native-language media encapsulate how Buryat cultural leaders in the post-Soviet era continue to pursue symbolic ethnonational visibility and native autonomy—to the extent possible—within the multicultural Friendship of the Peoples and existing political-discursive frameworks.

Assimilation by media was successful in the sense that at present, Buryat-language media support a minority language public that is a subpublic of Russian society. To the extent that some Buryats, like Badma, do not feel completely *rossiiskii*, however, the minority language public also holds the possibility of alternative belonging. Although the process of institutionalizing linguistic and cultural practices through native-language media has not led to the maintenance of a distinctive language and culture, it affords what resources there are for linguistic and cultural revitalization. Modernization over the twentieth century is now felt as a series of unnatural ruptures in what people take to be the naturally unfolding, organic process of sociocultural evolution (an assumption that is itself a legacy of Soviet social science). Likewise, the Buryat "nation," defined in the Soviet style, appears to many people today to have been artificially fractured and separated from its Mongolian kin or from Asia at large. Some people place the moment of disjuncture even earlier, at the moment of Russian contact, and speak offhandedly about a moment of Buryat self-determination that was simply "in the past" (*v proshlom*). These senses of rupture, and the search for their antidotes among the scraps of Siberia's half-completed modernizing projects, are the subject of the next chapter.

RUPTURE AND RECLAMATION

In 2006, when Larisa was twenty-two years old, she had a major epiphany. She realized that she had been living "incorrectly," which she explained to me a couple of years later in both psycho-spiritual and ethnolinguistic terms. She had been "living, speaking, and thinking like an (ethnically) Russian girl [*russkaia devushka*]," she said, as opposed to a member of her "own" Siberian ethnicity. Wishing to rectify this, she began visiting Buddhist lamas and shamans for advice, asked a lama for a traditional Buryat name to replace the Russian "Larisa" that her parents had given her, and set about learning her family's genealogy. She dragged out her family's heavy, burgundy-bound hardback dictionary of Buryat, which she claimed she had never before touched or seen anyone else open. And as Yanzhima, her new name, she used her breaks from work at a clothing shop selling Polish and French fashions to begin studying Buryat. At the time, she said, there were no organized classes for adult learners of Buryat, and most of her elderly, Buryat-language-dominant relatives had passed away. She struggled through newspaper articles with the aid of her dictionary and tried to make small talk with Buddhist lamas at the datsan. Her greatest hope was to be able to raise her own children to speak Buryat.

Over the past fifteen years, I have met many people like Larisa/Yanzhima, who feel either ashamed that they have lost touch with their Buryat roots or angry that they have been cheated out of that possibility by parents who did not teach them Buryat words and traditions. She was somewhat unusual in the zeal with which she pursued her reidentification as "Buryat," but she was entirely typical in expressing a longing for a kind of cultural reclamation. She was typical, too, in stressing that she was not learning Buryat as a new or foreign language. Rather, she was reclaiming her "own" (*svoi*) language. While Larisa/Yanzhima had not grown up speaking any Buryat and had never had any active control of the language, she identified it as her "native language." She is one of the many people in post-Soviet Russia who identify their native (*rodnoi*) language as their heritage or ancestral language, based on their cultural or ethnic identity, without claiming active or even passive knowledge of the language's grammar or lexicon. Larisa/Yanzhima is a poignant reminder that a person may care deeply about a language that she does not herself speak. In this respect, she has something in common with the members of diasporic populations who fund Irish and Armenian language immersion programs, or with American Jews who seek to "re"learn Hebrew later in life (Avineri 2019). She sees Buryat as her heritage, a semipropertized thing that has been lost and may be reclaimed.[1]

It is in this context of heritage ownership that language shift from Buryat to Russian feels, to the many people like Larisa/Yanzhima, like a rupture that needs to be healed. Racially and by family history, she belongs to the Buryat ethnonation, in the sense that both she and the people around her identify her as "Buryat." But she does not feel that this belonging is complete so long as she is not also part of the Buryat minority language public. Her dilemma is common in contexts of language shift, in which a community is moving from using mostly one language to mostly another. Language shift is often experienced as a matter of imposition, when the speakers of the new language B are so powerful, or speaking their language offers such enticing financial, political, or other material benefits, that speakers of A are all but forced to abandon A in favor of B. Indeed, Larisa/Yanzhima feels that Russian was imposed on her ancestors, and she blames unnamed Russians of the past for a kind of cultural imperialism—as well as her own family members for giving into it. Other people, however, see her loss not as anyone's fault per se, but as the inevitable result of tectonic economic, political, and sociocultural changes well beyond an individual's agency. What they have in common is a mode of explaining contemporary social divisions in terms of the past, by referring to generation gaps, "breaks" of various sorts, and times "before" and "after" upheavals in Russia's tumultuous history.

This chapter examines how a series of temporal and spatiocultural disjunctures over the course of the twentieth and twenty-first centuries have overdetermined language shift in the Buryat territories, even while the percentage of the population that is ethnically Buryat has been slowly growing. Language shift destabilizes existing notions of what it means to be a "real Buryat" and complicates efforts to reclaim that identification. Larisa, for instance, had a strong sense of a form of belonging that had been disrupted and that she wanted to reclaim as Yanzhima, but without the tools necessary to do it. She delimits the Buryat "culture" that she seeks to reclaim as historically antecedent to the perceived moment of rupture and invests it in a small group of authoritative cultural elites: lamas, professors, lexicographers, and television news anchors. But are these the only arbiters of "real Buryat"? Efforts to reclaim Buryat origins and revitalize one's personal relationships, particularly through language revitalization, must grapple with competing sources of authority and alternative visions of the future—and of the past. The last part of the chapter examines the varied, often contradictory ways that people pursue reclamation of Buryat belonging, from visiting shamans to watching Chinese television to emphasizing the sounds that Buryat has in common with English.

Temporal Disjunctures

The most common way in which contemporary Buryats express a sense of rupture is with reference to clearly delineated periods in Buryat history: before and after the Bolshevik revolution of 1917 (experienced in the 1920s in Buryatia), before and after World War II (1941–45), before and after the rapid urbanization and industrialization of the 1960s, and before and after the dissolution of the Soviet Union in 1991. Soviet modernization in Siberia was supposed to bring about a radical break (*perelom*) with the past, and the same word—*perelom*—is used to describe these "breaks" of other sorts. When men and women narrate their lives today, they refer particularly to times before and after the Soviet collapse (*raspad*, lit. break-up or disintegration).

The collapse of the Soviet Union in the early 1990s ushered in a period of extreme confusion and a total breakdown in most social services. While all Russians suffered, the disastrous effects of the *raspad* were arguably more pronounced in the poorer republics and native communities of Asian Russia, which are largely rural. When Soviet support systems were dismantled, villagers who had already been living close to the bone were suddenly isolated, and living standards fell as rates of alcoholism and violent death increased (Bogoyavlensky 1997; Ulturgasheva 2012; Vitebsky 2005).[2] In rural areas of Buryatia, especially along the borders of administrative districts from which the state has largely withdrawn, people live what Caroline Humphrey (2015, 2) has called a "literally de-modernised life."

These massive sociocultural transformations have created an acute sense that there is a significant ideological difference between generations. In the living memory of contemporary Buryats, there are two "generation gaps" that inform the way people view one another and themselves. One prominent gap emerged from a period of rapid industrialization and urbanization in the 1960s, when young Buryat workers moved into cities in droves and mingled with new "internal immigrants" from other parts of the Soviet Union, its satellite states, and western Russia (Chakars 2014). This gap falls between people who are currently older pensioners and their children, who are currently in their forties and fifties. The former are more likely to have been raised in rural areas and more likely to be fluent in Buryat, while their children (and grandchildren) are more likely to have been raised in Russian-dominant schools and with the expectation that Russian would be their primary language. A second major gap falls between people who came of age before and after the *raspad*. Young people with no particular attachment to Soviet-era institutions, television stars, or possibilities to travel in satellite states like Yugoslavia are more likely to seek cosmopolitan futures of a different sort. As a group, they identify much more readily with claims to indigeneity and are much more interested in reclaiming Buryat "roots." In both cases, however, parents and senior workers feel disconnected from their juniors, the possibilities of whose very existence differ radically from those of their parents.

As the 2000s unfold and the children of the early 1990s become adults, the generation gap between Russians who lived through the late Soviet period and those who did not is increasingly entering workplaces and affecting social relations. In 2009, I observed a group of journalists in their late thirties and forties as they edited text in their newsroom, a large collection of computer workstations facing one another, and chatted. Somehow the conversation turned to the nephew of a journalist who had innocently asked who Lenin was, after hearing the unknown word. "These kids don't know anything," one woman said absentmindedly, shaking her head and flipping over her notebook to continue typing up her report. "Well yeah, they eat 'SSSR' ice cream and don't know where the hell that name comes from," another reporter said with a smirk. (SSSR is the Russian-language version of the English USSR.) He referred to a brand of ice cream bar that drew on Soviet kitsch and was very popular in local stores and kiosks, for reasons similar to resurgent Soviet brands elsewhere (see Klumbytè 2010). "They know the SSSR only as an ice-cream brand." A couple of people chuckled dryly. In the room were a number of younger workers in their twenties, who were usually among the most talkative but stayed mute during this conversation. Later I asked one of these younger women, Marina, what she remembered about the Soviet period. Marina had memories of physical things, such as her desire to wear the red tie of a Young Pioneers uniform like her older sister, but she felt no ideological connection. She had just liked the color red, she said, and the tie was pretty. Marina noted that her parents had prospered under socialism and missed it—"like a kind of nostalgia [*nostal'giia*]"—but that she felt "liberated" (*svobodnaia*) to think outside the box. Echoing a division that I had heard invoked frequently by journalists in St. Petersburg in 2001, she drew a sharp contrast between herself and workers "of the old system [*sistema*]," including most (but not all) of her senior colleagues.

People often feel and show these temporal disjunctures and generation gaps through language use. Some of this is lexical. Words that had salience during the Soviet period, for instance, do not carry the same weight with a new generation. The semantic weakening and shift of "SSSR" is an extreme example of this. But the gaps often become salient to people through language choice as well—that is, the choice to use one language or code rather than another. Children who came of age in the industrializing, urbanizing 1960s were more likely to use Russian in their daily work lives than Buryat, and they had less reason to teach Buryat to their children.

Generation gaps are also clear in the way people narrate how the twentieth century's modernizing projects brought about temporal disjunctures between the present and a mythic past. When Yanzhima imagines the Buryatness that she hopes to reclaim, she speaks of her great-great-grandparents, whom she knows from a single black-and-white photograph. In the photograph, a young couple stands in front of a wooden yurt, or gèr,[3] the woman wearing some of the elaborate silver jewelry typical of the time, studded with semiprecious gemstones like coral and turquoise—very "ethnic" (*ètnicheskii*), Yanzhima points out to me with a tone of wonder. They both wear Buryat degels, thick robes buttoned on the side and cinched at the waist with a belt, and from the man's belt hangs a large knife sheath. He also wears a fedora. They stare seriously straight into the camera, their brows slightly furrowed. The portrait appears to have been posed in the 1910s or 1920s, perhaps for a visiting ethnographer, but the photographer is unknown and the photo is undated. It is notable that the past to which Yanzhima aspires is pre-Soviet—and possibly even predating Russian contact. She assumes that the great-great-grandparents pictured in the photograph spoke Buryat and knew nothing of Russian ways, though it is likely, given their origins near Irkutsk, that they and perhaps even their own great-great-grandparents had plenty of contact with Russians and Russian speakers.

Other senses of temporal disjuncture are themselves profoundly Soviet. Many Buryat scholars have explained to me, patiently and carefully, that over the course of the twentieth century, the Buryats skipped a natural stage in sociocultural development—that is, according to the appropriate stages of Marxist-Leninist sociocultural evolution. In the radical leap forward that they describe, Buryats were wrested from feudal conditions—paying tribute in the form of furs, meat, and other animal products to local headsmen or to Buddhist monasteries in exchange for military protection—and carried via rapid education, industrialization, and nation-building efforts into the modern era.[4] At the same time, in Buryatia, the teleological view of time underlying Marxist-Leninist theories of sociocultural evolution has always been in tension with the more cyclical view of time endemic to Buddhism. Based on fieldwork in Buryatia in the Soviet period, Humphrey (1989, 148) observed that the cyclical view of time "meant that the very notion of irreversible progress was, if not incomprehensible, not truly apprehended and internalized." Today Buryats largely view the Soviet period as an unnatural or "abnormal time" (*nenormal'noe vremia*), nostalgia for it notwithstanding, to be reached back over. People like Larisa/Yanzhima evince a sense of working against the imposition of a somehow false modernity to reclaim something that is rightfully theirs, located in a past that predates the Soviet period or even Russian contact. Likewise, activists for linguistic and cultural revitalization usually seek to reach back into the pre-Soviet period for what they see as intact linguistic and cultural practices that might be brought forward into the current era.

Such efforts rest on the fact that the Buryat language has become strongly indexical of a whole complex of related cultural practices—Buddhist and shamanic adherence, dwelling in yurts, animal husbandry, and related pastoral-nomadic lifeways—that are figured fundamentally as premodern. At Tolon, one of the newspaper's founders, whom I will call Dorzh, ruminated on this temporal problem in an interview with me in 2009. We were discussing the editorial board's reasons for recently deciding to open what had long been an exclusively Buryat-language publication to Russian-language material. This was something being done around the same time by other Buryat-language newspapers, including Buriaad ünèn. The Tolon editorial board's plan was to produce 60 percent of the newspaper in Buryat and 40 percent in Russian, with "contemporary" topics for young readers more in Russian and literary and artistic topics more in Buryat. Dorzh stressed that this was not a short-term response to changing politics or tight finances, but rather an inevitability borne of decisions made (or not made) long ago:

KG: So was it exactly a choice?
Dorzh: Yes, well it's of course connected, on the other hand, with the fact
        that today, of course, there are specific problems with the Buryat
        language. Today young people control the Buryat language poorly—
        you already know this yourself. And it's connected with the fact
        that—it's not because the state or the politics are such, but pre-
        cisely because the Buryat language is the language of our bygone
        nomadic civilization. Yes, because [it's a] conceptual apparatus. It's
        all conceptual. All of this old Buryat world of ours, that is, carries
        our language away with itself. Our language. And . . . also, in those
        times, well maybe thirty, forty, fifty, seventy years ago, we obviously

very poorly adapted our language to contemporary life, to the coming Western civilization. It was necessary to **adapt** the language, uh-huh, but our language remained **unadapted**. Therefore today we have to admit that it's very difficult to converse in Buryat on some contemporary topics, because there aren't the concepts, there isn't the terminology, uh-huh, there isn't—as they say, there's no verbal image.[5] Yes. Therefore today it's only possible to converse in Buryat somewhere on the quotidian level [*na bytovom urovne*]. On the quotidian level.

KG: Ah, you have in mind particularly the lexicon, yes?

Dorzh: Yes, today it's very ba—hard to even imagine holding meetings, or [scholarly or literary] sessions, or any kind of public events in Buryat. It's practically impossible.

KG: Mm.

Dorzh: Yes. Because both the leadership and the people who are today, uh, running, let's suppose, one or the other of the structures of power, they practically—they control such language very poorly. Well, they're able to carry on a conversation face-to-face about something quotidian, of course, but they're in no state to hold a conversation that's official, or businesslike, of course. It's—generally speaking, they're basically probably not even in a state for this. Maybe with the exception of a limited circle of people, yes, and these people, of course, will be [able to participate] if there's an official conversation. Of course they're there. But . . . in very large part, it will be made up of words that are, well, Russian—loan words.

KG: Mm.

Dorzh: Yes. Therefore, it's simply—it's not anyone's fault, it's just that life has apparently been ordered in such a way that we really have not been able to adapt our language, [and] our language is going away with our way of life. [*gestures toward his clothing: a blazer, turtleneck, and slacks*] Today we don't go to work in a Buryat dègèl, let's say, in Buryat clothing. Yes, I'll admit that at an official meeting or event, it's very hard for me to observe, let's say, my own folk traditions [*narodnye traditsii*]. [*mimes interaction, switching to informal second person*] "I'm senior by age, so here, you're junior by age, sit lower than me." But although [the director] is younger than me, all the same he should sit higher than me. Therefore, yes. It's because, well, our traditions, our original . . . that is, our folk traditions [*narodnye traditsii*], [and] that which existed earlier, it is of course, today, generally for the most part already more modernized. Already life has been covered over by Western civilization, of course. It's simply really impossible. And it's—in general, in principle, I think, there's nothing bad in that. **Although**, of course, with **language** [...] there is, of course, an axiom that with language goes spirituality [*s iazykom ukhodit dukhovnost'*]. Spir—spirituality. That is, yes, I think in general that this is true, it's probably true. All the same, language is a living organism, it's a living life, language. Yes. It is, I suppose, a part of our, as they say, **being**. Therefore, of course, if a people forgets, abandons their language, probably at the same time its foundations will fade. Therefore, from this perspective, of course, it's very **sad**, yes. I don't even know whether it will ever come back.

Like many Buryats, Dorzh expresses sadness about what he takes to be an inevitable conflict between maintaining distinctive Buryat practices and becoming modernized, which he expresses temporally. He divides cultural practices into a Russified, Westernized present and traditions that were observed in an unspecified past—"that which existed earlier" (*to, chto bylo ran'she*). In his commentary, language and other distinctively Buryat practices, such as national dress and politeness norms, are inextricably connected because language is the "foundation" for the rest. He moves seamlessly between them, suggesting that adopting one element of the larger semiotic complex of Westernization (a suit jacket, for instance) entails adopting others (the Russian language, for instance). Moreover, these practices appear to be in direct conflict with one another: you may dress in *either* a suit jacket or a dègèl, just as you may sit *either* here or there in a business meeting. As though to underscore the point, Dorzh chose Russian for our interview, although he knew that neither Russian nor Buryat was my native language, and although he assumed that I knew Buryat terms.

From Dorzh's perspective, the key hindrance to language maintenance is that Buryat is the language of a "bygone nomadic civilization." This is an argument about indexicality that avoids placing blame. Dorzh argues that Buryat too strongly indexes an obsolescent past, not because people associate it with that past, but because the language itself does not contain the correct words. He thus places causality in the *language itself*, rather than in its speakers. If it is the fault of speakers, it was speakers in the Soviet period, "maybe thirty, forty, fifty, seventy years ago," who did not adapt the language properly.

Here Soviet modernization appears, paradoxically, as a kind of endpoint for Buryat. While the overarching ethos of the era was one of forward progress, Dorzh's depiction of Buryat language and culture in the Soviet era is that they became stuck; it is an image of *not* advancing. This is a common way in which the Soviet period is presented, even by people who personally flourished during it, as a prolonged tragedy for Buryat culture, and as an interruption that must be reached back over to reclaim Buryat belonging.

Spatiocultural Rifts

Alongside these temporal disjunctures are notions that Buryats have been separated from their rightful kin across multiple scales: in Mongolia, in greater Asia, and from one Buryat territory to the next. While there was never a historical moment of perfect Buryat unity, it is true that modern political borders, missionary history, the machinations of powerful states, and the bounds of circulation within media markets have carved up Buryat social networks and prevented what might have been greater ethnonational coalescence.

Buryats have a potential "kin state" in Mongolia, with deep cultural connections and a shared history of Mahāyāna (Tibetan, or Lamaist) Buddhism. The Buryat language is closely related to Khalkh Mongolian, the standard language of Mongolia, and some dialects of Buryat and Khalkh are at least partially mutually intelligible, depending on a person's background and will to understand.[6] Yet Buryats and other Mongolic speakers have been separated by various subtle and not-so-subtle factors. The Russian-Mongolian political border running along the Buryat territories' southern edge has a very restricted number of crossing points. Although at the time of writing Russian and Mongolian citizens can travel across it visa-free, the border has periodically been closed to them—sometimes quite inexplicably in response to unnamed "security concerns," such as in 2010. More subtly, many Buryats feel ambivalent about their potential connections to Mongolia for the same reasons they feel ambivalent about their Asianness more generally. This ambivalence was evident in Érzhena's forceful declaration that in Russia (as opposed to China), "we don't spit on the floor." Most Buryat speakers insist that they do not understand Khalkh, especially if they are native speakers of one of the northern dialects far from the border, and they often comment that Khalkh Mongolian sounds "choppy" or "harsh," apparently referring to a lateral fricative [ɬ] that Buryat lacks [l]; use of [s] and [x] where Buryat has [h]; and a loss of endings that makes Mongolian sound "short" or abbreviated to listeners accustomed to Buryat.

Other spatial and cultural rifts are felt among the three Buryat territories, particularly between the west side of Baikal, including Ust'-Orda and the mountainous Tunka region, and the east side of Baikal, including most of the Republic of Buryatia, Ulan-Ude, Aga, and the eastern steppes. Generally, western Buryats are taken to be more Russified and integrated into the state, and eastern Buryats are taken to be more Buddhist, spiritual, and Mongolian. One of the first "social facts" that a visitor will be told about Buryats is that they are divided in these ways, west from east, and the division has taken on remarkable explanatory power in local self-conceptions.

There *are* significant cultural differences between the western and eastern edges of the Buryat territories, grounded in climatological differences and exacerbated by historical missionizing and state-building efforts. Ust'-Orda is mainly agricultural, with green, rolling hills and fertile soil. Traditionally home to western Buryat tribes including the Alar', Bulagat, and Ekhirit, Ust'-Orda's Buryat population adopted settled agriculture earlier than the Buryats east of Lake Baikal, trading round felt yurts for unique octagonal log dwellings with earthen roofs. Western Buryats converted to Russian Orthodoxy in greater numbers, and their cultural and linguistic Russification was both earlier and more extensive (Murray 2012). Today, this history is salient in the Russian and Orthodox personal names that many western Buryats possess, and in how linguistic knowledge is distributed (western Buryats are not expected to control Buryat well). Western Buryats overall also had less contact with Buddhist missionaries from the south and east in the eighteenth and nineteenth centuries, retaining instead more shamanic practices—although there are some Buddhist datsans in Ust'-Orda, including an outpost of Buryatia's prominent Ivolginsk datsan.

By contrast, Aga is known among Buryats as an "ark" of Buryat language and culture. Aga Buryats continued to practice pastoral nomadism for longer than their counterparts further west, with some families setting up winter and summer camps in addition to their "settled" homes as late as the 1950s.[7] Aga is mostly dry steppe land, mixed with stretches of larch forest and scattered groves of pine and birch, and is bordered on the south by the Onon River, legendary birthplace of Chinggis Khan. A harsh continental climate closer to that of Mongolia makes it best suited to animal husbandry, including cows, sheep, and camels. Like the Republic of Buryatia's eastern steppes, Aga was heavily missionized by Tibetan-Mongolian Buddhists, and the region is home to Buddhist monastic centers, such as Süügelei (Tsugol) datsan and Agyn (Aginskii) datsan, that were extremely powerful in the eighteenth and nineteenth centuries and are currently the focus of religious revitalization.

Cultural and political differences among the Buryat territories have been sharpened by a piecemeal "information field." At the regional level, the three primary Buryat territories are in separate media markets. What is called in Buryatia a "republic newspaper" (*respublikanskaia gazeta*) is mirrored in Ust'-Orda, Irkutsk Oblast, as an oblast-level newspaper (*oblastnaia gazeta*) and in Aga, Zabaikal'skii Krai, as a krai-level newspaper (*kraevaia gazeta*). The Buryat capital cities of Ulan-Ude, Ust'-Ordynskii, and Aginskoe are thus served by separate regional-level newspapers, whose news selection and distribution correspond to the boundaries of these regions much more closely than, say, the *New York Times* for New York state or the *San Francisco Chronicle* for California. Unless they can depend on word-of-mouth in social networks, residents of Zabaikal'skii Krai do not know what is occurring in Irkutsk Oblast. Similarly, the Republic of Buryatia's flagship Buryat-language newspaper, Buriaad ünèn, rarely covers events in Ust'-Orda, and Ust'-Orda's flagship Buryat-language newspaper, Ust'-Ordyn ünèn, rarely covers events in Ulan-Ude. This situation—what Galina Dyrkheeva has called the lack of a "unified information field" (2002, 66)—has resulted in Buryats of the three territories being remarkably disconnected from one another's news and linguistic practices. When I traveled to Ust'-Orda in 2009, journalists there peppered me with questions about their colleagues in Ulan-Ude and the state of the political merger in distant Aga. Information and linguistic practices travel, of course, through such circulations of *people* in face-to-face interactions, but Buryats are largely missing out on the possibilities of mass mediated communication to interlink Buryat linguistic practices in the three territories.

When people want to emphasize the difference between these territories, they do so most often with reference to language loss. A woman in Aginskoe asked me whether it was even possible to conduct anthropological research in Ulan-Ude, given that "[Buryats there] have lost their ethnic traditions" and are "Buryat only by face [*litso*]." When I pressed her on what she meant by "ethnic traditions"— thinking she might cite dances, clan names, dress, or some specific Buddhist and shamanic practices—she shook her head. They had lost their language, she said, and everything else had followed.

Language Shift

To judge by censuses, surveys, ethnography, or even idle observation, the language shift away from Buryat in post-Soviet Buryatia has indeed been swift. Over the longer, four-hundred-year history of contact with Russian, the language shift from Buryat to Russian would be better characterized as generally slow, punctuated by periods of faster shift. In living memory there have been *two* periods of dramatic shift, however, so a sense of decline permeates most people's perception. One accompanied rapid urbanization and industrialization in the 1960s, when large numbers of ethnic outsiders came into Buryatia from Ukraine, the Caucasus, and other western parts of the Soviet Union and everyone relied more heavily on Russian as a lingua franca. This period in particular produced what is felt now as a generation gap between knowledgeable Buryat elders and their Russian-dominant adult children (see, e.g., Babuev 2001, 2006).

The second occurred over the years covered in this book. In the 2002 all-Russian census, 72 percent of the total Buryat population of the Russian Federation reported knowledge of Buryat.[8] By the 2010 census, that number had fallen to 45 percent.[9] Within the Republic of Buryatia, the decline has been even sharper. In the same period, the proportion of the republic's Buryat population reporting knowledge of Buryat fell from 81 percent to 43 percent (although the percentage of Buryats reporting their "native language" as Buryat remained constant and high, at 82 percent).[10] The dizzying drop is probably due in part to changes in how linguistic knowledge is understood and reported on census forms. It is common in the former Soviet Union to consider one's "native language" to be one's "heritage" or "ancestral" language, regardless of actual competence, and Russian censuses have been uneven in how (or whether) they elicited the distinction between a language that one *knows* and a language that one *affiliates with*.[11] Still, in under a decade, the census figures suggest a significant shift away from Buryat.

More subtly, Buryat has been receding from public life, albeit unevenly. Despite a considerable amount of Buryat-language media production and well-institutionalized Buryat language education, the domains of usage are restricted (Dyrkheeva 2002, 2003). Sociolinguistic surveys that are more detailed than census questionnaires ask respondents to differentiate between social domains in which they *use* Buryat, as opposed to just whether they know it or not or consider it their native language. In such surveys, Buryat respondents have reported using Buryat at home in rates of 5–40 percent, with numbers as high as 68 percent only among Buryat teachers (Dyrkheeva, Darzhaeva, Bal'zhinimaeva, et al. 2009, 86–87). In a comparative survey of language attitudes and Buryat language use in Ulan-Ude, rural Buryatia, Ust'-Orda, and Aga, only 2.4 percent of respondents in Ulan-Ude reported using Buryat in work or at school (Khilkhanova 2007, 81). No one in Ust'-Orda reported using it in this context. Russian is particularly dominant in Ulan-Ude and in urbanized administrative centers, including the district capitals of some otherwise Buryat-dominant districts.

There are pockets of stable bilingualism. Many families in Ulan-Ude, including some of the families with whom I lived, do use Buryat at home. In parts of rural Buryatia and Aga, Buryat is widely used—so much so that resident ethnic Russians learn it. In Erzhen Khilkhanova's survey (2007, 81), 31.5 percent of respondents in rural Buryatia and 25.7 percent of respondents in Aga reported using Buryat at work and school. Though based only on self-reported data, these results are consonant with observable public Buryat use. In Aginskoe, Buryat is actively spoken on the street, and I have even had whole exchanges to buy shampoo or bread in which the speaker behind the counter initiated the interaction in Buryat and did not draw any metapragmatic attention to code choice or to the oddity that I spoke Buryat. These, however, are the exceptions that prove the rule: the principal language of public life in Buryatia is overwhelmingly Russian.

Why do people choose to speak one language rather than another? In part, ethnic Buryats' shift from Buryat to Russian is a matter of demographics. Despite their status as the titular nationality, ethnic Buryats have never been a statistical majority in the Republic of Buryatia. Since the first census with the current borders in 1939, their percentage of the total population has ranged between 20.2 and 30.0 percent, where it currently stands, versus an ethnically Russian population of 66.1 percent.[12] (By contrast, Ust'-Orda in the 2010 census was 39.8 percent Buryat versus 54.2 percent Russian, and Aga was 65.1 percent Buryat versus 32.5 percent Russian [Rosstat 2012–13].) Yet being statistically swamped by ethnic Russians cannot fully explain language choice, not least because the percentage of the population that is ethnically Buryat has actually been *increasing* over all three territories in the same years that Buryat linguistic knowledge has been declining. There must be other factors at work.

Linguistic anthropological work has demonstrated the importance of vectors of affiliation such as national and ethnic belonging (e.g., Bilaniuk 2005; Errington 1998; Gal 1988; King 2011) and gender (e.g., Cavanaugh 2006; Gal 1978; Kulick 1998; LeMaster 2006) in language choice, locating individual interactional choices within the context of broader economic, political, and sociocultural pressures. Studies of the sociocultural factors leading to language shift and obsolescence have focused on language choice as a means for managing social connections, networks, and social positioning, often analyzed in terms of the "prestige" afforded by alignment with a dominant social group (e.g., Bonner 1982; Gumperz 1982).

Many of the macrosociological reasons for Buryat-Russian language shift are common to cases of language shift, attrition, and obsolescence. Culprits include occupation, colonization, and migration but also more subtle political coercion and the economic and personal benefits made available to minority-language speakers for shifting in a hierarchy controlled by speakers of the majority tongue (e.g., Craig 1997; Dorian 1989b; Grenoble and Whaley 1998, 2006; Nettle and Romaine 2000). Certainly Buryat is in many ways low-prestige. Numbers like 2.4 percent of respondents in Ulan-Ude using Buryat in work or at school suggest that the language is not seen as necessary or practical for socioeconomic success. At the scale of the Russian nation-state, Buryat is decidedly marginalized. Although knowledge of Buryat offers many personal, psychological, and even socioeconomic advantages, they are not immediately apparent to most outsiders. The general attitude toward Buryat (and Buryatia) among Russian young people outside the Buryat territories was reflected in the response of a young woman stamping passports at a border crossing in Irkutsk. I had just arrived on a flight from Beijing, populated mainly by Chinese and Russian businessmen, and the bored girl at the entry desk looked up with interest on seeing my US passport. "What is your purpose in **Ulan-Ude?**" she asked, reading the address on my entry visa and smirking at the city listed. I was accustomed to this reaction, many well-meaning Russians in St. Petersburg and Moscow having protested, "But, Katya, that is in the **sticks!**" (*Èto v glushi!*) or "Siberia? You will surely die." Traveling in other parts of Russia, I have had to convince museum workers and even border guards that Ulan-Ude is, in fact, a part of the Russian Federation and not a city in Mongolia or China. This woman was in Irkutsk, however, so her skepticism was aimed not at the Siberia she called home but at the provincial cow-town across Lake Baikal. I responded that I was studying Buryat in Ulan-Ude. "**Buryat?**" she repeated, leaning forward with her eyebrows now sky-high. "For **what?**" (*Buriatskii iazyk? Zachem?*)

If dismissive attitudes like this indirectly lower a person's desire to learn or use Buryat, other factors actively discourage its use. As territorial, protectionist strains of nationalism gain prominence in western Russia, using Buryat in some spaces has become actively dangerous. Xenophobia toward Asian Russians is often a matter of mistaken identity, and it is grounded in the physical phenotype and reading of surfaces inherent to racism. Visual cues are only part of the picture, however, and Asianness, like foreignness, is constructed aurally as much as visually. Thus many Asian Russians take care to tailor their code choice and accent, particularly while traveling or living in Moscow or other parts of European Russia. In 2012, as I arrived in Ulan-Ude on a flight from Moscow, two middle-aged women whom I, by chance, knew from earlier fieldwork got into a lively debate over whether it was better, at that time, to speak Buryat on the streets of Moscow or Russian with a Buryat accent. Either, they agreed, was dangerous if you were also already a "persona of Asian extraction" (i.e., racially), because Muscovites would only recognize you as Asian, and that could only be remedied by speaking Russian natively. The threat of racially motivated violence may not be completely assuaged by language choice, given that attackers racially profile based on phenotype. But as one man who had been living in the St. Petersburg diaspora explained to me in 2009, speaking Russian on the street with a native accent could at least signal that one was a Russian citizen (*rossiianin*). He rarely spoke Buryat anyway, he said, but he continued to fear that his Russian was marked by a Buryat accent.

Regionally, Buryats' control of major political and cultural institutions and commitment to the Friendship of the Peoples protects them somewhat from overt racism. Some of the same macrosociological factors, however, privilege Russian over Buryat in public life. In particular, Buryat's temporal indexicalities make it easy to dismiss as socioeconomically useless.

Language shift entails temporal disjunctures. Periods of fast shift in particular are often experienced as a generation gap (or gaps) within families. In many contexts, such rupture is intimately linked to projects of modernization. For instance, Don Kulick (1992) describes a case of language shift in which Christian missionizing and development projects in Papua New Guinea created a stark contrast between "old" and "new" ways of speaking. Chronicling the village of Gapun's multigenerational language shift from a local language called Taiap to Papua New Guinea's lingua franca, Tok Pisin, Kulick found that the two codes were increasingly linked to different aspects of personhood. Speaking Taiap became indexical of irrationality, femininity, childishness, and a culturally specific conception of stubbornness, while speaking Tok Pisin became indexical of rationality, masculinity, adulthood, and modernity—along with the material trappings of development, such as roads and schools. Language shift proceeds due to the indexical meanings of using each language.

A similar devaluation of Buryat is clear in Dorzh's musing over the recent past. During the Soviet period, and to some extent during Russification efforts in the prerevolutionary period as well, Russian was successfully made indexical of progress, and Buryat of tradition and ancient ways. Because tradition was devalued in the twentieth century, Buryat was also devalued. Using Buryat has come to index rurality and a bygone era, connections which, whether viewed derisively or romantically, become self-fulfilling as language shift progresses.

Non-Buryat migration into the Buryat territories, encouraged by the Soviet state through work incentives and major projects like the Baikal-Amur Railway across northern Buryatia and a gigantic paper mill at Baikal'sk, further devalued Buryat linguistic knowledge by necessitating the use of Russian as a lingua franca. "Internal immigrants" from Ukraine, Armenia, and Azerbaijan arrived with the not-unreasonable expectation that they would use Russian, not Buryat, in public life. Buryat-medium education was slashed, and requirements for studying Buryat as a subject were slackened, ostensibly to accommodate the large new immigrant population. Official ideology stressed assimilation, with Buryat linguistics scholarship increasingly emphasizing the intermixing of all Soviet peoples and languages into a single Soviet people—and language. For decades, it was considered nationalistic, rude, and not only anti-Russian but also anti-social to speak Buryat on the streets of Ulan-Ude. Describing similar conditions in the Sakha Republic, Jenanne Ferguson (2019) points out that there does not need to be a law explicitly forbidding people from speaking a language (such as Sakha) in urban public space for people to nonetheless feel it is forbidden. In Buryatia, this sentiment seems to have peaked in the 1990s, when the possibility of Buryatia separating from Russia and becoming an independent nation (like Kazakhstan or Moldova) was over but still fresh in people's minds, such that interethnic relations were fragile. Over the course of the 2000s and 2010s, Chinese speakers have become more visible and audible with increasing immigration into Ulan-Ude and Aga, and the language they seek to master is usually (though not always) Russian. While census results suggest that thousands of non-Buryats and non-Russians do learn some Buryat, expecting this of adult immigrants might be unrealistic. As Armenian and Ukrainian college students pointed out to me many times, the triple burden of maintaining one's "own" language and of learning Buryat alongside the languages that one "must" know well for socioeconomic success—namely Russian, and secondarily English or Chinese—is often too much. They experienced Buryat State University's required course in Buryat mainly as an impingement on their ability to participate in dance ensembles and otherwise pursue their "own" ethnic traditions.

Historically, we can see how this notion of obsolescence encroached by observing the way that the role of Buryat-language media changed over the periods of rupture described above. Archival records of editorial meetings in the 1960s and 1970s show that media producers during this period were troubled by language attrition among their would-be audience members. Radio and television workers began to complain that they could not record quality interview materials due to a lack of competent speakers.[13] Buryat-language newspapers saw a continuous decline in the number of letters they received, especially in contrast to the perpetually overflowing mailbox of Russian-language *Pravda*, and they began to worry about the advanced age of their staff.[14] To publicly raise the inefficiency argument and suggest a curtailment of Buryat-language production would have been anathema to Soviet ideology, thrusting the dissonance between a policy of supporting two languages equally and the actual results of "intermixing" initiatives uncomfortably to the fore.[15] But periodically throughout the 1960s–80s, minority-language media personnel seem to have been subtly questioning their own raison d'être.

In terms of the sheer quantity of material produced, however, the postwar period through the early 1980s was a kind of golden age for Buryat-language media. Where was all of that newsprint and airtime going? One possibility is that this was a late Soviet institution simply going through the proverbial motions, for an audience of no one. But in fact, subscription and viewing rates appear to have remained high, even during a period of intense language shift. And people cared: in the late 1980s and early 1990s, as other media support structures disintegrated before people's eyes, Buryat politicians, editors, and activists within Buryatia fought successfully to save much of the Buryat-language television, radio, and press.

A more likely explanation for the paradox—and answer to the question of where all these media were going—is that over the late Soviet period, minority-language media were taking on a new role in Buryat society. Media were shifting from serving more informational and state-symbolic roles to serving a more culturally symbolic role (see also Graber 2012). Television, radio, and newspaper staffs had increasingly differentiated content and even style, implicitly acknowledging (or imagining) the different interests and demands of a Buryat versus Russian audience. Buryat-language media personnel were faced with an audience that increasingly could—and did—go to Russian sources for its news, and while Russian- and Buryat-language institutions were not exactly in competition with one another because of guaranteed state support, the shift did encourage specialization. As media producers increasingly assumed a bilingual audience, a division of labor emerged between Russian and Buryat, according to which Russian functioned more as the language of international politics, economics, and "hard news," while Buryat carried more "soft news," including human interest stories, history, and "cultural" topics such as music, dance, poetry, and tradition.[16] Thus a certain historical poetics emerged, according to which Buryat-language articles and broadcasts evoke the space-time of a mythic, unchanging Buryat past. Ironically, this quintessentially pre-Soviet, "Buryat" space-time that can be evoked discursively—what M. M. Bakhtin ([1934–35] 1981) terms a "chronotope"— is indebted to widespread Soviet efforts. At opposite ends of the former Soviet Union, Sigrid Rausing in Estonia (2004) and Bruce Grant on Sakhalin Island (1993) have argued that local history was effectively replaced by static Soviet representations of folk culture, when individuals' (mostly willing) participation in Soviet modernizing projects demanded it. The same could be said in Buryatia. But this does not make the chronotope any less powerful today. Indeed, it resonates all the more strongly as Buryat language use seems to recede into the countryside and from younger to older generations.

In rural areas, the language ideology linking Russian to urban spaces and Buryat to rural spaces helps drive language shift, as people turn aspirationally toward Russian. This was brought home to me when I visited the offices of Khori District's newspaper, *Udinskaia nov'* (The Uda news), in the district capital of Khorinsk, a town of about eight thousand people. The newspaper had been operating for many years in both Russian and Buryat but had recently switched exclusively to Russian. Two of the journalists explained that their sole staff journalist writing in Buryat had switched to writing exclusively in Russian. It was "no longer necessary" to write in Buryat for Khorinsk's population, they said, because they had become urban "city people" (*gorodskie*), so "naturally" everyone could now read Russian. On learning that I was a student of Buryat, one of the journalists expressed some interest, and I asked (in Buryat) whether she spoke Buryat. "Of course!" she responded in Russian, almost indignantly. "Of course I speak Buryat. I am a Buryat!" (*Konechno! Konechno govoriu po-buriatski. Ia buriatka!*) Most Buryats, as we have seen, do not speak Buryat. But for this woman, Buryat linguistic ability was so self-evidently a part of being Buryat that she could not separate the two. And the issue of her own linguistic ability or identity, it seemed, was unconnected to the question of whether or not writers in their offices would (or should) be writing in Buryat. From the perspective of these journalists, the purpose of Buryat-language content had been more informative than symbolic; and it had been a means to the ultimate ends of urbanizing and integrating Buryats into modern society. They viewed that transformation as complete, and they saw evidence for its completion in their ability to expect a Russian-dominant audience and shift their newspaper fully to Russian. Khorinsk's urbanity is tenuous, which accounts in part for these journalists' insistence. Before I left, they repeated that the people of Khorinsk were "city people." As though on cue, a small herd of goats wandered past the window.

The journalists' comments point to the power of language ideologies to "locate, interpret, and rationalize sociolinguistic complexity" (Irvine and Gal 2000, 36), making divisions and distinctions appear utterly natural (see also Eagleton 1991; Fairclough 1989, 1995). Such language ideologies are central to language preservation and revitalization efforts, as a growing amount of scholarship shows (see especially Meek 2010; Nevins 2013). The change at *Udinskaia nov'* illustrates the powerful forces that such efforts must counter if they are to succeed, as the communities that *could* produce Buryat-language media appear to simply value Russian more.

But prestige is more complicated than this. Linguistic value is unevenly distributed and determined in different segments of society, at different scales, and in different situations. Shagdar, a Buryat man of twenty-seven who was doing manual labor in Ulan-Ude during my fieldwork, said he never spoke Buryat around his Russian boss and had never had any particular reason to speak Buryat in the city, but he wished he spoke it *better* when he was unloading boxes with other young men from villages. He did not always understand what they were saying or get their jokes, he said. "Does it affect your pay?" I asked. "Yeah," he said, "I don't, you know, get good shifts or hear about extra work." There were also businesses where Buryat dominated, like the grocery stores noted in a preceding chapter, where Shagdar did not even hope to find work. The registers, dialects, and multifarious resources of Buryat, like those of any code, are fully accessible only to (some) speakers of the code, among whom a different set of values may apply than those found in the broader multilingual society of which they are a part. For many residents of the Republic of Buryatia—perhaps even the majority—Buryat, as a code, is decidedly low-status. Valuation is generally more positive, however, among those who actually control Buryat and consider themselves part of a larger Buryat language public, as well as among Russian-dominant speakers who self-identify as ethnically Buryat or are interpreted as such. Knowing Buryat indexes rurality and poverty, but it also indexes being Buryat, attachment to the "homeland" (R. *rodina*, B. <u>toonto niutag</u>), and belonging to a broader Mongolian and Asian sphere. By the same token, losing Buryat indexes a broader loss of cultural continuity.

Figuring one cultural practice as "high" and another as "low," or "local" events as nested within "global" events, is itself a semiotic accomplishment, not a given (Carr and Lempert 2016; Irvine and Gal 2000). Once forged, scalar distinctions and hierarchies are useful semiotic resources, to be capitalized on in interactions and, thereby, reinforced. Smart, well-educated language rights activists and literary editors like Dorzh are especially fond of invoking globalization, universal human rights, spiritual worlds, and the longue durée. Such invocation instantly makes a painting, a meeting, a folktale, or the choice of one word over another appear more meaningful and important, but the move works only because a scalar understanding privileging the global over the local, the macro over the micro, and the spiritual over the quotidian has already been well established.

Attending to this semiotic labor can help us understand the more nuanced reasons for cultural and linguistic change. At first blush, the reasons for language shift may seem quite obvious. Speakers of a "big" language such as Russian seem to have more social and economic power than speakers of, say, Buryat. Certainly at the scale of the Soviet Union or Russia, Russian has been the language of power. But there are senses in which speaking Buryat is extremely advantageous—not only for the aforementioned emotional and affective reasons but also for reasons of political economy. For example, much of Buryat social life revolves around the *zemliachestvo*, literally a community linked by 'earth' or 'homeplace' (R. *zemlia*, B. <u>niutag</u>), meaning people who may live scattered far and wide but who share the same ancestral district. As Buryatia has industrialized and urbanized, zemliachestvo gatherings in Ulan-Ude have become critical sites for reaffirming countryside connections, making business deals, and finding romance. Although public life in Ulan-Ude demands Russian, you will get farther at a gathering of the zemliachestvo by knowing Buryat. Likewise, Shagdar felt that speaking Buryat within his workplace would have improved his income and social position. What is often called in sociolinguistic literature "covert prestige" (Trudgill 1972) is positive evaluation of a way of speaking at these smaller scales of interaction, as opposed to ways of speaking deemed "prestigious" at larger scales of interaction.

The "Real" Thing

Language shift poses a problem for Buryatness because knowing and using the Buryat language has been the main criterion of ethnonational belonging. This is not the case everywhere: in some cases of language shift, speakers appear highly pragmatic about adhering to whatever language or languages seem to be most useful and letting others go, such that language shift poses no particular problem (e.g., McLendon 1978). Certainly, many Buryats echo the border guard in Irkutsk who saw no point in learning Buryat, or language shift would not be proceeding at such a rapid clip. Some scholars have argued that Buryats are (or should be) giving up on the language and moving toward alternative criteria for ethnonational belonging, such as biologized notions of ethnicity (Khilkhanova and Khilkhanov 2003). As a group, however, Buryats have strong political and emotional reasons not to give up Buryat, or at least to be troubled by its loss.

Reclamation has immediate geopolitical stakes. Moscow is currently engaged in a "regathering of the lands," a reference to Ivan III's campaigns to annex East Slavic lands and consolidate Russia in the fifteenth century. From outside of Russia, this is most visible in border disputes in the Caucasus and the 2014 annexation of Crimea, but consolidation has been a domestic priority too, in ways that threaten Buryat political autonomy. Administrative restructuring under President Dmitrii Medvedev and Prime Minister and President Vladimir Putin has deprivileged ethnic territories like Ust'-Orda and Aga, at least in terms of territorial and political sovereignty.[17] Ust'-Orda was officially merged with Irkutsk Oblast on January 1, 2008, and Aga—a harder sell—was merged with Chita Oblast to form a new Zabaikal'skii Krai on March 1, 2008. The mergers were passed by referendums, although they were contentious decisions and many onlookers at the time doubted the legitimacy of the votes (Graber and Long 2009)—not, it must be added, unreasonably, given that the voter turnout rates were reported as over 99 percent of eligible voters with 98 percent in favor of unification in Ust'-Orda in 2006 (Petrova 2006) and 90 percent of eligible voters with 94 percent in favor in Aga in 2007 (Khamaganov 2007). Both okrugs still technically exist, as administrative divisions with what is officially called "special status" (*osobyi status*), and Buryats in both regions retain this "special status" as well, with provisions for ongoing support for the preservation of Buryat language and culture. Culturally and in the geographic imaginations of the people described in this book, Ust'-Orda and Aga remain Buryat territories; some Buryat scholars use the term "ethnic Buryatia" to describe the once-unified lands. But their dissolution as federal subjects provoked heated discussion and no small amount of anxiety over the political future of the Republic of Buryatia. There have been fears in Buryatia that the republic itself would be dissolved, and underlying discussions of regional development in the past several years has been the possibility of an administrative super-region that would subsume the Republic of Buryatia, Irkutsk Oblast, and Zabaikal'skii Krai.

The dissolution of these two smaller territories has raised the political stakes of speaking—or not speaking—Buryat. In discussions leading up to the dissolution of Ust'-Orda, some proponents of dissolution claimed that the fact that most Buryats there no longer spoke Buryat proved that political autonomy had not ultimately worked to maintain an identifiable Buryat culture. Similar arguments have been circulated to justify dissolving the Republic of Buryatia. Although they remain mainly rumors, the threat of using language preservation as a criterion for ethnic political autonomy has inspired anxiety. Recentralization campaigns are balanced, however, by the growing majority of Russian citizens who live in provinces and smaller cities, rather than in the wealthy megalopolis of Moscow, and by mounting tensions along the Russian Federation's borders. Contemporary Russian politics is characterized in these senses by both centripetal and centrifugal pressures (Clowes 2016). Although separatist sentiments in Buryatia are very limited, central authorities do not appear secure about the future of Buryatia within the federation.

Reclamation also has emotional stakes. Language shift and endangerment are often wrapped up in personal sentiments and strong, sometimes contradictory emotions, and the literature on language shift, endangerment, obsolescence, and death is rife with examples of strong emotional attachment. For instance, Nancy Dorian (2014) has described the "language loyalty" of young Scottish fisherfolk who, despite being fluent in higher-prestige English and not speaking the local dialect of Scottish Gaelic well, nonetheless persist in using that dialect as best they can. Young people in a Kaska-speaking community in the Yukon invest their elders with feelings of respect, tenderness, and protectiveness that color their feelings for Kaska (Meek 2007, 2010). In the Colorado River delta, semispeakers of Cucapá feel disillusionment and malaise as they are "reduced" to being countable objects—last speakers (Muehlmann 2012). They respond, in part, by reserving the Cucapá language for vile swearing like "spread your ass cheeks," which, as Shaylih Muehlmann (2008) points out, is not something you're "supposed to say" in an endangered language.

Despite these many examples, when trying to explain and predict language change, researchers of language shift have tended to focus on political economy to the exclusion of strong emotional attachments. This is understandable given our collective focus on power and on understanding the imbrication of individual speakers and languages within larger social complexes. But by not taking seriously the depth and importance of emotion in language shift, we risk missing clues that would bridge the gap between a thousand daily, micro-level choices and broader social change. I, for example, immediately asked Shagdar about how his limitations in Buryat affected his income, but he had actually foregrounded his feelings of embarrassment and isolation from his coworkers. Taking those feelings seriously, and attending to the complex emotional responses of speakers (or would-be speakers) in contexts of language attrition, will help us understand the more subtle reasons for linguistic and cultural change.

Unfortunately for individuals like Larisa/Yanzhima, solving the problem is not as simple as relearning and reteaching some kind of prerupture Buryat (itself a tall order), because the language itself has changed. This change, and the way that Buryat speakers organize linguistic variation ideologically, make it very difficult to locate the "real" Buryat language, further destabilizing what it means to *be* a "real Buryat."

Over the course of multigenerational shift, the languages being shifted *to* and *from* can change a great deal. As fewer speakers use a language actively, words may be forgotten, its syntax may be simplified and restructured, and the phonological system may change (e.g., Dorian 1989b; Schmid 2011). Bilingual speakers may incorporate elements from one language into the other, such as intonation patterns and verb morphology, even creating new linguistic varieties (e.g., Bilaniuk 2005; Queen 2001; Rickford and McWhorter 1997; Thomason 2001; Thomason and Kaufman 1988). Buryat, for instance, has borrowed the sound [k] from Russian, as well as extensive vocabulary in multiple waves, and the literary language has borrowed elements of Russian literary style. In these and other ways, contact-induced change from Russian has made it a shifting target for revitalization.

While these linguistic phenomena are much more thoroughgoing than forgetting single words, it is lexical loss that is often the most noticeable, and therefore worrisome, to speakers themselves. As Michael Silverstein (1981) and others have pointed out, lexical variation—whether between languages, dialects, or registers—is the aspect of linguistic variation most salient to people and therefore most available for metalinguistic comment. For example, Paul Kroskrity (1998, 110) found that among the Arizona Tewa, anxiety over maintaining a clean, pure language was directed at the lexicon exclusively, not at grammatical convergence.[18] Likewise, the focus of many of my interlocutors in Buryatia was on lexical loss in Buryat-Russian shift, particularly in domains of the lexicon associated with traditional Buryat pastoral-nomadic culture, such as botanical terminology or specialized vocabulary from horseback riding and animal husbandry.

This kind of vocabulary is not, however, necessarily considered "real Buryat" by speakers themselves in all contexts. How my own language acquisition was assessed is a case in point. When I learned Buryat as an adult during fieldwork, my tutors focused on the standard literary language, drawing on their expertise in linguistics to explain verb morphology and having me translate long newspaper passages from Buryat into Russian. I memorized the Buryat names of trees, berries, and wildlife of the steppe and taiga, only a small portion of which are still actively used by the region's increasingly urbanized Buryat population.

Outside that narrow pedagogical context, other speakers of Buryat, who were mostly bilingual in Russian and who tended to use much more colloquial forms of Buryat with more Russian influence, assessed my acquisition differently in different instances. After my first appearance on Buryat-language television, acquaintances and strangers alike praised me for speaking what they called "real Buryat" (*nastoiashchii buriatskii iazyk*) with many Buryat-origin forms that native speakers claimed not to know themselves. One of my older Buryat-speaking friends, Bairma, was particularly proud of my performance, because she felt she had played a part in it, and she delighted in all the "ancient words" I had learned at the university. A few months later, however, chatting over tea in her kitchen, she turned suddenly to her cousin Sèsègma, visiting from their ancestral village, and switched from Russian into a rapid, colloquial Buryat that I could barely follow. They laughed heartily at a joke Bairma made, and she looked back at me, addressing me in her usual not-quite-native Russian: "Do you understand what I'm saying?" (*Ty ponimaesh', chto ia govoriu?*). I answered honestly that I had caught only a few words and did not get the joke. "Ha!" she exclaimed with satisfaction, thumping the table hard and making the teacups and jam jars rattle. "That's because we speak real Buryat here! Sure, it's not like . . . on **stage**." She swept her arm out grandly, as though on stage, to the merriment of her cousin. "It's not like . . . in the **newspaper**." She tapped a copy of <u>Buriaad ünèn</u> that was sitting close at hand. "But it's real Buryat, right?" For confirmation, she turned to Sèsègma, who tried to nod seriously but was laughing so hard that tears had sprung to her eyes. "You should be learning **here**, in the kitchen [*na kukhne*]! Ha ha! That's where you'll learn real Buryat!"[19]

What counts as "real Buryat" is a subset of all possible ways of speaking—and being—Buryat. This is not, in itself, surprising. Drawing on insights from Bakhtin, many anthropologists of language have observed a fundamental diversity of ways of speaking within what linguists or speakers themselves nonetheless identify as a single code. Jane and Kenneth Hill (1980, 1986) observed that the indigenous Mexican language Nahuatl, for instance, can seem like a discrete code and can be envisioned by its speakers as such, in an ideologically dyadic relationship with a dominant language, such as Spanish—what is sometimes called a "matrix language." But depending on social context, that code may be more or less open to the use of the dominant or matrix language. Nahuatl may be more or less open to Spanish, depending on the speaker, the addressee, and the context in which they find themselves. Buryat-Russian language shift, when phrased thusly, might seem to involve only two codes, but on closer inspection, speakers, writers, listeners, and readers draw on resources from a wide array of varieties along a spectrum between an idealized "clean," purist code of Buryat and an idealized "clean," purist code of Russian.

Paradoxically, the "real Buryat" that Bairma suggests is spoken in kitchens is highly *im*pure, in the sense that it shows a great deal of Russian influence. When she says that it is "real" (*nastoiashchii*), she means that it is how people actually speak, behind closed doors, as opposed to how they would speak on stage or in newspapers, when they have a more public audience. By contrast, Larisa/Yanzhima seeks a purist code of Buryat as the "real" language, which she imagines as predating Russian contact. She looks to the work of lexicographers and newspaper writers and to poetic genres of speech that scholars and speakers alike consider unassailably authentically Buryat: extended poetic greetings and blessings (B. üreėlnüüd, R. *pozhelaniia*), geneaological recitations (B. ug garbal, R. *rodoslovnaia*), and those "ancient words" for trees, berries, and the pieces of a horse's bridle.

In looking to these authoritative sources, Larisa/Yanzhima underscores the chronotopic power of particular mediums and genres. Mass media are, after all, materially important both for the kinds of relations they engender and for the time periods they come to represent. Radio and newspapers may be considered "old," for instance, while television or digital media are "new." Although building Buryat-language newspapers was a quintessentially Soviet modernization project, for Larisa/Yanzhima, they are old, and therefore authoritative on matters of Buryat linguistics. Poetic genres of Buryat have likewise become part of a chronotopic imagination of a "real" Buryat to be reclaimed. If Buryat as an "unadapted" purist code evokes the "ancient past" and "bygone nomadic civilization" to which Dorzh refers, poetic genres distill the listener's sense of nostalgia. Larisa/Yanzhima is nostalgic for these specific ways of speaking because they are indicative, to her, of a particular time period and of particular social alignments that have passed (Wilce 2009).[20] At the same time, as Bairma points out, they are not the ways of speaking that people employ in a kitchen over tea.

Reclaiming Origins, Revitalizing Relationships

Learning to recite üreėlnüüd in purist Buryat from the newspaper is not the only way to go about reclaiming what one sees as one's Buryat origins. Holidays, for instance, have been enthusiastically revived in the post-Soviet period, particularly when they are connected to religious observance. An important target of cultural revitalization is Sagaalgan, the Buryat Buddhist New Year, and the lunar month of Sagaan Har (the White Month), which usually begins in early or mid-February. Among the most popular forms of music in Buryatia are traditional songs with Buryat lyrics, updated with synthesizers and colorful sequined gowns. "ethno rock" is an emerging genre of music, as is "ethno fashion," which marries miniskirts and high heels with the studded leather helmets of Mongolian warriors of the Middle Ages. Thus Buryatness is celebrated and repopularized through a variety of semiotic modes. Yet language is part and parcel of songs and Sagaalgan and memories of Chinggis Khan's sartorial choices, and people often see language as the medium for all of these other kinds of reclamation.

In fact, what people are seeking by reclaiming language is rarely the language per se; rather, it is the lost social relations that are not only invoked by a way of speaking but directly enabled by it. For instance, on the Mongolian side of the border, Buryats have revived shamanic practices as a way of coping with postsocialist rupture and economic devastation (Buyandelger 2013). This is a matter not only of mending relations with your living kin but also of reconnecting to your ongons, ancestor spirits who might aid you (or make your life very difficult, if you have been ignoring them). On the Russian side of the border, my colleagues and I (Quijada, Graber, and Stephens 2015) found that some Buryats are pursuing other forms of cultural revitalization, such as tracking down their genealogies and trying to learn and use Buryat, as pragmatic means to mend relationships with their ongons. Once they have successfully channeled an ongon through a shaman, many supplicants cannot communicate with the spirit, needing to rely—sometimes desperately—on intermediaries to translate into Russian (see also Quijada 2019). When your ancestors speak Buryat and you do not, your lack of knowledge has painfully practical implications: you cannot understand your ancestral spirits' advice or appease them to improve your fortunes.

Many Buryats also seek to reclaim personal relationships with living relatives in ways that interweave language and other Buryat cultural practices. This is illustrated by a typical encounter I had with a group of university students in Ulan-Ude in August 2011. A friend had asked me to speak to her class in Buryat about Mongolian studies in the United States, for the same reasons I had been interviewed for newspapers, radio, and television: to model interest and ability. The students peppered me with the same questions I had grown accustomed to answering from journalists and many other students before them—formulaic, but telling in how they constitute almost a script for presenting Buryatia to outsiders. Did I like Buryatia? Had I been to Lake Baikal? Had I celebrated Sagaalgan? Had I danced ëkhor, the traditional Buryat circle dance? We were working our way down the list of places and items emblematic of Buryatia and Buryatness. Had I tried buuza? one of the students asked, referring to the Buryat national dish of steamed meat dumplings. Buuza (R. pozy) are formed by working dough, usually by hand, around a mixture of onions, garlic, and minced mutton, beef, and/or horsemeat.[21] Once we had established that, yes, I had dined on buuza many times and loved them very much, another student upped the ante: could I *make* buuza? It happens that although I am no great cook, many kind women over the years have taken it on themselves to teach me this central art, and I could answer honestly that, yes, I could make buuza. Afterward, one of the students told me that our meeting had inspired her to make buuza with her grandmother when she went home to her village for the holidays, adding with an embarrassed giggle that she might try to speak Buryat with her, too. She connected our meeting directly to intergenerational cultural transmission and preservation within her own family and to her failings on this count thus far. At issue here is not the survival of the Buryat language, culture, people, or public en masse but, rather, her relationship with her grandmother.

These personal reclamations are often made via mass media, and Buryat media personnel see it as part of their job to facilitate them. One of the most popular genres printed in local newspapers and broadcast on local television consists of personal historical accounts, usually chronicling Buryat families that suffered tragedy after tragedy during Russia's tumultuous twentieth century. Similarly, a short-lived "telebridge" (*telemost*) program on BGTRK linked audiences in television studios in Ulaanbaatar and Ulan-Ude, with hosts translating between Russian, Buryat, and Mongolian as necessary. Modeled after a popular Russian program that reunited families on air, the program traced the stories of families who had been separated by changing politics, World War II, the large-scale migration of Buryat families into Mongolia in the 1930s, and other historical traumas. Focusing on the personal tragedies wrought by political changes, it was phenomenally popular, but it was canceled—and its Buryat host fired—under circumstances that remained unclear to her journalist colleagues. Some thought she had grown too old for the camera and that letting her go was a "natural" outcome, while others believed the program was too politically sensitive, due to both its attention to contested periods of Soviet history and the way it encouraged Buryat-Mongols to think of themselves as such.

Some media personnel also attempt to "scale up" these personal reclamations to reconstitute a Buryat minority language public that they see as having been divided. The most thoroughgoing example of this is Tolon. In 1989, a group of Buryat nationalists and intellectuals in Aga began this independent media experiment as a way to reach and interlink ethnic Buryats living across Russia's widespread Buryat territories. By conceiving of it as an "all-Buryat" (*vseburiatskaia*) newspaper—first in the sense that it was only in Buryat, and then in the sense that it would cover events and be distributed across the Buryat territories—Dorzh and the other founders of Tolon sought to mend the Buryats' political fragmentation and the piecemeal information field described above (Graber 2016). Tolon has succeeded in the sense that it has survived Aga's dissolution and Russia's recentralization and renationalization efforts, but efforts to link the Buryat territories through mass media like this have been rare.

Rarer still, and pursued on an even more ad hoc basis, are efforts to reclaim Mongolianness via mass media. The fate of the "telebridge" program between Ulaanbaatar and Ulan-Ude, as well as quashed efforts to write and publish in mutually intelligible border dialects (described in the chapters to come), suggest some reasons why. Yet people have more subtle spiritual and linguistic ways of ignoring—or transcending—the political border between Russia and Mongolia. Humphrey (2015) has argued that although the border's constraints are a main way that Buryats' remoteness is constructed vis-à-vis the Russian state, Buryats living on the border locate themselves in a more mobile social and spiritual world that transcends politics (see also Bernstein 2013). Linguistically, some Buryats reclaim Mongolianness by emphasizing the similarities rather than differences between Khalkh Mongolian and Buryat, or by self-identifying with Mongolians and "Buryat-Mongolia." Dorzh, for instance, calls himself a "Buryat-Mongol," as do many other Buryat journalists like Bayandalai, a retired newspaper, radio, and television journalist who devoted his retirement years to writing Buddhist poetry. Bayandalai remarked during one of our many wide-ranging conversations about his career, the future of Buryatia, and his growing spirituality that as he grew older, he felt increasingly Mongolian. He described this as happening largely through his personal reclamation of Buddhist practices that he had learned as a child, as well as through his increasingly frequent movements back and forth across the Russian-Mongolian border.

References to Mongolia that invoke a shared past can enjoy ideological and commercial success. The television station Arig Us, for instance, has an extremely successful brand in Buryatia. The Khalkh name means 'clear water' and refers to the origin place of a mythical figure in the *Secret History of the Mongols*, ten generations before Chinggis Khan. The same company owns a chain of convenience stores under the same name, with the same logo, drawing on a pun on "clear water" and "clear broadcasting," as well as on romantic impressions of the Mongolian countryside as a clean, pure, healthy landscape.

For different reasons, Chinese television's depictions of life in Inner Mongolia resonate with many Buryat viewers and provide alternative imagined futures—as well as pasts—of Buryat belonging. China's flagship television station, CCTV, is available in Buryatia in standard cable packages, and it has grown quite popular with many Buryat viewers. Anti-Chinese sentiment in Buryatia is significant and has increased over the course of the 2000s, following an influx of undocumented Chinese workers and rising tensions over the lumber, oil, and natural gas flowing out to fuel China's growing economy. To judge from my interviewees' comments about CCTV, however, the broadcasts from Inner Mongolia succeed in ameliorating negative sentiment. The channel broadcasts stage performances of traditional song and dance, with on-screen text in classical Mongolian script—which exceedingly few viewers in Russia can read, but which strongly indexes Mongolian tradition visually. While they might appear cheesy and over-produced to some, these performances are in a format that makes sense within post-Soviet Russia, and CCTV gives Russian viewers the impression that Mongolic languages and cultures have been well preserved in Inner Mongolia. These representations are not consonant with what most observers from outside China report, but CCTV has succeeded in suggesting to Buryats that their language and culture might have fared better under Chinese colonization than under Russian colonization (or "integration," depending on how you look at it).

When I asked a BGTRK journalist, Tsymzhidma, why she thought China had been, as she put it, a better "host" or "caretaker" (*khoziain*) of Buryat, she suggested that it was because the state had taken this role more seriously. In Russia, she suggested, language preservation had long since become the responsibility of individual families, with everything depending on grandmothers. Grandmothers often play an important role as cultural and linguistic standard-bearers, not only in Buryatia but in other communities experiencing language loss as well (e.g., Dorian 2014). Among Buryat speakers, some of the most heavily circulated metalinguistic commentary, including jokes about language loss, is transmitted intergenerationally primarily through women (Graber 2017). (Grandmothers are also among the individuals most likely to chide young people about not speaking well, which has its own unintended consequences.) Despite the fact that this is a common situation, Tsymzhidma took it as the aberrational result of the state abdicating its natural responsibility. In her view, language preservation and revitalization should be pursued primarily through institutions and formatted cultural performance—something on constant display on CCTV.

In practice, Buryat language revitalization efforts are going on both in state-run or state-funded institutions like BGTRK and the Republic's Ministry of Education and in an ad hoc fashion among interested private individuals. Efforts to increase the number of hours of Buryat-language instruction in K–12 education and to introduce Buryat-medium schools beyond the national boarding school have mostly failed—and in any case, those institutions were never meant to serve adult learners. For the past several years, at least two small groups of adult learners of Buryat in Ulan-Ude have informally organized language classes that they attend on their own time. On YouTube, Buryat learners can find lessons by a popular teacher and Mongolist, Jargal Badagarov, teaching Buryat grammar through song lyrics. Buriaad ünèn has periodically run short language lessons for adult learners of Buryat, alongside news stories that assume existing mastery. In the past, these lessons have sometimes focused on the terminology and expressions that one would need to buy a loaf of bread or have a dress tailored, but today they more often focus on those "ancient words" that are both more consonant with

Buryat's current indexicality and, sometimes, more practical, in that they are more likely to be necessary when speaking with one's ongon (if not one's grandmother). In these ways, language revitalizers often try to reteach cultural traditions simultaneously with language, by focusing on domains in which Buryat is, as editors and writers often put it to me, particularly "rich" (B. baian, R. *bogatyi*). Features in Buriaad ünèn have explained, for example, specialized Buryat terms for male and female horses of different ages, as well as animal coat colors.

Buryat language revitalization efforts thus far have probably been less successful at producing new fluent speakers than at improving the social status of Buryat and reestablishing a link between contemporary Buryats and what they feel is "their" ancestral language. But this is no small thing and indeed is the most many new revitalization projects can hope for (Grinevald 2005). While using Buryat smacks of rurality and often the poverty that goes along with it, it also increasingly indexes pride in Buryat culture, which has become, in a word, cool. Over the course of the 2000s, it has become noticeably more acceptable to speak Buryat in the streets of Ulan-Ude, partly because of extreme post-Soviet migration from rural areas to the city and partly because the tide of public sentiment regarding Buryat has turned. As the (then) senior editor of Buriaad ünèn, Ardan Angarkhaev, suggested to me in 2009, young people are now "interested in their own culture," and they no longer "feel a complex." In fact many young people spoke to me, and to each other, of feeling a complex (*kompleks*), and it was reflected in the way people of all ages reacted to the television broadcasts I described in the preface. How remarkable, they said, that a young person with a European face could speak Buryat on camera "without a complex" (*bez kompleksa*). But this is different from the complex to which Angarkhaev referred. Angarkhaev referred to a feeling that many Buryats describe as having felt in the recent past (and sometimes still feel), that it is unseemly and low-class to speak Russian poorly or with a Buryat accent. By contrast, many young people now have a strong complex about speaking *Buryat* poorly or with a Russian accent. Although this is not entirely new, there has indeed been a change in attitude.

Paradoxically, the subtle change in attitude to which Angarkhaev refers is closely connected to many Buryats' intense interest in learning English, Chinese, and other "world languages," because both are rooted in a desire for cosmopolitanism in what they see as an increasingly globalized context. Through the late Soviet period, Russian-speaking populations treated Russian in much the same way English-speaking populations in the United States treat English now: they assumed that it would continue to be a useful lingua franca, likely well outside the borders of the state. While foreign language study was an important part of school curricula, Russian was so far and away the dominant language of social and economic advancement that many students did not see the need to learn

other languages.[22] With the dissolution of the Soviet Union and rapid globalization, this impression has changed, and being multilingual has taken on new prestige. Thus Buryat language revitalization efforts in Buryatia are most successful
when they capitalize on young people's interest in *foreign* languages.

Rapidly growing numbers of younger residents study English. Spanish, Polish, and Japanese have also been popular languages to study, in part due to the
availability of exchange programs. A number of elementary schools in Ulan-Ude
and neighboring districts have introduced mandatory English and Chinese into
their curricula. English is increasingly seen as a way to travel and to succeed in
Mongolia, China, or Europe, as well as in Russia, while Chinese offers employment opportunities in China or in Russia's booming oil, gas, and forestry industries. These foreign languages (all of which are considered more foreign than, say,
Armenian and other languages of the former Soviet Union) often offer neutral
ground in the value-laden terrain between Russian and Buryat. English, in particular, has become the language of cosmopolitanism. A Buryat writer offered a
compelling example of this when he explained why he wanted to translate his
book—an enormous, detailed mytho-historical study of Aga's Süügèl datsan—
directly from Buryat into English. It was very important to him *not* to translate
via Russian, he said, because it would corrupt his meaning, and because he had
no interest in presenting his work to a Russian-speaking audience. He sought
to reach beyond the Russian-speaking country in which he found himself to a
cosmopolitan audience (and specifically to the Dalai Lama).

In pursuit of cosmopolitanism, many Buryats thus see intensified foreign language study as means of reclaiming Buryat belonging. While one might imagine
that Buryat language advocates would protest losing instructional hours to other
languages, I have rarely encountered this argument in Buryatia. Most journalists and other cultural elites with whom I spoke advocated learning as many
languages as possible. A group of newspaper journalists in Aga claimed that they
had learned, from their children and younger relatives, that English and Buryat
had much in common. For instance, they share the laryngeal /h/ [h], which Russian lacks. This might seem like very little common ground, but it is salient to
speakers because the speech of native speakers of Russian who learn Buryat in
school or later in life is marked by their pronunciation of /h/ instead as velar
[x]. Pronouncing /h/ as [x] is likewise one of the central features of a Russian
accent in English. (Think of the stereotypical way Boris and Natasha of Rocky
and Bullwinkle pronounce the word *house*—"xaus"—or *I have a plan*—"I xev
a plan.") Indeed, Buryat speakers often express surprise at my "native" pronunciation of /h/ because it differs from the [x] they expect out of the mouth of a
"person of European origin." One of the reporters mocked the way children now
encounter Buryat only after having learned some English. She impersonated a

child, pantomiming reading a line of the Buryat-language newspaper in front of her with a finger and finding a letter. "*Chto ėto*—[**h**]?" (What is this—[**h**]?) she said, raising her eyebrows and emphasizing the laryngeal [h] sound hard so that everyone in the room laughed. "They are learning Buryat through English!" By the same token, some people hoped that Buryat college students would become interested in their "own" (*svoi*) language by first becoming interested in Mongolian—a language potentially considered more fashionable by virtue of being foreign.

Looking Sideways as well as Back

Healing temporal and spatiocultural ruptures by looking sideways—to English [h], say, or to Inner Mongolia—is not so odd. Efforts to reclaim something from the past rest on a kind of nostalgia. As Svetlana Boym (2001) has observed, nostalgia is always a matter not only of looking backwards and into the past but also of looking sideways, at an alternative present. We can see this attitude in language revitalizers describing a need to "re"insert Buryat into the public sphere and onto the streets of Ulan-Ude. Ulan-Ude was never a Buryat-dominant city. It grew up as a Russian trading post, Verkhneudinsk, and while Buryat appears to have been an important language of commerce and daily interaction, the city's most powerful institutions—including the government, schools, and mass media—were overwhelmingly run in Russian. Verkhneudinsk's early newspapers were run and printed almost entirely by Jewish men who championed public education and other progressive social causes. The city's current name, Ulan-Ude (B. Ulaan Üdė, lit. red Uda, for the Uda River) was a not-so-subtle Bolshevik attempt at indigenizing it and displaying the new state's anti-imperialist agenda. Certainly Buryat nationalists and their Bolshevik allies in the early twentieth century wished for this to *become* an alternative native capital, but that is not exactly what happened. This is what is captured today by wistful suggestions of "returning" to a Buryat Ulan-Ude—or by musing over whether Buryat would have been better preserved under Chinese rule: an alternative history, and an alternative path, still running tantalizingly alongside the present.

Under political pressure to maintain cultural distinctiveness, possessing knowledge and authority in the context of language shift becomes a moral concern. The moral implications of preserving Buryat are visible in how linguistic knowledge of Buryat is attached to neighboring domains of cultural knowledge. Speaking Buryat has taken on a personal, ethical importance like that of ordering prayers for your relatives at the datsan, observing Sagaalgan with friends and family, healing relations with your ongons, or being able to make buuza with your aunt.

The sense of rupture and loss evinced by many contemporary Buryats, and the ways in which people now work to reclaim a Buryat selfhood, suggest a cyclical view of time in which languages, like other cultural practices, are more likely to sleep and awaken than become forever "extinct" (Leonard 2008). But the sideways views are also admissions that Buryat cannot be simply plucked out of the past and imported into the present. Larisa/Yanzhima locates Buryat belonging in a time "before," but she does not find an easy source. Relocating the "real" Buryat language—and "real Buryats"—in the post-Soviet era has been made difficult by extreme language shift, by contact-induced change within Buryat, and by the way Buryats understand and organize linguistic variation ideologically.

Dorzh deftly places Buryat belonging instead on a spiritual, metaphysical level, transcending daily experience and physical political borders.[23] This is one of the more interesting and provocative moves of contemporary Buryat cultural politics, as it suggests that many of the existing trappings of ethnonational belonging, such as physical territory, are unnecessary. Yet in tying language to the spiritual well-being of a people, he still foregrounds linguistic knowledge as key to cultural continuity.

Larisa/Yanzhima, for her part, was finding learning Buryat a difficult task—particularly because she sought to learn it "correctly," through dictionaries, newspapers, and cultural elites whom she took to be linguistically authoritative, and in whom she sees the "real" language. For all her efforts, she may not be taken as a real speaker of Buryat in the kitchen. She is learning the literary standard, which some of her relatives may not even understand. How and why Buryat as "a" language is ideologically bifurcated in this way, and how mass media experts perpetuate their own linguistic and cultural authority, are the subject of Part II.

Part II
MEDIATED STANDARDS

A LITERARY STANDARD AND ITS DISCONTENTS

Masha squinted at the page, puzzling out the last few lines of a Buryat news-paper article that she was reading aloud. She reached the end and shook her head, sighing heavily. "Oh, it's **tot**ally incomprehensible. **Totally!**" (*Oi, èto sovsem ne poniatno. Sovsem!*) Another participant in our focus group, Ayuur, looked swiftly up at Masha in disbelief. "Really? You don't understand anything?" (*A da? Nichego ne ponimaesh'?*) He knew that Masha was fluent in Buryat, though they spoke only Russian with one another. They had just argued over the differences between their respective dialects, with Masha maintaining that the differences were extreme, and Ayuur maintaining that they were not. All native speakers, he had said, could "basically" understand the standard literary language. Now Masha was saying that she could not grasp anything from an article that he understood "completely," and he looked less surprised than skeptical. "Well," said Masha, "maybe I understand . . . 10 or 20 percent. But no more." (*Nu, ia mozhet byt' ponimaiu protsentov . . . 10–20. A bol'she, net.*) She asked Ayuur about several specific words and passages. He tried to pick through an especially long particip-ial phrase, finally laughing and admitting that he had not understood everything either. "Let's say 90 percent." (*Skazhem 90 protsentov.*)

At the end of our focus group, Masha was visibly shaken, depressed by her newfound feeling that she had, as she put it, a "low-level knowledge" (*nizkii uroven' znanii*) of her native language. Another participant pointed out, by way of consolation, that even her own grandmother could not read <u>Buriaad ünèn</u>, and she had spoken only Buryat her entire life. They returned to the topic of dialect variation, continuing to speak Russian and further absolving Masha of any expectation to understand (or produce) the standard literary language. But the damage had been done. Masha had a strong Buryat accent in Russian, so although she used Russian in most of her daily interactions and reading, she was not taken as a full native speaker of Russian. She had felt secure in her knowledge of Buryat based on her control of the spoken language, and here she was confronted with the possibility that she might be a semispeaker—that is, what she herself would consider someone with incomplete knowledge, despite her oral fluency—of what she considered her first language and native tongue.

Several different factors—native dialect, literary standards, the desire to understand—affect a person's comprehension of what I call Standard Literary Buryat (SLB).[1] Speakers of Buryat who grew up with exposure to conversational Buryat in their home, village, or neighborhood are highly aware—even hyperaware—of the multiple gaps between their native "colloquial," "vernacular," or "conversational" linguistic forms and the SLB that they encounter in institutions such as schools, libraries, or mass media. Native speakers of Buryat like Masha and Ayuur consistently report radically different comprehension of the written Buryat of newspapers, and very few speakers under the age of about forty-five report understanding everything.[2] I had been hearing about this phenomenon of incomprehensibility from native speakers of Buryat for several years before I formally documented and explored it in a series of focus groups.

The gaps are not new; there have been serious and consequential discrepancies between SLB and other ways of speaking Buryat since the beginnings of state-sponsored standardization in the 1920s–30s. As the register of literature, institutional discourse, and interdialectal communication, SLB was created by analogy to literary Russian and the principle that nations should have literary standards, without any expectation that it would mimic everyday speech. However, the contrasts are particularly poignant for Buryat speakers at this moment in cultural and linguistic history. Language shift over the late Soviet and post-Soviet periods did not only mean shifting from more Buryat use to more Russian use; it has also manifested itself in an intergenerational shift from print literacy in both Buryat and Russian to print literacy in Russian and oral comprehension in Buryat. This phenomenon is not unique to Buryatia. A similar pattern of shift has been at work to greater and lesser degrees throughout Russia's ethnic territories, as Russian is increasingly used in most domains of public life and native regional tongues are relegated to use at home. While still widely spoken, languages like Tatar, Udmurt, and Buryat are often dismissed by their speakers as too poor, too colloquial, or otherwise unfit for use outside the kitchen. As these native languages become restricted to increasingly narrow functional domains, they are popularly referred to as *kukhonnye iazyki*, or "kitchen languages" (Ar-Sergi 2007; Pustai 2005, 11; Wertheim 2009, 274).

This might sound like a straightforward case of diglossia, in which Buryat is the low-status language of the kitchen and Russian is the high-status language of the workplace, official discourse, and the newspaper. Thus far, most scholarship on post-Soviet bilingualism has suggested such a diglossic split between local languages and Russian, focusing on the phenomenon exclusively at the level of code (e.g., Khilkhanova 2009). But linguistic bifurcation in these cases is not limited to a functional diglossic split between Russian and the native language. There is also functional bifurcation within the native language, such as between Soviet Stage Romani and standard Romani (Lemon 2002) or between more and less purist ways of speaking Tatar (Wertheim 2003), Ukrainian (Bilaniuk 2004), or Belarusian (Woolhiser 2001).[3] Rapid erosion in native language literacy in the post-Soviet period has exacerbated these gaps. Although a standardized form of the native language is used in institutions and in texts printed and speeches read for symbolic political purposes, average speakers like Masha are not necessarily competent in this standard and may use a variety of dialects, colloquialisms, and syncretic forms outside of official or ritualized contexts.[4]

This chapter traces the origins of Masha's problem to standardization efforts in the Soviet period, advanced primarily through mass media production and education, that remain incomplete. Creating a strong literary standard was part of the Buryat modernizing project, but as bilingualism in Russian grew and as the state increasingly pursued the development of Russian as a Soviet lingua franca, Buryat standardization efforts became more symbolic than substantive. Today, media makers and other language elites nonetheless persist in trying to use SLB, because it so strongly indexes modern nationhood and is the code of an idealized, unified Buryat minority public. Consequently, contemporary audiences who control colloquial forms of Buryat have a hard time understanding Buryat-language media, particularly news media, which further encourages them to default to Russian-language sources—and to remain silent when interviewers come knocking at their door.

Even under the best circumstances, language standardization necessarily creates divisions and hierarchies. Enregistering a strong literary standard—that is, creating it and making it "stick" as a well-defined way of speaking—does not necessarily denigrate other registers, dialects, and ways of speaking across all domains of use. The first two sections of this chapter examine linguistic resources, namely dialects and Russian-Buryat mixed forms, that are not part of the literary standard but that nonetheless serve important social functions in certain contexts. Language standardization does, however, hierarchize ways of communicating in formal or public domains such as newspapers, courts, classrooms, or wherever the literary standard is to be employed. Once an orthography is standardized, for instance, spelling conventions become *rules*, adherence to which can show that one knows about "proper" form, that one cares about it, and that one shares the ideological commitments embedded within it (Johnson 2005; Suslak 2003). The ideology of standardization also rests on—and brings with it—a number of assumptions about how language works, including that languages *should be* uniform (Milroy 2000, 2001), and that part of a linguistic landscape can stand in for the whole. Logically, relying on a part:whole relationship is necessary when choosing one dialect on which to base a standard, such as Parisian French for standard French or Lhasa Tibetan for standard Tibetan. Because a standard must be based on one variety and not on others, standardization grants existing speakers differential access to the new code of public power.

Within the sociolinguistic hierarchy inherited by contemporary Buryats, SLB is publicly venerated over colloquial ways of speaking. Ideologically, the literary standard has been made so successfully to stand in for the whole range of what might count as "Buryat" that native speakers see their collective knowledge of SLB slipping away as their collective knowledge of *Buryat* slipping away. Yet the standard has always been tenuous. Moreover, in practice, people use linguistic resources to achieve multiple, overlapping goals at the same time. A given linguistic feature can be evaluated differently in different contexts and imbued with either the values ascribed to the supposedly "high" variety or those ascribed to the supposedly "low" variety—or both, since a single resource might simultaneously belong to two codes (Woolard 1998b). Additionally, although SLB and colloquial ways of speaking stand in a diglossic relationship to one another, variation among those colloquial ways of speaking precludes this being a neat opposition between two discrete registers.[5] All of this multiplicity belies a more general truth about linguistic possibility: most Buryats have far more than two options available to them in their interactions. They do not merely inherit analytically separable languages and varieties. Rather, they work to create and maintain a diglossic relationship between discrete pools of linguistic resources: Russian and/versus Buryat, and SLB and/versus the various ways of speaking colloquially to which we now turn.

Ways of Being *Razgovornyi*

Colloquial or vernacular language tends to be defined negatively, as whatever the official, standardized, or prestige language is *not*. Colloquially, what people count as Buryat can include a great deal of Russian borrowings and mixed Buryat-Russian forms, and it includes a wide range of dialects, some of which are only irregularly mutually intelligible. Within Buryat, deviation from the written standard can happen in multiple ways, but such deviation is often expressed or identified as simply *razgovornyi*.[6] The term literally means 'conversational' or 'colloquial,' but it encompasses a range of linguistic forms that are only loosely unified in being somehow different from the literary standard.

Broadly, *razgovornye* ways of speaking fall into two categories, examined in this section and the one following: (1) dialects, tied to specific geographic areas; and (2) Buryat-Russian mixed forms. In both cases, the *razgovornye* resources are decidedly inferior in a publicly validated sociolinguistic hierarchy, but they nonetheless play important roles in a wide range of socially significant activities, from making business deals and cursing to building friendships and finding a marriage partner.

Dialects are especially important in this respect. If one-third to a half of the Republic of Buryatia's residents live legally or illegally in Ulan-Ude, the other half to two-thirds live in the republic's diverse districts (*raions*), the contemporary descendants of pre-Soviet administrative districts based very loosely on Mongol-era tribal grounds (aimags).[7] The historical connection between tribe and territory is relevant for how linguistic diversity is understood in the contemporary period, because regional Buryat dialects are now taken as indexical of territorial and familial belonging. And the districts do function as geolinguistic units in some ways: they are relatively isolated; they provide key sites of intergenerational language transmission from grandparents to citified grandchildren; and with their own newspapers, they represent important local media markets. Although the districts have many semiurban administrative centers, they are often spoken about in opposition to Ulan-Ude: things happen either "in the city" (*v gorode*) or "in the districts" (*v raionakh*), and the latter are figured as slightly wild places— poor and quiet, but also as beautiful, pure, and closer to nature and to Buryat traditional life.

Standard Literary Buryat is based on a single eastern dialect, Khori. But several districts are considered home to what people call, oxymoronically, the "literary dialects." Speakers from Aga and from the eastern steppe districts of the Republic of Buryatia, including Khori (R. Khorinskii), Iaruuna (R. Eravninskii), Khėzhėngė (R. Kizhinginskii), Zagarai (R. Zaigraevskii), Mukhar-Shėbėr (R. Mukhorshibirskii), and Bėshüür (R. Bichurskii), are generally considered speakers of the literary standard (*nositeli literaturnogo iazyka*). Among these, Khorinskii, Eravninskii, and Kizhinginskii are the three dialects best known to average speakers as the "literary language," perhaps because such a large percentage of the Buryat cultural elite hails from these regions and Aga.[8] (See figure 10.)

Contemporary dictionaries, when they include dialectisms at all, often mark lexical deviation from SLB by specifying dialect. For example, a comprehensive electronic dictionary created by buryadxelen.org for the Republic of Buryatia

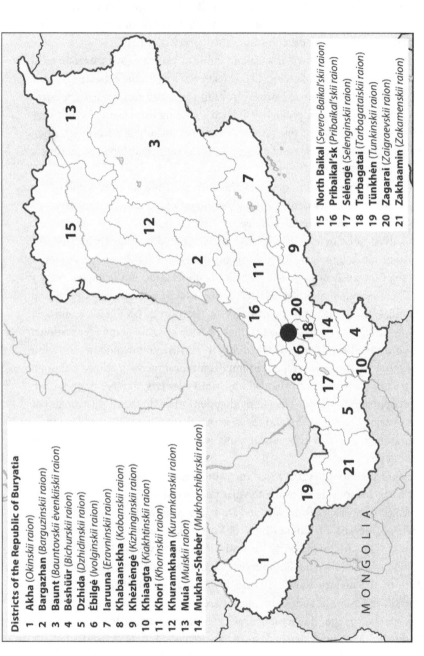

Districts of the Republic of Buryatia

1 **Akha** (*Okinskii raion*)
2 **Bargazhan** (*Barguzinskii raion*)
3 **Baunt** (*Bauntovskii évenkiiskii raion*)
4 **Bëshüür** (*Bichurskii raion*)
5 **Dzhida** (*Dzhidinskii raion*)
6 **Ébilgé** (*Ivolginskii raion*)
7 **Iaruuna** (*Eravninskii raion*)
8 **Khabaanskha** (*Kabanskii raion*)
9 **Khëzhëngé** (*Kizhinginskii raion*)
10 **Khiaagta** (*Kiakhtinskii raion*)
11 **Khori** (*Khorinskii raion*)
12 **Khuramkhaan** (*Kurumkanskii raion*)
13 **Muia** (*Muiskii raion*)
14 **Mukhar-Shëbër** (*Mukhorshibirskii raion*)

15 **North Baikal** (*Severo-Baikal'skii raion*)
16 **Pribaikal'sk** (*Pribaikal'skii raion*)
17 **Selëngé** (*Selenginskii raion*)
18 **Tarbagatai** (*Tarbagataiskii raion*)
19 **Tünkhën** (*Tunkinskii raion*)
20 **Zagarai** (*Zaigraevskii raion*)
21 **Zakhaamin** (*Zakamenskii raion*)

MONGOLIA

FIGURE 10. Administrative districts of the Republic of Buryatia. The dot marks Ulan-Ude. Some districts have alternative Buryat names: Dzhida is also known as Zédé, for example, and Baunt is also known as Babanta. Note that this is *not* a dialect map, though district affiliations and dialects are often taken as indexical of each other. (Map by author and Emma Percival; base layer from Viktor V.)

Ministry of Education and Science (2006) catalogues several Buryat variants for Russian *lob* (forehead), including dukha, sokho, magnai, and mangilai. Dukha, the variant used in SLB, appears unmarked. Sokho is listed as meaning (1) 'forehead' "in several dialects and rarely literary" and (2) 'temple' or 'temples' in Okinskii dialect. Magnai is recorded as *ustnaia rech'* (oral speech), to mean 'forehead' or 'brow.' Mangilai is marked as belonging to western dialects, specifically Ëkhiritskii. Finally, in a separate entry for dukha, the dictionary distinguishes between a Khorinskii usage, 'forehead,' and an Aginskii usage, 'back of the head.' Variants for 'forehead' are one of the more famous examples of Buryat dialectal variation, and when I informally elicited a person's word (or words) for 'forehead,' it often sparked lengthy discussion of dialect differences.

Dialectal variation in Buryat is a popular topic, not only among linguists perched in urban institutions but also among the speakers they study. Single words have long been a way of determining a person's background and attachments to place, or of locating him/her in the larger Mongolic-speaking world. And the popularity of the topic is long-standing: Humphrey (1989, 169) observed in the late Soviet period that when Buryats from different regions gathered, long discussions of dialectal variation sometimes ensued. In similar conversations that I observed in the 2000s, words like those for 'forehead' became discursive focal points for working out the indexical meanings of variation. Most people did not produce all four forms cited above, but they would often know two or three, one of which was almost always dukha. Among everyone except trained linguists, sokho, magnai, and mangilai were all deemed "local" (*mestnye*) or "dialectal" (*dialektnye*).

While the definition of the standard is quite narrow, *razgovornyi* acts as a sort of catch-all category for a wide range of dialectal, contact-induced, and accentual deviation. When a form is identified as *dialektnyi* informally, it most often means that it is from one of the nonliterary (western or southern) Buryat dialects, like sokho and mangilai. However, *dialektnyi* also sometimes means that the form is from one of the "literary dialects" but is not part of the literary standard (i.e., as recorded unmarked in dictionaries), like magnai. These items, neither dialectal nor literary as defined by linguists, are often described as belonging to the spoken language (*ustnaia rech'*), as in the dictionary entry. Yet in everyday metalinguistic discourse, *ustnaia rech'* is part of the larger *razgovornyi* ascription. To complicate matters further, the concept of *razgovornyi* often conflates variation between dialects with variation in Russian influence. Similarly, an individual's speech can be identified as *neliteraturnyi* (nonliterary) based on a Russian accent.

These various ways of being *razgovornyi* serve a number of important social functions, when used in the right context and for the right audience. Buryat dialects in particular are very powerful linguistic resources, owing to the regional, local, familial, and emotional affiliations that they index.

Many Buryats, particularly in older generations, describe a strong emotional connection to their <u>toonto niutag</u>, or 'birthplace' (lit. the place where one's after-birth was buried). Some members of Buryatia's current over-seventy generation were born in traditional felt yurts on the steppes of Khėzhėngė, Iaruuna, and Aga. Bayandalai, for instance, was born in a mobile felt yurt in Aga and remembers an early childhood populated by sheep, horses, and herdsmen. A pastoral-nomadic lifestyle that privileged the <u>toonto niutag</u> as an intimate, personal place of rest, return, and stability persists in living memory. In the late Soviet and post-Soviet periods, this lifestyle has been romanticized, and it has become popular among some hip, urbanized youth to identify their hometowns and ancestral villages (rather than the birthing hospitals where most babies are actually born) as their <u>toonto niutag</u>. Birthplace is so important that Buryats living in diaspora in European Russia even occasionally relocate to Buryatia to have children in the *rodina* (homeland or motherland, lit. birthland).

Dovetailing with this intensely felt personal connection with land are interpersonal connections to clan and zemliachestvo. Clan, in this context, is a patrilineal descent group, the members of which are treated as a discrete unit with its own name. A surprising number of rural Russian Buryats still know their clan or lineage affiliations, particularly if they are from one of the older, better known lineages such as the Galzuud, if their families practice shamanism intensively, or if their recent ancestors hail from the steppe regions of Aga, Iaruuna, and Khori (see also Humphrey and Sneath 1999, 27–30). Reciting one's genealogy through the male line, the <u>ug garbal</u> (R. *rodoslovnaia*), is an extremely important and prestigious ability, and genealogies are currently one of the most popular genres in newspapers, academic papers, and cultural shows like the annual pan-Buryat Dangina-Gėsėr competition, a combination beauty pageant and variety show. Clan descent is also important in the ascription of shamanic abilities, which are supposed to be largely hereditary. However, the practical strictures associated with clan and lineage affiliations, such as marriage rules, largely disappeared during the twentieth century. District affiliations, in contrast, are still important—and have arguably grown in importance in the post-Soviet period with increased migration into cities. District affiliations loosely reflect historical tribal affiliations and apply to both families and individuals, based on a combination of birthplace and heredity. Masha and Ayuur, for example, identify respectively as *aginskaia* and *kizhinginskii*, based on their birthplaces, while Bairma's cousin Sėsėgma identifies as *aginskaia* based on her heredity, despite having been born in a Russian factory town. Within the sprawling industrial capital of Ulan-Ude, these affiliations link up huge networks of village transplants, who have been migrating to the city seasonally or permanently over the past several decades.

Zemliachestvo connections become especially visible during the Buryat Buddhist New Year, Sagaalgan, and the "White Month" that follows it. Annually during this season, the members of a zemliachestvo (R. *zemliaki*, B. niutagaarkhid) gather for a holiday theatrical performance, Soviet-style awards ceremony, and celebratory banquet. These zemliachestvo gatherings provide a host of important opportunities: developing business connections, strengthening social ties, gaining public recognition, reaffirming regional identity and pride, and networking to find marriage partners.

In this context, there are social and economic benefits to speaking the dialect(s) of your parents' district(s). Dialect in Buryat is often identified as niutag khêlên (lit. place language, meaning 'the way we talk around here')—and there are few better ways to evoke your roots in the niutag than to speak a few words of niutag khêlên. Linguistic knowledge of your ancestral village's dialect suggests that even if you were raised mainly in Ulan-Ude or a Russian-speaking district capital, you probably spent significant time in the countryside with your grandparents or village relatives during your childhood and summers—a very common and valorized practice throughout the Buryat regions.[9] As an adult, this knowledge shows not only your bloodlines and your irreproachable countryside background, but also your commitment to fostering traditional Buryat culture. Vasilii, a well-heeled but romantically challenged Buryat man of about thirty, made a point of attending the annual zemliachestvo gatherings of both his mother and father, who come respectively from southern and western districts, to look for a wife. After striking out for the third year in a row in 2009, he complained bitterly to me that his relatives were hypocrites for encouraging him to pursue a university education in the city but then favoring the "most country-hick" of all the village boys for marriage to the available girls.[10] He had learned only rudimentary "school Buryat" when required, and he felt quite sure that he was excluded from consideration because he could not perform linguistically at zemliachestvo events. His friends advised him to learn some nice traditional poetic wishes, üreêlnüüd (R. *pozhelaniia*), and, "for fuck's sake," just go spend a summer in the village learning "a few words, resting and picking flowers."

Vasilii may have been overstating the importance of linguistic competence to the exclusion of other factors, but his desire to fit in not only as a member of the *Buryat* community but more specifically as a member of multiple *district* communities shows how dialectal variation can be socially and politically (not to mention romantically) meaningful. Crucially, dialect identification does not necessarily require knowledge of a whole system; as is evident from Vasilii's friends' advice, a few resources may be enough to index knowledge of the dialect or one's willingness to accommodate a dialect-speaking interlocutor.[11] For all the absence of a "unified information field" among Buryats, the same famous few examples of dialectal differences are repeated and circulated over and over again, so that specific linguistic features of dialects become metonymic for entire districts. Aga, for example, is sometimes humorously cited as the place "where 'forehead' [dukha] means the opposite"—that is, where <u>dukha</u> refers not to 'forehead,' as in SLB, but to the 'back of the head.'

Dialectal features perform another important geographic and political function in indexing relative nearness to Mongolia. Watching an evening Buryat-language news program, Oyuuna, an older woman from a Buryat district of Zabaikal'skii Krai, giggled with delight at the Khalkh Mongol pronunciation of a Buryat man being interviewed. She identified him as *aginskii* but concluded from his pronunciation of certain words that he must spend a lot of time in Mongolia. "It's clear," she said, nodding sagely, "that he feels himself to be Mongolian." (*Iasno, chto on chuvstvuet sebia mongol'skim.*) I happened to know the man in question, and she was correct: He is from Aga, but he frequently travels back and forth between Ulaanbaatar and Ulan-Ude, apprises himself of historical scholarship emphasizing the Mongolic origins of Buryats,[12] identifies not as a "Buryat" but as a "Buryat-Mongol," and indeed considers himself Mongolian in his personal and political leanings.

Further evidence of the social importance of dialectal variation can be found very simply in its popularity as a topic of casual conversation and in the weight placed on it in regional linguistics. Dialectology in the Baikal area has played a central role in Buryat linguistics since 1961, when the eminent linguist Trofim Alekseevich Bertagaev urged greater comparative attention to Buryat and Mongolian dialects and opened a booming subdiscipline. Buryat dialects were extensively documented in the late Soviet period, and a good knowledge of dialectology is currently considered part of basic education at NGI, where students are required to complete a summer field practicum in dialect documentation.[13]

Returning from one of these field programs, two NGI students noted to me how difficult it had been for them to elicit dialectal data from village *babushki*—elderly women—who did not themselves distinguish between dialectal forms and another type of *razgovornye* resources, mixed Buryat-Russian forms.[14] Lexical or grammatical use of Russian in speech otherwise framed as Buryat is often identified as "dialectal" by speakers not trained in linguistics. In a sense, this is a valid appellation, in that some dialects—most famously in western Buryatia around Irkutsk—have incorporated more Russian-origin lexical items and grammatical features, so that relative Russian influence marks dialectal variation. However, it also shows slippage in how dialectal forms and mixed forms are conceived of and suggests that for some speakers, Russian-contact-induced forms and dialectal forms make up a kind of grab bag of *razgovornye* features or resources.

"You Just Said It Right"

Language standardization efforts are often directed not only at delimiting the language to a single dialect but also at cordoning it off from undesirable external influence. Thus the second way to be nonstandard in one's use of Buryat is to use lots of Russian borrowings, codeswitch frequently into Russian, or otherwise use what speakers deride as "mixed language."

"Mixed language" (*smeshannyi iazyk*) can include subtle phonological features such as Russian prosody, shortened vowels, or Russian (and foreign) [k], when it is not nativized to [x]. Syntax and morphology are also sometimes "mixed," such as by adding Russian grammatical gender and adjectival endings to Buryat nouns, which otherwise lack grammatical gender. Most salient for speakers, however, are lexical borrowings, and this is usually what is meant when a person evaluates a stretch of discourse as "mixed." Using such language can index several things about a speaker. Most obviously, mixed forms index the relative Russification of a speaker's family, home district, or personal upbringing. Because Russian influence is so widespread, however, Russification is not always a remarkable fact; sometimes it is taken more as a given condition, albeit one to be struggled against. So mixed forms do not necessarily preclude a person from being judged a competent native speaker of Buryat. In fact, metalinguistic jokes ridiculing an extremely Russian-lexified way of speaking that people often call "pidgin" suggest that this is the "real Buryat" Bairma had in mind when opposing her kitchen to the stage and the newspaper (Graber 2017).

It is possible in many informal contexts to "speak Buryat" while using a huge number of Russian borrowings or codeswitching frequently into Russian.[15] This was the form in which most of my Buryat-speaking research consultants—and teachers—conversed with me, especially as my knowledge of SLB grew and they attended less to my acquisition of "correct" (*pravil'nyi*), "pure" (R. *chistyi*, B. sėbėr) Buryat. Whether our *smeshannyi* (mixed) conversation could be labeled "Buryat" was often unclear to me, and I wanted to verify its status. I was hesitant, however, to discuss the Russianisms of our own conversations, because that particular metalinguistic discourse often prompted embarrassment. I instead seized opportunities to discuss "mixed language" in the language of strangers on television and in public spaces.

One evening on a crowded public minibus in Ulan-Ude, I overheard the following from a teenager, violating Russian public transportation etiquette by talking loudly on his cellphone (which was, according to an urbanized friend, a "sure sign" that he had recently arrived from a village). He was engaged in a friendly conversation, apparently about two attractive girls that he and his interlocutor had recently met. At one point he said:

Ügy, *chego? Net!* [laughs] Ügy, shi *prosto norma:l'no* khėlėėsh . . . *No.*

Ügy,	chego?		Net!		
NEG	what.GEN		NEG		
Ügy,	shi	prosto	norma:l'no	khėl-ėė-sh . . .	No.
NEG	2SG	simply	normally	speak-PST-2SG	yes[16]

Gloss: 'No, what the heck? No! [laughs] No, you just said it right . . . Yeah.'

This utterance showcases both codeswitching (emphasizing Buryat negation, Ügy, with a codeswitch into Russian and the exclamation, *Net!*, followed by another Buryat negation and return to Buryat) and borrowing with phonological nativization (using Russian *prosto* and *normal'no* as adverbs in a Buryat grammatical construction). One of the most common means of nativizing new Russian borrowings is to apply Buryat vowel length, which is phonemic, to the stressed vowels of Russian-origin words. This practice is exemplified above in the lengthened *a:* of *norma:l'no.*[17] *Prosto* and *normal'no* are Russian words and do not appear in Buryat dictionaries, but they are easily borrowed into *razgovornye* ways of speaking Buryat, as this teenager's utterance shows. *Normal'no* literally means 'normally' but is used colloquially to mean 'correctly,' 'OK,' or 'well,' as in the common expression "to live *normal'no*"—that is, as one should, without crisis or abnormality. In this case, the speaker may have been referring to the form of his interlocutor's speech or to his evaluation of the girls.

Over the next few days, I repeated his beautifully bilingual sentence—shi *prosto norma:l'no* khėlėėsh—to several linguists and writers, carefully reproducing his Buryat pronunciation. "Well yes, that's how we talk" (*Nu da, tak govorim*), one poet said with a chuckle. His companion, a Buryat language teacher, agreed. "It's quotidian, but . . ." (*Èto bytovoi, no . . .*) She raised her eyebrows and shoulders, sighing slightly and shaking her head: ". . . totally the real language" (. . . *sovsem nastoiashchii iazyk*).[18]

Whether speech like this will be considered quotidian, real, solidarity-building, funny, bumpkin, or stupid depends on the context and participants of the interaction, on the interaction's scale, and on the intersectionality of statuses and identities. For instance, Pierre Bourdieu ([1982] 1991) describes the mayor of a French town, who speaks in the local dialect to index his regional affiliation. While the dialect is stigmatized within the larger "marketplace" of the French nation-state, speaking in dialect does not threaten his social capital because that status is secure for other reasons—namely, his role as mayor. Moreover, the mayor speaks at the scale of the town, not the nation-state. Without such social capital to protect him, the young man on the minibus was more likely to affirm his outsiderness in the city by mixing Russian and Buryat. But neither I nor my urbanized friend nor the reader of this book was his audience. He spoke at the scale of his friendship, and perhaps of his village or age cohort, within which such mixing could successfully show solidarity.

In short, with the right listeners in the right context, codeswitching and rampant new borrowing from Russian may not only "count" as Buryat but be perfectly appropriate to the situation. Mixed forms may suggest that a person is a fine native speaker but is ignorant of SLB, meaning that she was probably educated mostly or entirely through Russian and did not have access to formal education in Buryat, or that she is a heritage speaker who does not use Buryat much in her adult life. Both situations are extremely common, although they do not always get a person off the hook for using mixed forms. This is partly because, more subtly, mixed forms can be taken as evidence of a speaker's lack of commitment to preserving the Buryat language and culture, or—perhaps worse—as evidence of ignorance, degradation, or stupidity.

While these possibilities are all negatives within the contemporary Buryat cultural sphere, mixed forms are widely used anyway—including by language elites, such as journalists, teachers, and stage performers—because they have other benefits. They are, first and foremost, more comprehensible to semispeakers of Buryat, allowing framing of an interaction in Buryat without sacrificing intelligibility. Despite periodic attempts to purify Buryat and purge Russianisms, Buryat shows a great deal of Russian lexical influence, even in SLB, and it is not always feasible to reassert older Mongolian-origin forms or introduce neologisms. Television and radio workers, for example, consistently reject Buryat neologisms in domains like medicine, science, and (to a lesser extent) government, in favor of what they consider internationalisms (Graber 2019). Mixed forms can be more approachable for semispeakers of Buryat, allowing them to frame an interaction in Buryat without risking alienating their interlocutor(s). Some focus group participants were put off by a radio anchor who used "big NGI words," identifying him as an arrogant member of the cultural elite. Russian codeswitches can likewise serve to distance the speaker from his or her own words, the most prevalent case being swearing, which is strongly prohibited by both Russian and Buryat code-internal language ideologies but seems to be more acceptable if a speaker switches from Buryat to Russian (or vice versa) to deliver the expletive.[19]

At least as often, however, codeswitching offers opportunities for emphasis, humor, and familiarity (Myers-Scotton 1997). The loud-talking teenager emphasized his "no," for instance, by using both Buryat and Russian. To the extent that mixed Russian-Buryat forms, like other *razgovornye* forms, are associated with private, domestic spaces, they can be used to demarcate a personal space in an otherwise formal event, indexing authenticity, genuineness, sincerity, or familiarity. For example, formal awards ceremonies at zemliachestvo gatherings are usually carefully framed in formal, literary Buryat but are often peppered with humorous Russian interjections from emcees that are made all the funnier because of the disjuncture between the poetic formality of SLB and Russian familiarity. An emcee at a 2007 award ceremony for the Khèzhèngè zemliachestvo received a tremendous laugh when he interrupted his poetic, high-style Buryat-language presentation to merrily beckon an old friend to the stage in Russian. "*Ira!*" he cried, using the familiar nickname for Irina, her Russian first name. "*Idi siuda!*" (Come here!)

In sum, *razgovornye* ways of speaking Buryat perform a number of discursive functions and can index a host of social positions: district affiliation, bloodlines, tribal or familial background, education level, or stance toward Buryat cultural preservation, as well as one's relationship to whole nation-states. These are the forms of Buryat that might be said to have "covert prestige," in the sense that certain contexts, such as children's playground interactions and friendly conversation between familiars, demand colloquial language use, while the standard literary language would sound pompous, standoffish, and out of place. What is at stake is less prestige, however, than building solidarity and fellow-feeling, and there is nothing covert or hidden about it, except that a person needs a fair amount of cultural knowledge to make sense of what is being indexed by using one form or another. Only loosely organized, *razgovornye* ways of speaking include a wide array of dialectal and mixed Russian-Buryat resources, the identification and indexical values of which depend largely on context and on the position(s) and knowledge of speakers and their audiences. As a class, they appear unified only in opposition to the much more tightly defined literary standard.

Standardizing Buryat

Language standardization is a quintessentially modern project in that it requires the coordinated efforts of many different knowledge institutions: bureaucratic offices to undertake the censuses and surveys that will describe the population (Anderson 1991; Hirsch 2005); scholars to make sense of them and develop a basis for the standard; media institutions to create and distribute grammars, dictionaries, primers, and other schoolbooks; educational institutions to use them and regiment future linguistic action (Peery 2012); and bureaucratic offices again to employ the new standard as a language of state—or at least of practice (Errington 1998, 2008).

Standard Literary Buryat bears many of the marks of concerted institutional efforts: a unitary dialect basis (Khorinskii), an official script (Cyrillic), standard spellings recorded in dictionaries, and literary and cultural references derived from a robust native literature. The literary standard has been extensively described in dictionaries, grammars, textbooks, and monographs and is supported by a substantial network of language elites working in scientific and educational institutions—including, most centrally, NGI at Buryat State University and BNTs at SO RAN. This is why Siberianists generally consider Buryat one of the strongest and most viable native Siberian languages, second only to Sakha/Yakut, despite its functional restriction (Grenoble and Whaley 2006). More subtly, literary Buryat occupies the ideological position targeted by institutional elites who derived their conception of a "modern literary Buryat language" (*sovremennyi literaturnyi buriatskii iazyk*) from their conception of literary Russian: a language of literature, education, and public life that would represent *the* language (R. *iazyk*, B. khèlèn) of the Buryat people. In this respect, literary Buryat is ideologically convergent with literary Russian, though Russian's stylistic variation and corresponding functional domains have been much more extensively codified.

Some of the earliest ways that Buryat was standardized appear in nineteenth-century descriptions of Mongolic varieties spoken in the Baikal area, in the sense that early (mostly amateur) linguists emphasized what these divergent ways of speaking had in common. James Milroy (2000) argues that when people—including well-meaning linguists and other scholars—have exclusive experience with highly standardized languages, they are more likely to expect to see uniformity in the ways of speaking that they describe. This was certainly the case for the Finnish, Russian, and Russian-educated missionary linguists and scholars who initially described Buryat in print and first attempted to develop primers, grammars, and translations. Both for practical reasons—such as translating liturgies, developing mutually intelligible scripts, and reinforcing the Russian political border—and based on their comparisons with Russian and European languages, these early linguists increasingly looked for what Mongolic varieties in the region had in common and for what might distinguish them, as a group, from Mongolian proper (Graber and Murray 2015).

Some of the earliest efforts at standardizing Buryat came during the late tsarist period. In the late nineteenth century, several missionary linguists developed their own systems for writing western dialects of Buryat in Cyrillic, particularly associated with the Irkutsk Translation Society. Missionaries' writing systems appear to have been used in Russian schools for Buryats, especially in Irkutsk, although their efforts to translate meaningful liturgies and win converts were plagued by misunderstandings (Graber and Murray 2015; Murray 2012). Other efforts were more conceptual than practical. In 1910, Nikolai Amagaev, a Buryat schoolteacher, and Ėlbek-Dorzhi Rinchino, a young scholar and nationalist revolutionary writing under the pseudonym Alamzhi-Mėrgėn, issued an impassioned plea for the adoption of a modified vertical Mongolian script to represent what they called the "Mongolo-Buryat" language. Amagaev and Rinchino were inspired in part by notions of common affinity and ethnolinguistic nationalism that had been percolating in the Austro-Hungarian Empire. They argued that existing systems for writing Buryat—including Cyrillic, Latin, and vertical Mongolian—had kept Buryats apart by exacerbating the differences between dialects and by cutting Cyrillic-educated western Buryats off from eastern Buryats who were more likely to be literate in the vertical (classical) Mongolian script. The orthographic reforms they proposed would "create the soil and conditions for the emergence of a new general Mongolian [obshchemongol'skii] literary language" that would be widely used not only by well-educated elites but also by the "masses," who the authors implied were mostly illiterate (Amagaev and Alamzhi-Mėrgėn 1910, 38). For these activists, language standardization was a matter of moral necessity. Western cultural influences had corrupted local Buryats, they argued, engendering alcoholism, other social ills, and general moral decline. Cultural contact had destroyed traditional, patriarchal Buryat society without leaving a replacement. In their view, a unified, standardized language would allow Buryats to overcome these problems by fostering a common cultural identity based in shared cultural heritage and Buddhist texts.[20] But their plans were doomed to languish as interesting but unrealizable ideas, without the kind of sustained institutional support that language standardization generally requires.

The Soviet state provided such institutional support in the 1920s and 1930s, when enregistering a strong literary standard became part of an ideological project to facilitate Buryat national development. Over the course of the 1930s, Soviet authorities in Ulan-Ude, Irkutsk, Moscow, and Baku, Azerbaijan (the site of lengthy alphabet debates for various parts of the Soviet Union), settled on what would arguably be the two most important elements of the literary standard as it is used now: the script and the dialect basis. Both decisions show how language standardization efforts mediated struggles for political power in Soviet Siberia.

The immediate motivation to standardize the script was to produce primers, textbooks, and other educational materials for literacy campaigns. It is difficult to determine what the literacy rate in the Baikal region in the 1920s might have been. A significant number of Buryats had attended Russian Orthodox schools, some had attended native Buryat schools, and there were large monastic communities and traveling Buddhist monks who provided basic education to the children of seminomadic families, including in classical Mongolian and Tibetan. The 1897 all-Russian census and the 1926 all-Union census ostensibly gathered data on literacy among ethnic Buryats (Demoskop Weekly 2009; Hirsch 2005; Troinitskii 1905), but the reported results are difficult to trust.[21] By any account, few ethnic Buryats would have been able to read texts in either Buryat or Russian. So they needed a script that would be both easy to learn and easy to teach.

Advocates for the classical Mongolian (vertical) script often point out that it is culturally distinctive and that it underspecifies vowels, such that any of the wide-ranging Mongolic dialects may be well represented by it. Classical Mongolian script has, however, a large number of positional variants, meaning that a [g] sound will be represented differently depending on where it falls in a word. Advocates for the Cyrillic and Latin scripts emphasize the difficulty of learning multiple positional variants, and the relative simplicity of an alphabetic system. Amagaev and Rinchino, for instance, argued that the classical Mongolian script needed only to be simplified and brought closer to Buryat pronunciation. They based their own unified alphabet on a writing system devised by Agvan Dorzhiev—an accomplished lama, politician, and liaison between Russia and Tibet—which he designed to be easier to learn (Dugarova-Montgomery and Montgomery 1999; Kara 2005, 173–76).

Beyond pedagogy, there were other practical and ideological reasons to abandon the vertical script. In the 1920s, repeated efforts to establish Buryat-language newspapers or Buryat-language bilingual service within existing newspapers stalled out on the issue of typesetting in the classical Mongolian script (Graber 2012). Limited linotype sets for the Mongolian script were heavily used, resulting in terrible print quality in the 1920s. Some of the newspapers that survive from this period are all but illegible. Letter sets had to be ordered from abroad and specially trained typesetters employed (*Buriat-Mongol'skaia pravda* 1928). Moreover, classical Mongolian was, alongside classical Tibetan, the language of Buddhist monasteries and lamas. In addition to potentially sidelining non-Buddhist Buryats, the vertical script indexed these alternative sites and persons of authority in a way that threatened the new Soviet Union's tenuous authority in Buddhist areas.

In other parts of the Soviet Union, some languages with established literary traditions kept their prerevolutionary scripts. Yiddish, Georgian, and Armenian, for example, continued to be written in Hebrew, Georgian, and Armenian scripts (Comrie 1996, 782). The Mongolian script, however, was treated like Arabic and replaced. The motivation might have been similar: to thwart pan-Turkism and pan-Mongolism, both serious political threats along the Soviet state's tenuous borders.

Cyrillic would have been the obvious practical choice. Alternative Cyrillic scripts for writing Buryat were already in use among Russian Orthodox missionaries and the generation of Buryats who had attended Russian schools, especially west of Baikal (Graber and Murray 2015). But that had the significant problem that it was associated with Russian Orthodoxy, and adopting Cyrillic—the script of Russian and Russification—to write Buryat smacked of what was known at the time as "Great Russian chauvinism."

Latin emerged as the solution to these problems, and the BMASSR officially introduced a new Latin script for Buryat in September 1926. The Buryat script change was part of a sweeping new "internationalist" policy to Latinize the native Siberian languages and many of the smaller languages of the Soviet Union, thus making them more transparent to one another and to the outside world, minimizing linguistic barriers (or so the logic went). A Latin alphabet was introduced in 1927 for Kalmyk, and in 1930 for Tuvan. Robert Rupen (1966) has interpreted the Tuvan Latinization in particular as an attempt to linguistically isolate the region from the Mongolian People's Republic (MPR), though the MPR also tried (and failed) to Latinize Mongolian in 1930–32.[22] In practice, many literate Buryats probably continued writing in classical Mongolian script (Shagdarov 1974), and the lag in implementing the change in media institutions was extreme: the first publications in the new Latin script appeared in 1931, *five years* after the script's official adoption.

This solution was short-lived. With the purges of the 1930s and increasing emphasis on developing Russian as a Soviet lingua franca, the Latin script and the internationalist ideals it embodied died a quick death, and a Cyrillic alphabet was implemented for Buryat in 1939–40. By that point, much of Buryatia's intelligentsia—including Agvan Dorzhiev, Amagaev, and Rinchino—had been killed or exiled from the Communist Party under accusations of "bourgeois nationalism" or pan-Mongolism or for coming from families who owned too many cattle to be trusted.

Choosing a dialect basis was likewise inextricably connected to political matters. In the 1920s, the renowned Mongolist Nicholas Poppe and other scholars recommended southern Buryat dialects as the basis for a new standard Buryat, scripted in Latin (Bazarova 2006; Montgomery 2005). But in the 1930s, central authorities became increasingly concerned about pan-Mongolism, and in that context, these dialects became dangerous for precisely the same reason they had been recommended: they were intermediary between northern Buryats and southern Khalkhs.

As a political ideology, pan-Mongolism reflects a broad desire to reunite the peoples of the former Mongol Empire. Some proponents have concentrated explicitly on the concept of territorial reunification, advocating combining parts of the vast territory between the Caspian Sea and Lake Baikal into a single contiguous nation-state. More often, however, pan-Mongolists have stressed the reunification of Mongol peoples—variously conceptualized as Mongolic- or Mongolian-speaking, or as Mongolian based on cultural, historical, ethnic, or religious criteria.[23] From the Soviet perspective, pan-Mongolism was dangerous not so much because a united Mongolia would become powerful *in itself* as because a united Mongolia could expand into and alongside existing Soviet territories and then be allied with Chinese or Japanese interests. Soviet authorities instead hoped to use a smaller and more controllable Outer Mongolia as a friendly buffer state insulating Russia from China and as a satellite from which to spread socialist interests in the Far East. In this context, speakers of the southern, more "Mongolian" of the Buryat dialects have periodically been considered dangerous for their mutual intelligibility with Khalkh.

In 1936, the Buryat ASSR's Supreme Soviet announced that it was changing the dialect basis for standard Buryat to Khorinskii, an eastern dialect that was not yet well described in the academic literature.[24] The decision remains somewhat controversial: both linguists and nonacademics in Buryatia periodically suggest that this move northward was made intentionally to exaggerate the distinction between standard Buryat and Khalkh Mongolian.[25] Linguistic debates of the era are often overshadowed by the decimation of the Buryat national intelligentsia and Buddhist monastic communities in the purges. In the absence of clear historical evidence, it is not clear that Soviet authorities chose the Khorinskii dialect expressly to distance standard Buryat from standard Mongolian and thwart pan-Mongolism. The decision might well have been motivated more by practical considerations: the Khori had historically inhabited a politically powerful region; much of the Buryat intelligentsia was composed of Khori; and in dealings with the Russians and Soviets, they had long been one of the most prominent Buryat tribes. For example, when Tsar Peter I received a diplomatic delegation from Baikal to secure nomadic land rights and protections along the Mongolian border, it was a group of Khori who came on behalf of the Buryats (Baldano 2003; Mitypov 2003; Zhimbiev and Chimitdorzhiev 2000).[26] Ultimately, however, moving the dialect basis did emphasize Buryats' difference from Mongols and from each other, not only shifting the Buryat "homeland" northward and away from the Mongolian border, but also grounding it more firmly in the eastern steppe regions, away from western Buryats and the western Russian capital of Irkutsk.

Through pedagogical materials, mass media, books of poetry and literature, and linguistic treatises, Standard Literary Buryat was successfully differentiated, both functionally and stylistically, from colloquial ways of speaking Buryat (Shagdarov 1974). The standard became a metonym for the Buryat people's progress on the road to nationhood and for the right to self-determination and cultural sovereignty. It has so successfully taken on this role, in fact, that the historical process of language standardization itself has become the target of debate over national development, as can be seen in how it was reconceptualized in the 1990s. During the Soviet period, Soviet authorities took full credit for creating a literary standard for Buryat. Standardization was officially said to have begun in the late 1930s, after the dialect basis was decided—a date repeated in the compulsory prefaces gracing Soviet works of linguistics (e.g., Tsydendambaev 1972, 3). In the early 1990s, Buryat philologists began placing the beginnings of language standardization earlier. L. D. Shagdarov (1993) argued that standardization began in the 1920s with efforts to modify the vertical Mongolian script for Buryat. Emphasizing textuality and mutual intelligibility, he pointed to the mass production of texts for a national audience, mainly in the form of newspapers. D. D. Dorzhiev (1994) argued that literary Buryat should properly be understood as beginning with folklore, some oral markers of which are "above" the level of dialect and therefore indicate that a literary standard was already being formed in the nineteenth century—notably before any Soviet efforts at all. And a high judgment of SLB is not limited to elites or to those who command SLB well; Buryats from different socioeconomic and cultural segments of society proudly refer to "the literary language" as a crowning achievement of the Buryat people.

Reforming the script and choosing a dialect basis were highly visible, tactile, overt ways to go about standardizing Buryat. But most elements of standardization are considerably more subtle than this. Although it might seem that a language is standardized from the moment it is codified, in practice standardization is always an ongoing process. Dictionaries must be updated, after all, and languages change. It is in how people use the codified standard (or do not use it) on a day-to-day basis that we can see where it works, where it is still under active negotiation, and where it fails.

Truncated Standardization

Individual speakers are always competent in different registers and ways of speaking (or reading and writing) to different degrees. As Jan Blommaert (2010) has pointed out, people are keen observers of where someone falls short, particularly regarding written standards. English, for instance, is often learned as a second, third, or fourth (etc.) language by adults who never acquire its formal registers, conventions, or idioms fully enough to be considered competent by native speakers. This is why a Nigerian email scam appears suspicious to many of its readers: there are subtle mistakes and infelicities in the form of a "business proposal" or request for funds, which reveal the writer's "truncated repertoire" in English (Blommaert 2010). In the end, Masha worried, based on her partial understanding of SLB, that she did not know her "native language" sufficiently well, which was an emotionally trying experience. Ayuur, by contrast, seemed happy to persist in feeling that he had total linguistic knowledge but lacked experience with a few specialized cultural terms. For both of them, their linguistic and cultural knowledge were—necessarily—incomplete, and to that extent, they had truncated repertoires. But Masha's problem is as much truncated *standardization* and the failure of the literary standard to be used as a lingua franca or consistently taught in the schools with which it is so strongly—almost exclusively—associated.

Despite state-driven standardization, a strong ideology opposing the literary standard to colloquial forms, and its success in representing national development, Standard Literary Buryat never fully emerged as a regional lingua franca for the Buryat territories. Dialects remain in wide use, and Russian continues to take over many of the functional domains for which a standardized Buryat was so carefully fashioned. Dialects are disparate and mutually *un*intelligible enough that Buryat should be considered a macrolanguage. Astute Buryat speakers often note that, within living memory, using Russian as a separate lingua franca in Buryat regions has allowed internal geographical variation within Buryat to continue, and even increase. The sociolinguist Galina Dyrkheeva has likewise argued that the multidialectalism (*mnogodialektnost'*), "relatively weak" normativity, and "narrowness of the social basis" for the literary form of Buryat continue to hinder the development of Buryat national and cultural politics (Dyrkheeva 2002, 156; see also Dyrkheeva 2003). In this light, dialectal variation appears to be a negative phenomenon, indexical of the failure of the literary standard to function as a language of "the" Buryat nation.

Failure of the written standard to function as a lingua franca between dialects is one of the most commonly cited reasons for ongoing language shift to Russian, because Buryats who natively speak two divergent dialects will speak Russian together instead of trying in Buryat. This explanation points to a feedback loop in which the use of Russian enables avoidance of Buryat and the perpetuation of internal variation, which in turn encourages the use of Russian, and so on. This situation has structural analogues in cases elsewhere in which the absence of a lingua franca in the lower-status minority code encourages faster adoption of the dominant code. Harold Schiffman (1993), for instance, has argued that many German-American communities shifted fully to English (as opposed to maintaining stable bi- or trilingualism) in part because they spoke multifarious unrecognized German dialects and lacked the more visible *Hochdeutsch* standard. German-American language maintenance efforts focused on the *Hochdeutsch* standard, a doomed enterprise that resulted in accidental English monolingualism when *Hochdeutsch* was replaced by English.

Russian could easily replace both SLB and the *razgovornye* ways of speaking laid out here in a similar way. This, however, is a large-scale, long-term possibility that does not take into account the micro-changes implicit in individual interactions. In particular, it does not take into account the role of *choice* and *effort* on the part of speakers. Cognizant of the importance of such effort, some Buryat-language journalists see their task as interrupting the feedback loop of variation and shift by providing the linguistic resources necessary "to at least **try** to speak Buryat together—to show what a unified information field [*edinoe informatsionnoe pole*] could be," as one young newspaper reporter put it. Thus, while SLB is seen by many as the exclusive province of institutional elites, the supposed elites themselves tend to see their role as pedagogical and inclusive, and the literary standard, in their view, is less a gold standard to be defended than an example to set.[27] Their attitude serves as a reminder that the standardizing process does not end with the publication of a grammar and dictionary. For all their apparent stasis, literary standards are constantly being renegotiated.

Literacy, specifically institutionalized literacy education, is one of the primary domains in which standards are dynamically reproduced and renegotiated (Cody 2013). In the contemporary educational system, the norms and goals of Buryat language classes (i.e., classes in which Buryat is a subject, not the medium of education) are mostly set by university elites in Ulan-Ude, who not only set official benchmarks for the teaching of "Buryat as a state language" (*buriatskii iazyk kak gosudarstvennyi*) but also teach the majority of teachers.[28] The domains of linguistic education and mass media overlap to a remarkable extent in maintaining a language elite: the overwhelming majority of journalists working in Buryat-language media today have been trained at either NGI or its predecessors, the departments of Buryat philology at Buryat State University and Irkutsk State University. Moreover, because NGI only recently instituted a journalism track within Buryat language education, the majority of currently practicing Buryat-language journalists were formally trained not as journalists but as schoolteachers and philologists. Pedagogy and language ideologies of the classroom therefore have an unusually direct impact on language ideologies of the newsroom.

Within the classroom, Standard Literary Buryat is the exclusive target of literacy education, and, simultaneously, there is a pervasive belief that one can acquire literacy in SLB exclusively within the classroom. As a *medium* of education, however, many different ways of speaking Buryat may be used. Because Russian is officially the medium of education in public schools (with the notable exception of the national boarding school in Ulan-Ude, which is supposed to provide Buryat-language immersion), the occasional use of Buryat is informal, cropping up when teachers and students share some competence in the same dialect. It thus tends not to be subject to the standard strictures. For instance, after a geology lesson that I observed being partly conducted in Buryat at a high school, the teacher apologized to me for what she called her "terrible" Buryat, which she contrasted with what she imagined I must be learning at Buryat State University. "Oh well," she laughed, "we're not teaching Buryat here!"

This role is taken very seriously by linguists at the primary institutions of linguistic and pedagogical training, NGI and BNTs.[29] Training their graduates for cultural work as educators, journalists, and performers, NGI instructors stress knowledge of regional history, the historical development of Buryat studies, and native Buryat literature, particularly from the Soviet period; competence in Buryat-Mongolian philology, linguistic documentation, and folklore studies (folkloristics); and mastery of Buryat as it is codified in pedagogical materials produced and published mainly by NGI. Above all, they emphasize reading and writing. Nonfiction report-style assignments are common, and the highest goal is to write "scientific" (*nauchnyi*, 'academic' or 'scholarly') prose in Buryat. Students are encouraged to write their final graduation papers in Buryat—a feat made all the more unusual and amazing because most of their secondary and higher education coursework, including classes at NGI, has been conducted in Russian. SLB is fundamentally thought of as a written register, and mastery of its oral forms—on stage and in radio programming, for example—is supposed to proceed from a solid foundation in writing. Thus, despite a historical emphasis on oral storytellers as the repositories of Buryat cultural wisdom (Abaeva and Zhukovskaia 2004), culture work in the contemporary period depends very heavily on institutionalized training in written registers.

The peculiarity of this training in the literary standard was particularly clear to me as a rare foreign student of Buryat—not only because my student status prompted continuous commentary about the vicissitudes of the literary language, dialects, bilingualism, the imminent death of Buryat, and so on, but also because I felt the gap that Masha feels, only in the opposite direction. Over the years that I studied Buryat at NGI, 2005–9, it became painfully clear to me that I was learning a purist literary standard that few speakers actually control. I was increasingly frustrated with my difficulty understanding—and making myself understood by—Buryat speakers who had not themselves been explicitly trained in SLB. However, comments from native speakers that this was somehow not "real" Buryat, or that it belonged only in limited domains, like Bairma's comment about the newspaper and the stage, were exceptional; for the most part, native Buryat speakers were not only tolerant of what I felt was a weird and partial acquisition but even actively encouraged it. When, at the apparent pinnacle of my NGI education, I wrote and delivered a short academic paper in Buryat, my friend Mėdėgma asked to hear it. A dignified, opinionated woman of sixty-two, Mėdėgma was usually not hesitant to level criticism at younger women, and she had told me more than once while we were speaking Buryat that she did not know "what the hell" I was "trying to say." I took a very deep breath before reading. Mėdėgma closed her eyes, listened to the end, then quietly busied herself making tea while I awaited her appraisal. "Beautiful" (Goë), she finally said softly. "Goë, goë. Ekhė goë khėlėn." (Beautiful, beautiful. Very beautiful language.) She refused to identify any errors, deferred to the linguistic expertise of the "talented, knowledgeable scholars" (bėrkhė, ėrdėmtėi uchėnye) at the university, and praised my teacher (whom she had never met) for teaching me excellent grammar and the "completely pure literary language, a beautiful language" (sovsem chistyi literaturnyi iazyk, goë khėlėn). Since I could write in Buryat, she said gravely, I must now know Buryat even better than she.

Mėdėgma, like Bairma and many other proud speakers of Buryat, believed it only proper that a non-Buryat outsider should learn the literary standard, at least at first (later, Bairma said, I could find a Buryat husband and learn it "to completion" [do kontsa]). But she did not exactly expect the same of her own children, who understood Buryat but claimed not to be able to read it. They had grown up in Ulan-Ude, and in the difficult 1990s, their schools had not offered any native-language education at all. Like many otherwise well-educated Buryats, they were illiterate in Buryat and found Buriaad ünėn and Tolon impenetrable. When they left handwritten notes for their mother lying around the house, they used idiosyncratic phonetic spelling that reflected no formal knowledge of Buryat grammar.

When native or heritage speakers like Masha claim to be illiterate in Buryat, they often attribute their illiteracy to late Soviet and post-Soviet breakdowns in Buryat language education, particularly if they are members of the "lost generation" like Mėdėgma's children, currently in their thirties and forties, that missed out entirely on native-language education. This was apparent in focus groups like hers. Participants who reported being native speakers of the "literary dialects" of Buryat read fluidly, even poetically, and nativized some of the Russian-origin terms. The word fotozuraguud (photographs), for instance, became [fo:tozuragu:d], with a lengthened Buryat [o:] where there is a stressed [o] in Russian. Others stumbled over words, some stopping entirely. Like Masha, many interviewees and focus group participants who reported speaking Buryat on a regular or semiregular basis nonetheless had difficulty with newspaper prose. A common report was being able to understand the "general idea" (*smysl' obshaia*) or topic (*tema*) but not specific words. "Welllll, I see *khrabryi* [brave]," one girl said carefully, biting her lip as she looked over a newspaper article about World War II veterans and tried to make sense of it. "Zorigtoi." (She recognized it, she said, because her cousin had recently had a little boy, and they had named him Zorigto on the advice of a lama in Aga—not because she had read it before.) At length, another participant explained that ilalta meant 'victory' (R. *pobeda*), and she understood the topic.

Dialects were by far the most common reason people reported not being able to understand SLB, including these texts. Speakers from the Khèzhèngè and Iaruuna districts had, on average, the least trouble, and speakers of other dialects tended to complain—or simply note with a shrug—that the newspaper text was "all Khorinskii." But education mattered too; an interviewee from Dzhida, for instance, claimed that she had *not* spoken Buryat very often as a child but had studied it as a subject in school for seven years, giving her a better understanding of the literary language (*literaturnyi iazyk*) than the conversational (*razgovornyi*) Buryat she ascribed to her village friends at the technological university in Ulan-Ude. Comprehension of the newspaper samples depended, in sum, on a combination of dialect background and educational background.

This was consonant with what I had been informally told before conducting research to specifically investigate it. On being introduced to me, Buryat speakers would often immediately volunteer that they could not read the newspaper themselves, which they usually explained as the product of having never received formal education in Buryat, and which they sometimes contrasted with their understanding of song lyrics, *rech'* (speech), or the *razgovornyi iazyk* (conversational language). "I can't read," they would say simply, "because I didn't study it in school."

Lack of native-language education, in sum, is by far the most commonly cited reason for not understanding the SLB of newspapers, and it is also sometimes invoked as a reason for not understanding radio and television speech. These explanations show just how strong the connection between formal education and SLB acquisition—both written and oral—is in the minds of Buryat speakers. Weak state support for literacy education in Buryat has been blamed variously on public apathy, Russocentric state ideology, a general lack of funds, and the personal commitments of local politicians. Regardless of its proximal and ultimate causes, the literacy breakdown has a disastrous psychological effect: in a conflation of the literary standard with the whole range of what usually counts as "Buryat," native speakers see their collective knowledge of SLB slipping away as their collective knowledge of *Buryat* slipping away—even though the standard was always tenuous.

Linguistic Labor

Language standardization is often well-intentioned in the sense that its ultimate goal—especially in multilingual, colonial or postcolonial contexts—is to elevate a code that is otherwise stigmatized.[30] In the early Soviet period, standardizing Siberia's native languages for mass media, propaganda, and nation building was a priority largely to strengthen the new state, but it also reflected the idealism of early socialism. Amid shifting priorities over the course of the twentieth century, however, and the chaos and changing politics of the 1990s and 2000s, institutional commitment to this project waned. Today native speakers of Buryat do not uniformly understand their "own" literary standard.

The contemporary legacies of Soviet standardization efforts include not only this truncated standard but also pride in a literary standard as evidence of Buryat nationhood, which paradoxically appears to impede use of the standard. The literary standard remains a key part of the popular Herderian triumvirate aligning one territory with one language and one people, which made its way into Buryat intellectuals' thinking both through Soviet nation building and through pre-Soviet intellectual flows from Austria-Hungary. Although contemporary Buryatia is very diverse and effectively spread across three territories, the idea of it continues to draw on this Enlightenment-era model of the nation as instantiating cultural and linguistic unity. Thus speakers value what they see as a strong, well-institutionalized literary standard and hold diverse linguistic resources in contrast to it. Because that standard never fully emerged as a lingua franca, however, in practice speakers default to their dialects and other *razgovornye* resources—or they simply give up on Buryat altogether and use Russian.

Mass media play a central role in the truncated standardization characterizing the Soviet period and in the standardization process ongoing today. They work together with other knowledge institutions, particularly educational institutions, to reproduce both the form of the literary standard and the ideology that keeps diverse *razgovornye* ways of speaking rigidly separated from it. The sheer amount of labor involved in this, and the degrees of misunderstanding and incomprehensibility that plague Buryat speakers' attempts to glean content from Buryat mass media, make Anderson's (1991) depiction of readers picking up novels to discover that they all already speak French ring a bit untrue. Picking up one of the early novels he describes was almost certainly like an American English speaker in the twenty-first century picking up something written in Flemish, or like a speaker of a western Buryat dialect picking up something written in an eastern dialect. Without an account of the political legitimation work being undertaken in media circulations, Anderson falls into the trap of imagining that standardized vernacular languages such as "French" already exist, without the standardization efforts necessary to make widespread dialects mutually intelligible (see also Silverstein 2000). Standardizing a language takes *work*.

Average speakers of Buryat capitalize on the institutional character of SLB to offload the labor of language maintenance into institutions. In this chapter, we have seen ways of speaking that speakers ideologically separate for use, on one hand, in the home and with family (i.e., "in the kitchen") and, on the other hand, by well-educated elites in official domains of language production and performance. Faced with a long newspaper passage using specialized shamanic vocabulary, one interviewee cried, "You'd only know this if you went to NGI!" She pointed to her sister, who had performed on stage in Buryat cultural ensembles and "knew these things." By laughing and saying, "Oh well, we're not teaching Buryat here!" or observing that a radio anchor uses "big NGI words," speakers invoke their own position *outside* institutions and subtly absolve themselves of responsibility for certain kinds of linguistic and cultural knowledge.

Today the literary standard is the much-preferred (though not exclusive) target of Buryat mass media. Standard Literary Buryat's stalwarts, including many newspaper journalists, also allow less contact-based influence from Russian and even incorporate some Mongolic-origin borrowings to "erase" such influence.

This is not without its problems. Some Buryat media personnel, especially print journalists, target the literary standard so hard that they do not even try to pull in native speakers of colloquial Buryat like Masha. When I reported her low comprehension rate to Bair, a Buryat-language newspaper reporter in his fifties, I expected him to lament the difficult participial phrases or the nearly insurmountable distances between dialects of Buryat. Instead, he shrugged and said that she should try harder. That's the problem with our young people, he said. They don't try. Bair emphasized the pedagogical role of newspapers in language maintenance and believed that his existing audience consisted basically of older Buryats who already knew the language well. While he welcomed new readers, he did not seek them out or try to accommodate them; that, he thought, was the job of the student.

At issue are different notions of the minority language public. Like Bair, most Buryat-language journalists adhere to an ideology of standardization within which SLB is a bastion of pure, non-Russified, Khori Buryat. Their job, according to this logic, is to struggle against the rampant Russian influence coming from bilingual Buryat-Russian speakers who are increasingly shifting to Russian. Although the minority language public that they thus evoke is small, it is dedicated and cohesive. Others, particularly in television, see younger semispeakers of Buryat as prospective members of an expanded Buryat language public whom they must recruit. They reach out to semispeakers by consciously using more Russian words, phrases, transitions, phatics, and dialectisms—in short, more of the *razgovornye* resources that are supposed (by their own training and purist ideology) to be excluded from the literary standard. The next chapter examines the motivations and practices of these Buryat journalists, the people tasked with upholding, preserving, and developing language standards in the most public way possible.

ANCHORS OF AUTHORITY

Tsk, tsk. Soyolma made a clicking noise with her tongue and shook her head. We were watching television, and Soyolma, a Buryat woman in her forties, was criticizing a young television reporter for mixing too much Russian into his Buryat-language report—although she herself was criticizing him mainly in Russian. I asked whether she could give any specific examples. "Well, I don't know," she said. "He just doesn't speak in the literary language. He's just—well, he's young, and he just doesn't speak really excellently [*otlichno*], not like, for example . . . Bator." "Yeah, Bator!" one of the other people present, a younger man named Dugar, exclaimed. "He speaks the literary Buryat language beautifully [*krasivo*]. You know, he worked for the newspaper for a long time. He knows all the ancient Buryat words and that's how—and he speaks like that on television. He raises the level of the language."

Journalists are language workers, expected to uphold language standards even (or especially) when the rest of us do not. Readers look to reporters and editors for grammatical sentences and well-crafted arguments, and viewers look to news anchors for "proper speech." In fact, journalists' practices vary widely, and a single journalist may not be consistent from year to year or from medium to medium. Bator, for instance, did not speak on BGTRK television in the standard literary language that he had employed decades earlier in the newspaper <u>Buriaad ünèn</u>. He argued that the medium of television demanded a more colloquial style so that viewers could understand quickly, which meant using more Russian borrowings and avoiding neologisms and "convoluted" literary expressions. Nonetheless, Soyolma and Dugar assume Bator to be a consistent speaker of the literary standard across time and space, imputing authority into his person as well as the institution he represents. Standard-bearing is an *ideal* to which viewers hold journalists, and to which they hold themselves.

While this relationship between journalists and their audiences holds in many sociocultural contexts, minority-language journalists often occupy an even more complex and value-laden position. When the language in which journalists work is itself a strong marker of ethnonational identity, their status as language workers takes on new importance and scrutiny—especially when that language is in jeopardy. Journalists producing material in Buryat have become authoritative arbiters of cultural and linguistic reproduction in the midst of more general Russification. They are not the only Buryat speakers invested by fellow speakers with strong linguistic authority; senior Buryat women, Buddhist lamas, and certain shamanic teachers also play important roles as cultural and linguistic standard-bearers. But they represent the *institutional* center of Buryat. As described in chapter 2, republic legislation and existing state institutions have guaranteed the use of Buryat in news media over and above other genres of media or forms of minority cultural production. Together, these factors have made minority-language journalism in Buryatia a bastion of linguistic and cultural standards, a hyperideologized domain of practice to which other Buryats, like Soyolma and Dugar, orient as the source not only of trustworthy and authoritative information but also of correct ways of speaking and being Buryat.

This chapter examines the practice of minority-language journalism in Buryatia as a central way in which particular stances toward Buryat belonging are institutionalized. Focusing on journalists themselves, we can see how this native language elite is recruited and reproduced, including who Buryat-language journalists are demographically and how individual journalists are socialized into a tight-knit "community of practice" (Lave and Wenger 1991). Archival documents from the newspapers and television and radio companies, as well as the career trajectories of contemporary native-language media workers, show how this elite has developed out of ideological commitments to different kinds of professional journalism in the late Soviet and post-Soviet periods. This is not a completed, historical instance of professionalization but rather an ongoing process of creating and maintaining a minority ethnonational elite within institutions of power that will be recognizable to the larger state and to Russian society. In the absence of good pay or mobility in Russia at large, Buryat journalists emphasize the "transcendence" that journalism can offer, the satisfaction of creative labor, and their unique role in linguistic and cultural preservation and development.

Some of these values are held by journalists more generally, but the preservational imperative that Buryat-language journalists feel is unique to minority-language contexts. Buryat-language journalists have various strategies for meeting the preservational imperative at work, where they are experts in purism. But as they trek between workplaces and home, between their role as journalists and their roles as wives, mothers, brothers, and sons, the image of the journalist as consistent Buryat standard-bearer falls apart. As we will see, junior journalists are socialized not only into the journalistic craft at large but more specifically into bilingual office environments in which their language abilities and coverage of different topics and materials are evaluated within different—and sometimes competing—value systems.

Being a Buryat-language Journalist

As members of a professional cadre of trusted knowledge workers, news journalists enjoy a particularly authoritative role in public discourse. They can give the institutional imprimatur of authority to impressions and vague ideas already circulating in society, sedimenting and accrediting social knowledge (Boyer 2000). They can reproduce and reinforce existing language ideologies, both through metalinguistic instruction and by example. But anthropologists and linguists know surprisingly little about how journalistic texts are constructed or what journalists do—as opposed to what they say they do, or what audiences think they do—on a daily basis (Bell 1991; Cotter 2010). This is especially true of non-English environments and journalism as practiced outside the United States and Europe (Bird 2010b). Some sociolinguists have followed Allan Bell's lead, turning attention to the discursive practices that shape news production (e.g., Bell and Garrett 1998; Carvalho 2008; Catenaccio et al. 2011; Cotter 2011; Deacon, Fenton, and Bryman 1999; Perrin 2003; Philo 2007; Schrøder 2007; Van Hout and Macgilchrist 2010). Ethnographic studies of journalism (e.g., Bird 2010a; Boyer 2000, 2001, 2005; Hannerz 2002, 2004; Hasty 2005; Pedelty 1995; Peterson 2001, 2003; Ståhlberg 2013) have opened a new field of sociocultural study and have brought additional ethnographic rigor to the work of news sociologists, who pioneered the careful observation of production processes within news organizations in the 1970s and 1980s (e.g., Gans [1979] 2004; Golding and Elliott 1979; Schlesinger 1987; Tuchman 1978). But examining news production processes ethnographically is still a strikingly new enterprise.

By looking at news institutions ethnographically, we can see how journalists inhabit and renegotiate their roles as cultural brokers. During research for this book, I was often struck by the discrepancies between what audiences assumed to be journalists' motivations, goals, and lives; what the journalists themselves professed; and what their actions suggested. For instance, although television news often comes across (indeed, producers strive to come across) as spontaneous and fresh, scripting and editing written texts is a central part of the production process. The fact that the speech of anchors and reporters like Bator is so much more linguistically complex than that of their interviewees is due not only to their competence, after all, but also to the fact that they script and pre-edit almost all of the speech that they ultimately broadcast. Similarly, audience members were quick to ascribe political views and motivations to journalists—and to the media institutions employing them—that the journalists seldom shared; much of what was politically or ideologically driven from the perspective of audiences grew out of, from the perspective of the journalists, more pragmatic concerns.

In interviews and in side conversations while on the job, native-language journalists talked about their work in terms of two imperatives. The first was to uphold the professional standards of journalism. Journalism is hyperprofessionalized in Russia, and native-language journalism is no exception. Senior journalists emphasize mentoring junior journalists on the job to "develop" themselves as "professionals" and to treat journalism as a career rather than simply a job. They are also building young cadres through increasing specialization within the local educational system. A journalism track is available in Buryat State University's Department of Russian Language and Literature, on the basis of which the NGI, a key training ground for the Buryat language elite, established a journalism track for its own students—meaning that it is possible to acquire a university education specifically in Buryat-language journalism.

Additionally, and just as passionately, Buryat-language journalists cited an imperative to preserve (*sokhranit'*) the language and culture, according to a literary standard they felt it incumbent on themselves to uphold. This too is a form of professionalism, but one in which the journalists articulate their role less in terms of investigation, the referential content of the news, and enabling good citizenship than in terms of pedagogy, the *form* of the news, and enabling proper speech and action.

Because native-language journalists are held to both of these imperatives, their role as culture brokers is broader, more politicized, and arguably more consequential than that of their Russian-language counterparts. To the extent that cultural and linguistic change in Buryatia is currently being felt primarily as *loss*, however, the same journalists experience their work as failure or as a losing battle. Both imperatives weigh heavily in the self-understanding of Buryat journalists as culture brokers. And both imperatives have historical roots, in the way that native-language journalism was institutionalized in the Soviet period to serve particular sociopolitical ends, and in the changing role of minority media within the Russian Federation of the twenty-first century.[1]

Contemporary journalism in the Buryat territories bears a complex and often ambivalent relationship to Soviet journalism, for both journalists and their audiences. Journalism enjoyed a privileged position in Soviet life (Gorham 2003; Smith 1998; Wolfe 2005). To be sure, Soviet journalism was not static or uniform, although post-Soviet journalists and ex-journalists seeking to distance themselves from their earlier work sometimes speak of it as though it was. Principles of journalism and the role of the journalist in Soviet rhetoric changed considerably over time, and those shifts were very much reflected in the statements of local Buryat journalists. In 1939, a young reporter at *Buriat-Mongol'skaia pravda* echoed the literary emphasis of the time when he lamented that he did not feel himself sufficiently developed "as a literary worker."[2] In 1959, by contrast, a radio and television director roundly criticized an editor for his irresponsibility and "political short-sightedness:" "An editor should be, before all else, a politician."[3] By 1982, during the late Soviet period when many now-living journalists and pensioners were working, the standards by which journalists were measured had shifted again. This is reflected in a subsequent director's succinct encouragement: "A good journalist is an investigator."[4] He exhorted his staff to be harder and sharper in their reporting and more critical of problems and injustices in the existing sociopolitical system.

Investigative journalism was increasingly prized during the last decade of the Soviet Union—even before Gorbachev explicitly encouraged it under glasnost, a policy of openness and transparency in the late 1980s, as the above quotation from 1982 shows. Nonetheless, even this period is sometimes conflated with the preceding decades and remembered, in the post-Soviet period, as redolent with ideology (*ideologiia*). Bayandalai, for instance, wrote off his entire career—more than three decades of labor—as "ideology." He said the word with venom, screwing up his normally pacific face. Here, the word retains connotations familiar from the Cold War, of a person—an *ideolog*—so committed to rote political principles propping up the state that he is blind to the truth.[5] Late in life, Bayandalai seemed to have found *ideologiia's* cure in writing poetry and deepening his understanding of Buddhism, both of which he pursued with great passion. He rejected the notion that journalism could be overhauled in the post-Soviet period to reflect ideals other than the pursuit of money and profit—ideals that were, from his perspective, equally morally bankrupt.

Westernizers took a different approach. North American and West German newspapers and NGOs were particularly active in training Russian and

East/Central European journalists in the immediate postsocialist period (Boyer 2000, 2001, 2005). Several of the newspaper editors who appear in this book were invited at one point or another to conferences or development seminars in the United States, and additionally some administrative personnel took part in management seminars and *trenings* in Moscow and New York. Some of these measures succeeded, in the sense that the discourse of "Western" twentieth-century journalism could be found in circulation in Buryatia. Journalism textbooks in use at Buryat State University discussed familiar principles of reporting (objectivity, verifiability, protection of sources, and so on), and some of my interviewees referred to mass media as the "fourth branch of power" (*chetvërtaia vetv' vlasti*)—that is, the Fourth Estate. Yet Buryat journalism rarely instantiated the principles and ideals of journalism that were presumably intended by agents of democratic development. It had developed according to its own path. The only times I heard American ideals of journalism, such as independence, directly parroted in Russian were in connection with *Inform polis*, a popular weekly commercial newspaper explicitly founded on an American model. Buryatia's most popular and successful commercial newspaper since the 1990s, *Inform polis* prides itself on investigative journalism and has positioned itself against the state, as a "friend of the people" helping them navigate a dizzying consumer market, changing public transportation routes, and the complexities of bureaucracy. The paper also runs beauty contests, extended advertisements, and local celebrity gossip and has a reputation for printing unfounded rumors. Many of my research participants reported not liking it but reading it anyway because it is such an indispensable source of information for surviving daily life in Ulan-Ude. For his part, Bayan-dalai eschewed the Westernized post-Soviet journalism of the 1990s and 2000s as worthless as well, now simply driven by advertising, rather than ideology, into "trash and nonsense" (*erunda*).

While the role of journalists and media institutions in Russian society has changed, the Soviet period left a very important legacy in native-language journalism specifically. Ethnic Buryats in the republic consistently argue—or take for granted—that it is a responsibility of the state to provide media in the Buryat language, even or *especially* as the percentage of Buryat-dominant speakers shrinks. This view is shared not only by activists for linguistic, cultural, and minority rights, who have an interest in garnering resources, but also by people who have no particular interest in Buryat cultural development but who have grown up in an ethnic republic that identifies itself as such. By now there have been enough generations of native-language journalists, and enough generations of people exposed to native-language journalism, that it has become entrenched. It is an expectation on the part of the public that the state provides native-language media, particularly news. Native-language media institutions are also frequently pointed to as bastions of Buryat cultural and linguistic knowledge, although the situation inside them is considerably more complex.

Reproducing an Ethnonational Elite

At any given moment, across all of the Buryat territories in Russia, there are approximately thirty-five journalists producing Buryat-language media. This makes Buryat-language journalism roughly equivalent to Irish-language journalism in the size of its community of practice. The personal backgrounds of Buryat-language journalists show how this ethnonational elite is reproduced institutionally through multiple selection processes, particularly in the higher educational system and through emphasis on the standard literary language. Language ability is of paramount importance, not only because linguistic felicity is important for all journalists, but more specifically because native-language journalists feel the preservational imperative so strongly, drawing special attention to the form of their work. Educational institutions and on-the-job training stress writing above all else, even in radio and television.

Media offices in Buryatia are bilingual spaces that require frequent switching between Russian and Buryat on the part of Buryat-language journalists. The degree of Russian versus Buryat use differs systematically by media platform and by type of work. Some workplaces, such as the offices of the state publishing house Buriaad Ünèn, maintain almost exclusively Buryat-language communication by employing Buryat-speaking secretarial staff and fostering interaction with the Buryat-dominant workers of Russian-language publications who share the same building. Journalists in more Russian-dominated environments, such as the state television company's newsroom, employ a number of strategies to cordon off space for Buryat-only interactions. Even the most Buryat-intensive environments, however, require Russian for administrative purposes, so there is a de facto dual language requirement for Buryat-language journalists—and not for Russian-language journalists.[6] This de facto dual language requirement stretches back to the founding of the Buryat-language press, when, despite the indigenization (*korenizatsiia*) and Buryatization (*oburiachivanie*) of institutions, reports and records of activities needed to be generated in Russian for the sake of transparency to higher, non-Buryat-speaking organs of power.[7] Today, landing a job in a Buryat media institution requires good Russian language ability, though not necessarily skills in the literary and "publicistic" (*publisticheskii*) styles required of Russian-language journalists, because journalists are generally hired to produce material in one language or the other.

In fact, the ability to produce acceptable news material in both Russian and Buryat is rare. Occasionally a bilingual speaker will do a story in the "other" language on an ad hoc basis, either to economize on the time spent eliciting interviews in the field, as a favor to a colleague, or for personal interest. Usually this is a Buryat-language journalist producing a Russian-language story, but occasionally journalists who were hired into Russian-language departments produce material in Buryat. Nikolai, for instance, a young Buryat Russian-language journalist at BGTRK's television station, was actively trying to produce Buryat stories, largely out of his personal investment in relearning and reteaching his native language. He had recently returned to Buryatia with his wife and children after living most of his life in the Sakha Republic and abroad, and this was part of his reclamation of a feeling of belonging. Bilingual ability provided some job security during the "optimization measures" and financial crisis of 2008–9, when media institutions were more likely to lay off monolingual than bilingual journalists because they were legally required to continue producing material in two languages on less money. Anna, a Buryat radio journalist at BGTRK, described actively trying to improve her command of *publisticheskii* Russian because the radio station was facing cuts. Her boss reasoned that it would be cheaper to have bilingual Anna double up than keep a monolingual Russian speaker on staff in addition to her. The cuts were stressful, Anna said, but it was even more stressful to produce material in Russian, and the extra time that it took meant that the radio station was depending even more than it already had on rebroadcasting archival materials in Buryat rather than generating new stories.

Buryat-language journalists like Anna also control multiple ways of speaking Buryat. They almost universally have advanced knowledge of the literary standard from a formal college-level education at NGI; its predecessor, Buryat State University's Department of Buryat Philology; or this department's predecessor at Irkutsk State University in Irkutsk. A brief look at the educational background of working journalists shows just how strong this trend is. The number of staff journalists working throughout ethnic Buryatia is always in flux—particularly in times of economic crisis like that experienced in 2008–9—so I refer here to a demographic snapshot. In August 2009, approximately fifty staff journalists were working in bilingual offices in Ulan-Ude, Aga, and Ust'-Orda.[8] From May to August 2009, I collected basic demographic information, including educational background, from voluntary surveys and interviews among this group. This generated education information on thirty-six working journalists, twenty-nine of whom were working primarily, if not exclusively, in Buryat-language media. Of those twenty-nine, twenty-four had been trained specifically in Buryat-language pedagogy and/or philology, and an astounding twenty-eight had come from the same department at Irkutsk State University and its institutional descendants within the Buryat State Pedagogical Institute and Buryat State University.[9] The only exception was a new Buryat-language intern, freshly hired at the state television company, with a background in theater and the performing arts—a background common among young Russian-language television journalists and possibly a harbinger of things to come.[10]

When compared with their Russian-producing colleagues, the Buryat-language journalists showed a remarkably exclusive focus on native-language philology and pedagogy in their educational backgrounds. By contrast, Russian-language journalists had been trained primarily in journalism programs and foreign language departments, not only in Irkutsk and Ulan-Ude but also in cities as far-flung as St. Petersburg and Ekaterinburg. In interviews and surveys, Russian-language journalists also appeared much more mobile and ambitious at the scale of the federation. They placed less emphasis on their pedagogical and linguistic roles vis-à-vis Russian and more emphasis on informing the public, demonstrating professionalism, expanding commercial possibilities, and attaining personal upward mobility into the media markets of Novosibirsk, St. Petersburg, and Moscow.

In addition to a higher educational background, Buryat-language journalists tend to possess above-average knowledge of the literary standard on the basis of their native dialects. The majority of Buryat-language journalists included in the demographic snapshot—twenty-one of twenty-nine, or 72 percent—hailed from the eastern steppe regions of Khėzhėngė, Iaruuna, Mukhar-Shėbėr, and Aga.[11] While birthplace does not always fully reflect a person's native dialect, as we have seen, it is an extremely strong indicator in Buryatia. Demographic data thus strongly suggest that the majority of Buryat-language journalists are already speakers of "literary" dialects—those dialects most closely related to Khori—before they begin their formal education.[12]

In sum, the backgrounds of Buryat-language journalists suggest that to succeed, a person needs to have had training both in writing, pedagogy, or journalism in general and in specifically Buryat language and culture practices. The most fundamental requirement, however, appears to be a strong command of the literary language. A background in dance, for instance, shows depth of prestigious cultural knowledge and prized artistic ability, but it must be combined with knowledge of standard Buryat.

When I interviewed editors about hiring practices, no one denied that prospective candidates' native abilities in the Khori dialect played a role—although everyone was quick to point out that final hiring decisions were determined by standardized competitions. Young workers from the rural steppe regions were simply more likely to be fluent Buryat speakers, and if they controlled one of the "literary dialects" natively, so much the better. One editor additionally suggested that the high incidence of journalists from a small number of regions was the "natural" (*estestvennyi*) result of recruiting journalists from outlying Buryat villages to work in Ulan-Ude. He noted the "strong connections" among Buryat families from the same district, referring obliquely to the widespread nepotism that is often angrily decried by non-Buryat workers of the republic but is essential to the smooth functioning of Buryat kinship networks. Journalists working in both Russian- and Buryat-language formats often report becoming interested in journalism through a parent, aunt or uncle, or other older family member, and many journalists do get their start through a family connection; as a profession, it tends to run in families. These connections, however, are not the main recruitment strategy for media institutions.

New journalists are recruited through periodic competitions, consisting of written examinations in combination with additional medium-specific requirements like screen tests for television, and by extending application invitations to specific candidates—usually at competing media institutions, NGI, or the East Siberian State Academy of Culture and Arts (VSGAKI). The recruitment process reflects the priorities of media institutions, including some medium-specific criteria. Ability in the standard literary language, specifically in written prose, is at a premium in media offices—including in radio and television offices, because the initial scripting and editing phases are conducted in writing. The quality of voice (*golos*) is prized in radio, and television journalism is distinguished by placing additional emphasis on "face," "image," and "personality" (often summarized as *litso*), which results in a slightly different pool of candidates. Compared to print and radio platforms, there are more non-NGI grads in the Buryat television sphere, and more people without specific linguistic or pedagogical training, because presentational style is at such a premium.

Of primary importance across all platforms, however, was writing. Many of the more technical skills and finer points of presentation were taught on the job, whereas writing skills were largely seen as already formed. While editors sometimes engaged in "teaching moments" regarding the texts of their junior coworkers, young journalists were supposed to already be decent writers. While this criterion applied across the board, it was all the more the case for Buryat-language journalists, whose standard register is more tenuous than that of Russian, and who are supposed to be (and *are*, in most cases) drawing on extensive experience with literary standards on the basis of both education and dialect background.

Paychecks and Poetry

Why do people pursue this career? Journalists like Bator, Nikolai, and Anna note their career path's often negative impact on personal finances and family life, but they are quick to cite the satisfaction of creative labor as well. Throughout interviews, surveys, personal histories, and free-ranging conversations, the journalists with whom I spoke balanced their need to have bread on the table with poetry, other literary and creative pursuits, and the value of their work for Buryat cultural continuity.

When I asked one senior newspaper editor, Minzhur, what he found most fulfilling about the work that he clearly enjoyed, he pointed to the ubiquity of newspapers in people's daily lives. There could be no doubt, for him, that his work reached a wide audience, because he saw the newspapers stacked onto trucks and driven off for distribution. "But," he continued, "what is most wonderful [*chudesnyi*] about working in journalism is the possibility to transcend the limits of everyday thinking [*vyiti za predely bytovogo mysleniia*]." Minzhur was himself a poet and given to grand, philosophical statements. Like Dorzh at <u>Tolon</u>, he spoke at great length about the importance of the journalist's role in changing an individual's perspective and outlook. His greatest achievement, he said, were those moments "when a person comes to knowledge of something that he didn't know before . . . that helps him understand his situation, or himself, as a **person** [*kak chelovek*]." In other contexts, other newspaper editors and writers also used terms like *prevoskhodnyi* and *vydaiushchiisia*—'transcendent'—to describe their work and their potential effect on people.

Print journalists sometimes emphasized the literary aspect of the literary standard. Some of the authority granted to (and claimed by) print journalists comes by virtue of institutional position and ideological attachments to writing as a literary practice. They were more predisposed than their colleagues in radio and television to worry over—and take pleasure in—the minutiae of language. They took language and linguistic issues seriously, and their status as literary standard-bearers seemed to imbue them with a great sense of linguistic responsibility.

There are reasons within Buryat media institutions to not consider the work particularly artistic. Drudgery and meaningless story assignments are not-infrequent complaints, and there is not a great deal of creative control in the lower ranks. Authorship in newsrooms is dispersed, ultimate responsibility often lying with the institution rather than individual authors (Bell 1991; Cotter 2010). But Buryat journalists tend to think of themselves mainly as literary workers, not as technical workers or as cogs in a machine.

In part, this is because the material conditions of their workplace environment encourage it. Writing is a very solitary pursuit, even in busy news offices. In contrast with many of the European and American newsrooms that have been studied (e.g., Gans [1979] 2004; Gürsel 2010), and in contrast with the open-concept newsrooms of television studios, Buryatia's print news production takes place largely in individual offices down long hallways, each with a door that is often shut.[13] Because most post-Soviet media institutions inherited central Soviet media buildings and equipment, the production of news is still geographically very centralized. The majority of Ulan-Ude's newspapers, for instance, are housed in a single building in the city center. This serves mainly to collect the editors into one place, but the daily (or weekly) news production process is spatially very dispersed, in that much of the text generated for a publication like Buriaad ünèn, *Inform polis*, or *Buriatiia-7* is written offsite by correspondents, historians, letter writers, and government office workers.

Buryat-language journalists are particularly inclined to think of themselves as literary writers due to the historical and structural peculiarities of minority-language journalism in the Soviet Union and Russian Federation. Journalism and literary production have long been intertwined in Soviet and post-Soviet Russia, especially for minority-language writers. During the Soviet period, there was a great deal of crossover between the pages of Buryatia's literary journals and newspapers. Cadres of young language specialists were trained to work both as journalists and as literary translators—translating Gorky, Pushkin, and classics of Russian literature, which occupied much of newspapers' print space and radio stations' broadcasting time. Many of the members of the prestigious regional Writers' Union also worked as journalists. Most importantly, perhaps, the institutional structure of the centralized publishing house meant that books, newspapers, and literary journals were all published out of the same collective, namely *Pravda Buriatii*/Buriaad ünèn, such that there were very tight networks of "literary people" within a small ethnic republic like the Republic of Buryatia. The same, in fact, holds today, although more publishing houses and projects have appeared in Ulan-Ude, and self-publishing (*samizdat'*) has become a very popular way to produce small collections of poetry and fiction. With the ongoing shift in Buryat-language newspapers from "hard" news to cultural topics, the connection between minority-language literature and minority-language journalism only stands to grow.

The political economy of newspaper journalism—and especially of minority-language journalism—in Russia also gives those who pursue a career in it a sense of higher purpose or of idealism in the face of financial obstacles. Print journalism does not, after all, pay particularly well. For young native speakers of Buryat growing up in the late Soviet period, a career in journalism or even literature was a viable life path (Chakars 2014). Today, pursuing such a career is financially risky. In 2008–9, full-time reporters in Ulan-Ude and Aginskoe were paid between 6,000 and 12,000 rubles per month, which at the time was $180 to $360 US, with the average hovering around 9,000 to 10,000 ($270 to $300 US).[14] This is more than a new college graduate could expect to be paid as a rural Buryat-language schoolteacher, but it also provides less job security. And it is much less than she might make as, say, a manager in a local firm, with greater chance of long-term financial gain—but also with less chance of using Buryat. Indeed, two of the young newspaper journalists I interviewed were currently working in Buryat-language editorial collectives but were in the midst of earning degrees to begin careers in other fields that would not use their Buryat language skills. One young man had begun taking management and business classes in the evenings, aspiring to begin a business on Lake Baikal catering to German and Russian tourists. (Developing tourism, he argued, would further Buryat cultural preservation and encourage young people to learn Buryat, though he did not foresee using any Buryat in the company beyond, perhaps, a Buryat name.) Another man in his late twenties was in school to become a jurist, a popular field for steady employment in Russia at the time. He had a fiancée, he explained, and they wanted to start a family.

The implication here—that a career in newspaper journalism would not, over the long term, provide adequately for a family, in a context in which men continue to be seen as primary breadwinners—helps explain why print journalism in Buryatia is increasingly dominated by women. Senior reporters and editors, including nearly all of the current and retired newspaper editors described in this book, tended to be men, in part perhaps due to strongly held local beliefs (among both Russians and Buryats) in men's superior leadership abilities. But there were also some highly placed women who had risen through the ranks of their institutions in the 1980s and 1990s, and women dominated the younger cadres of newspaper journalists. According to local gender expectations, men are very much figured as the "providers" within families, embodying a traditional male role that has, if anything, intensified with Russia's "demographic crisis" and rhetorical return to traditional family values. In this context, our aspiring jurist implies that something must be sacrificed (namely, a man's ability to provide for his family) to pursue a career in journalism. Women, too, give something up to be journalists, in that privileging a career in writing (or at all) can be viewed as unfeminine. One ambitious woman in her mid-thirties working at a large newspaper in Ulan-Ude ascribed her failure to find a husband to potential mates' fear of her work. They were scared off, she claimed, by her independence, intelligence, and self-confidence; she pointed to colleagues who were also unmarried, divorced, and/or childless. In fact, most of the female journalists I interviewed were married with children, but regardless of the veracity of her claims, it is important that she *felt* she had relinquished a possible future to pursue her career as a reporter. Newspaper employees thus sometimes shared with literary writers a sense of personal self-sacrifice to their work.

Additionally, much of the content printed in newspapers is produced by writers beyond those employees on the payrolls. Occasional contributors are paid much less than full-time employees ("nickels and dimes" [*meloch'*], as one frequent correspondent put it), generally using the income to supplement that from another job or jobs. Scores of poets, short-story writers, students, and historians and other academics also contributed material to newspapers for free, for various personal and professional reasons.

All of this points to there being reasons other than financial to pursue a career in Buryat-language journalism, or to contribute material to the newspapers. When I asked about hopes, dreams, future plans, and employment satisfaction in interviews and surveys, newspaper writers most often cited the reasons laid out above: they liked contributing to language preservation, they said, or "developing our Buryat language." After these, however, they most often cited their love of "creative work" (*tvorchestvo*). The number of newspaper journalists with literary aspirations, especially as compared with radio and television workers, was striking. I did not meet a single editor who did not also pursue some kind of creative writing—usually poetry, and sometimes novels or short stories. (Some identified *first* as poets, in fact, and only secondarily as journalists.) One staff reporter at a district newspaper was a lyricist for a regional ensemble. Bayandalai and Minzhur were typical, among Buryat-language newspaper journalists, in turning to creative writing upon retirement.

Literary labor may not be financially rewarded, but journalists have standing in the Buryat community. Their prestige is found, in part, in the stable, enduring institutions they work for and the long local history of the minority-language journalist. The Buryat-language elite in Buryatia in the early twentieth century was relatively small, and bilingual and bi-literate Buryats often worked as intercessors between the Russian state and Buryat society. Throughout the Soviet era, Buryat-language newspaper editors served political functions besides heading the newspapers and producing propaganda. They were also frequently called on to head other seemingly unrelated committees, judge contests, go on fact-finding missions (especially to Buryat-speaking regions), and provide trustworthy linguistic expertise.[15] In the contemporary period, journalists working in the "native language" marshal their institutional positions to pursue literary dreams, once again combining linguistic roles and staying at the forefront of the Buryat language elite.

The Preservational Imperative at Work and at Home

Minority-language media, as opposed to mainstream media in the lingua franca, are often marked by linguistic insecurity, which foregrounds code and form

(Woolard 1995; Woolard, Ribot Bencomo, and Soler Carbonell 2013). Thus while all journalists are to some extent language workers, Buryat-language journalists spend more of their time scrutinizing their linguistic decisions, often over referential content, as a condition of their work. In my survey of journalists working in bilingual news offices, the Buryat- and Ewenki-language journalists stated goals that were markedly different from those of their majority-language counterparts, a discrepancy echoed in my interviews and observations. While the writers and editors of Russian-language newspapers in Buryatia tended to speak of their societal roles in terms of "enlightenment" and "informing the public," the writers and editors of Buryat-language publications talked about their role as being primarily one of linguistic and cultural development (*razvitie*) and, above all, preservation (*sokhranenie*). Perhaps these different goals are why they did not evince the extreme cynicism so common among Russian-language journalists working in the Putin (and Medvedev) eras. What Natalia Roudakova (2017) found among mainstream Russian journalists in the same time period—totally disillusioned workers who felt forced to abandon professional ethics and who described themselves as prostitutes—was remarkably absent from my study. I would argue that this is not because Buryatia is radically different from the rest of Russia, but rather because the goals of minority media are so different. Indeed, the different language ideologies journalists are working with—that is, what they imagine their words *do*—produce different stances toward the practice of journalism in the Putin era. Buryat-language journalists saw themselves not primarily as stymied truthtellers but as pedagogues and preservationists. When they were cynical, it was for other reasons.

At work, the preservational imperative of minority-language journalism underlies some basic principles of linguistic decision making—namely, to avoid Russian influence where possible, and to avoid dialectal forms in favor of the literary standard. Employing dialectisms, mixed forms, and other *razgovornye* resources is a live possibility on television and to a lesser extent radio, especially through interview material. But in their own linguistic production, minority-language journalists remain almost universally committed to the literary standard, at least ideologically. Echoing Mėdėgma's elevation of written over spoken language, this commitment is particularly steadfast in print. There is little doubt that Buryat-language media are more easily comprehended by native speakers like Masha, struggling through the prose of <u>Buriaad ünėn</u>, when they incorporate dialectal forms. Using dialects is actively encouraged at Buriaad FM, which broadcasts in different dialects on different days of the month, and by one of its greatest supporters—the influential Khambo Lama (leader of the Buddhist Traditional Sangha of Russia) Damba Aiusheev. But these dialectal forms are generally discouraged in newspapers.

Two notable exceptions prove the rule. Ust'-Orda's Buryat-language newspaper, Ust'-Ordyn ünèn, owes much to a woman from the mountainous region of Akha, whom I will call Dolgora. Language shift in Ust'-Orda is extreme: Buryat has all but left the streets and public life, few children are acquiring it, and few adults show interest in it. Those who speak it control a dialect that diverges strongly from the standard literary language and its basis, Khori. Dolgora married a man from Ust'-Orda and arrived in the area with knowledge of her native dialect and an education in Standard Literary Buryat. Recognizing the difficulty that Ust'-Orda's Buryat speakers encounter with the literary standard, Dolgora learned the area's western Buryat dialect and makes a habit of collecting local words and phrases, which she intentionally uses in her writing. With a keen ear and natural interest in linguistics, she has thought a great deal about the relationship between dialects and the standard language. Dolgora is a language activist and would like to appeal to dialect speakers to encourage language revitalization. But, she argued, they could not publish the newspaper "only in dialect" because there "would not be enough words." The remaining lexical store (*zapas*, 'vocabulary') is, in her view, insufficient to produce a Buryat-language paper—the implication being that it would be so Russified as to not count as Buryat. Dolgora and her colleagues use some words and phrases from the local dialect "for comprehension," in hopes of easing the local readership into SLB and making it accessible to potential new learners. Their ultimate goal, however, is integration into the larger Buryat language public via the literary language, "with some of their own local particularities [*svoi mestnye osobennosti*]."

Dialectal forms have also been unwelcome in print for political reasons. The most prominent of these cases involved the Buryat-language newspaper for Sèlèngè, a district south of Ulan-Ude on the Russian-Mongolian border where a dialect more intermediate between standard Buryat and standard (Khalkh) Mongolian is spoken. When the editor there published content in the local dialect, local officials intervened and (according to journalists later in Ulan-Ude) threatened to shut down the newspaper. Their demand reportedly hinged on an argument that the "Buryat language" that is covered in the Constitution of the Republic of Buryatia is SLB, the literary standard, not miscellaneous, unstandardized dialects. The extent of the threat was unclear—some people believed it was a real threat made under pressure from the republic's government, while others thought it was a suggestion from local leaders fearing reprisal, and a lot of it might have been rumor—but other Buryat-language journalists took it seriously as a cautionary tale, and to that extent it was successful in quashing further deviation from the standard.

Thus while few journalists would argue against their own right to decide what to publish, most print journalists do—whether explicitly or implicitly—support the view that Buryat is best off with a strong, single literary standard. Some repeat something that I have heard often in Ulan-Ude's language institutions: that the dialects should not be written at all. When the argument is elaborated, it is usually in appeal to the notion of a living (*zhivoi*) language and its proper attributes. Healthy linguistic variation should include, according to this view, a *written* standard and *unwritten* speech (*rech'*), dialects, oral (*ustnye*) forms, and so on, with the written standard being the target of preservation.

Meeting the preservational imperative becomes more complex as journalists trek between workplaces and home, or between their role as journalists and their roles as wives, mothers, brothers, sons, and so on. For all the workplace emphasis on the standard literary language, Buryat-language media personnel also control colloquial, informal, and dialectal ways of speaking. Like their Russian-language counterparts, they tend to have some command of different registers of Russian, such as "official," "publicistic," or "academic" styles, by virtue of having attained a higher education primarily through Russian—even if they do not produce journalistic material in these styles or feel comfortable using them. They did not necessarily grow up speaking colloquial Russian; in fact, many Buryat-speaking journalists report being monolingual in Buryat until starting school. But they have grown up in mixed Russian-Buryat environments, speaking with frequent codeswitching, Russian borrowings both new and old, and various mixed forms.

Attending to how minority-language journalists use Russian and Buryat in their daily lives reveals the practical difficulty of being a bulwark against cultural and linguistic change. As adults, Buryat journalists based in Ulan-Ude and in the capital of Ust'-Orda find themselves living in Russian-language-dominant public environments, in which Buryat-language offices serve as rare linguistic oases.[16] At home, the "kitchen language" for many journalists is actually Russian. Buryat-language journalists working in Ulan-Ude report using Russian at home with their spouses, children, and grandchildren to a surprising extent. This admission came up in many of my interviews and interactions with journalists, teachers, and other language workers, among whom it caused a great deal of pain, dissembling, and sometimes humor. The irony of being a Buryat language worker with descendants monolingual in Russian was not lost on anyone, and I found myself repeatedly reassuring my interlocutors that many of the other language elites with whom I had worked had lamented the same thing. The phenomenon appears ascribable to three main factors: (1) linguistically mixed marriages in which Russian becomes the default, (2) ease of communication with children who spend most of their time in Russian-dominant environments, and (3) the widespread practice, mentioned above, of off-loading Buryat language acquisition onto grandparents and "country" (*derevenskie*) relatives living in ancestral villages, where children can spend their summers immersed in Buryat.

The net effect is that some Buryat-language journalists use Russian more than Buryat in their daily lives, bringing their daily linguistic experience closer to that of their audience. Writing texts out with the aid of a dictionary can erase the Russian influence on one's journalistic prose, but sometimes unintended Russianisms emerge as "mistakes" (*oshibki*). "B̀ès̀h̀e̋! [No!] *Oi*," one radio announcer exclaimed, forcefully stopping her handheld recorder. She was exasperated with her first attempt at a recording, when she had strayed from her text and tried to ad lib a passage. "Sometimes the Russian phrase just comes to mind first."

In other contexts, using mixed Russian-Buryat forms and other nonstandard resources can be quite intentional. These resources are crucial, in fact, to the daily work of media production, for many of the reasons examined in the preceding chapter. Eliciting naturalistic interviews and making collegial conversation in the office requires knowledge of conversational registers for building rapport. District affiliations in particular can work wonders for journalistic networking and access; since they are most easily indexed by using regional dialect, a dialect can be an important work tool. Workers in radio and television formats also use their knowledge of dialectal differences to decide how to treat interviews. If an interviewee is likely to be incomprehensible to most viewers based on an unusual dialect, the interview will be cut (which is the only solution in radio), translated with running subtitles (an unusual solution for news, but not uncommon for cultural programs), or edited to show the original video with a new voiceover in clearer Buryat (a common solution in television broadcasting for all kinds of problems). At newspapers, editors and writers use their extensive knowledge of dialects to decide what to translate or gloss for readers. These are also some of the ways journalists use their linguistic and cultural expertise to produce purist Buryat.

Experts in Purism

In their daily work, Buryat-language journalists adhere to a strong language ideology of purism and practice a tremendous amount of "verbal hygiene" (Cameron 2005): cleaning up their own speech, erasing Russian influence, coaching and correcting their interviewees, and excising unwanted tidbits in the editorial process. This is mostly done on an ad hoc basis. Journalists, always under time pressure to meet deadlines, rely heavily on their pedagogical training in SLB (as well as former teachers and dictionaries) to decide what they should count as "good" Buryat. In this way, the institutions of linguistics, language education, and media remain tightly integrated; although they contain a diversity of opinions, they form a nearly closed loop. When innovations and new material do make their way into that loop, they can quickly be taken up into SLB, given the implicit stamp of approval by a television anchor or newspaper reporter.

Most Buryat-language journalists, particularly print journalists, try to use Russian-origin forms and dialectal forms as little as possible. When they catch Russian influence in their own speech or writing, they prefer to "correct" it, inventing a neologism if necessary, or more often excavating and reintroducing an existing Buryat word.

Neologisms, argued one former Buriaad ünèn reporter, are good for the language and encourage pride among speakers. Journalists did not, in my experience, regularly invent their own neologisms, but they did appeal to their former teachers and linguists to suggest them. Print journalists and former print journalists have been prominently involved in various failed attempts to create a Buryat language academy on the model of the Académie Française, from at least the 1960s to the present (Shagdarov 1967). One of the primary functions of such a body would be to recommend neologisms to be used in media and official discourse. In the absence of a dedicated language authority, the right to come up with neologisms is diffuse, as is discussion over what might count as a "real" Buryat term or a Russian borrowing, an acceptable internationalism or an instance of unacceptable Russian influence. When, late in my research, one of my language consultants suggested I write an abstract of my project in Buryat, we encountered an unexpected problem immediately: there was no accepted term in Buryat for 'language shift' (R. iazykovoi sdvig). We consulted dictionaries, and I scoured the library's collection on Buryat linguistics. Finding nothing, I began to ask the sociolinguists I knew in Buryatia, carrying my abstract with me and whipping it out in conference rooms and chance meetings on the street. Surely there was some term for moving from place to place? Could we use a verb for overwintering cattle or setting up summer camp? Would a hybrid Buryat-Russian form suffice, like "khèlènèi sdvig"? No one liked these ideas. How about "shift" from English? I asked. Couldn't that be an internationalism? Like "image" or "jeans"? No. My well-connected friend, a Buryat language activist, called his friend in Mongolia, who suggested "shèlzhèltèdèkhi." What does that even mean? asked a skeptical sociolinguist. No one will recognize it, said another scholar from BNTs. Why is he always suggesting Mongolian terms? cried a third from NGI.

Eventually, the question became less about how to represent 'language shift' in Buryat in general than about what it would mean for me to represent it in Buryat. The choices before me all seemed laden with implications for ideological positioning between NGI and BNTs, between locating the seat of Buryat in the proto-Mongolic history of the steppe and locating it in a dictionary, between resisting the object that I was trying to describe and admitting that it was extremely advanced. Perhaps, I suggested at one point, it would be most honest to write *iazykovoi sdvig*—in Russian. My interlocutor chuckled at the irony but argued vociferously against "giving up," telling me it was important to set a "good example." Some of my colleagues were invested in how I would write 'language shift' because this would be the first usage. But would a lexicographer care what *I* wrote? This is why some Buryat journalists want an Académie Française for Buryat.

More often than inventing neologisms, journalists excavate and reintroduce existing Buryat and Mongolian words. The reporter who encouraged neologisms for the sake of pride also encouraged the use of sènkhir èkran for 'television,' literally meaning 'light blue screen,' to replace the Russian-origin *televizor*. Other journalists shook their head over this, arguing that because *èkran* also comes from Russian, it was not demonstrably better, and possibly worse because at least *televizor* was an "internationalism."[17]

The main sources for excavating forms are dictionaries, both Russian-Buryat and Russian-Mongolian (though the latter are used more like thesauruses or for jogging one's memory than for finding original forms). In effect, this produces a loop between the institutions of linguistics, language education, and media. Lexicographers document newspaper usages, which language educators in turn teach their students, who become journalists and write the learned usages into print, which is in turn documented by lexicographers. The prescriptive (and proscriptive) ability of institutions like NGI and BNTs depends on authority derived in large part *from* their descriptive work, and they are thus caught in the usual paradox of institutions of linguistic science: they document linguistic behavior while influencing that behavior in the process. The same loop would exist, in principle, anywhere (see Taylor 1990), but in the small world of Buryat-language affairs with only a handful of institutions, it is especially close, if not closed.[18]

One of the reasons it does not become utterly redundant and self-fulfilling is that all of the language elites involved in Buryatia also valorize "outside" opinions from village babushki. As sources for old Buryat terms, journalists rely on their friends, former teachers, spouses, or parents, and especially grandparents or other older relatives. This means that mass media, particularly newspapers, are a crucial site in which older spoken forms may enter the standard literary language, given the imprimatur of print. Sènkhir èkran, for instance, circulates in the spoken language; I have heard it from a number of older Aga Buryats.

Another reason is that Buryat has gone through so many unique stages of concerted language planning that there are now many diverse eras on which to draw. In the post-Soviet period, newspaper journalists have reintroduced into SLB many Buryat words that had previously lost out to Russian alternatives. The older Buryat (and Mongolian) word oiuutan (student), for example, had entirely lost out to *student* (student) by the end of the Soviet period. Since the 1980s, however, <u>oiuutan</u> has been reintroduced into SLB and is now expected by default in print. Other forms coexist. Issues of <u>Buriaad ünèn</u> published in 2007 included three coexisting ways of writing 'in the Soviet period' (lit. in the era of Soviet government):

(1) *sovetskè* zasagai üedè
(2) *sovet* zasagai üedè
(3) zübièltè zasagai üedè

These forms represent a continuum of Russian influence, from more to less. *Sovetskè* and *sovet* are both borrowings from Russian *sovetskii* (Soviet), nativized here into Buryat either phonologically, by turning the final Russian *ii* into ẹ, or morphologically, by dropping the Russian *–skii* adjectival ending entirely. The most purist option is the third. Zübièltè is a more obscure term that coexisted with *sovetskè* in the early twentieth century but has fallen out of favor—except, occasionally, in newsprint (cf. Budaev 1992; Humphrey 1989). One of the journalists for <u>Buriaad ünèn</u> that my interlocutors have repeatedly pointed to as using a particularly "difficult" style, "high style," but also "very beautiful" style frequently uses the "more Buryat" Buryat alternatives, such as zübièltè zasagai üedè. She is, not surprisingly, a graduate of NGI and a careful student of Buryat linguistic history, and she makes these decisions quite carefully on the basis of a strong purist ideology.

Journalists have greatest control over their own language, of course, but they also make purist decisions by "cleaning up" interview material and other reported speech. It is a fact of Buryat-language journalism that the overwhelming majority of material is collected in Russian and translated by the journalist, either on the fly or later in the conversion of notes into a prose story. In fact, newspaper reporters rarely even attempt to elicit quotations in Buryat. In my interviews, journalists reported that they collected most of their material in Russian, and shadowing reporters quickly confirmed that the reports were accurate. (This was even true in Aginskoe, where Buryat usage in public is generally more common.) Given, then, that journalists *expect* to translate the events and interviews that they record into original prose, it almost goes without saying that they feel Russian usage in interviews or reported speech can and should be "cleaned up" and made into fluent Buryat. No one found this even worth comment. When I was interviewed for <u>Tolon</u> and <u>Ust'-Ordyn ünèn</u>, the reporters seemed charmed that I even suggested that I be interviewed in Buryat. I reminded the reporters, in both cases, that I was not a native Russian speaker anyway; neither language was *easy* for me. But ultimately I gave in to the expectation that most people are dominant in Russian, and the fact that, as one of the reporters put it, it was basically the same to them. Indeed, as I spoke (in Russian), she recorded our conversation and jotted down notes in Buryat, repeating the elicitation method that I witnessed most often. In this very fast and diffused translation process, little effort is made to retain an individual's voice or style, though the style of the Russian will often be replicated in the Buryat, with, for instance, an official political proclamation in Russian appearing in the same style in Buryat. It is usually impossible to tell, from a finished product, what language or languages, registers, or conversational resources were employed in the reported utterances. We all become fluent speakers of SLB in the newspaper.

Brokering Buryatness

On a daily basis, minority-language journalists negotiate how to hold themselves and their interviewees to an idealized literary standard while still meeting the demands of intelligibility and relevance to an audience that speaks and understands "mixed" language better. As we might expect from the capacious multilingualism of journalists, the language of news media is considerably more complex than simply reproducing a purist literary standard. Media institutions contain varying stances toward the "balance" between Russian and Buryat, and between SLB and *razgovornye* resources. The experience of journalists who produce praiseworthy literary Buryat prose at work and then speak in Russian and mixed Russian-Buryat at home suggests that ways of speaking are "attached" less to persons than to contexts of use. Regardless of this fludity and dynamism, however, people *ascribe* language standards to media makers, and monolithic authority to news journalists in particular.

By embodying this social role, Buryat-language media instantiate and institutionalize "proper" relationships between language use and ethnonational belonging. When journalists like Dolgora decide between referring to an object in the world by using a dialectal form, a standard Buryat phrase that her readers might not understand, or its more common Russian version, they (re)set the bar for other Buryats. When they showcase certain content as particularly Buryat and worthy of inclusion in Buryat cultural programming, they reaffirm what should and should not be considered part of Buryat—as opposed to general Russian (*rossiiskaia*)—culture. In this sense, they are the ultimate brokers of both language and culture.

This is not an easy role. In their recruitment and socialization into an ethnonational elite, they work within value systems that are sometimes at odds with one another. On one hand, they strive toward the professionalism and hyperinstitutionalization of journalism within the majority society, as all journalists do. On the other hand, their role as *native-language* journalists grants a narrower elite status within the minority that draws on rural authenticity and *non*institution-alization. The "real Buryat," after all, is in the village or out on the steppe. Or is it? To the extent that *korenizatsiia* and the movement of Buryat cultural distinc-tiveness into institutions of power have succeeded, the "real Buryat" should be discoverable among journalists. Indeed, activists among smaller ethnic minori-ties in Russia often claim that the existence of Buryat-language media grants Buryats unassailable cultural prestige or power, as though to have a newspaper in one's language is to assert enough cultural difference. Yet the "real Buryat" is still pictured in popular culture not as an intellectual, urban-dwelling reporter but as an archer on his horse or as a woman in traditional dress standing in a field of tall grasses. The halls of media institutions are populated by people who grew up without indoor plumbing and distrust those who did. There is a profound ten-sion between these two competing sources of cultural power and authority—the cosmopolitan and the hyperlocal, the concrete and the ephemeral, the institu-tional and the expressly uninstitutionalizable—which members of the minority elite must negotiate on a daily basis.

Journalists circulating between their newsrooms and their living rooms remind us that just as there is no neat separation between a literary standard and colloquial ways of speaking, so too there is no neat separation between media producers and consumers. In this book thus far, we have seen sites of media consumption, with examples of people watching television, listening to the radio, and reading (or trying to read) the newspaper; and key sites of media production, such as newsrooms. Media consumption and production come together in the context of interviews, letters to the editor, blogs, chatrooms, YouTube, and other forms of audience participation in media production. In these interactions, audi-ences collaborate with more institutionalized media makers to demonstrate their participation not only in the Buryat minority language public but, by extension, in the nation as well. Such interactions can be opportunities to renegotiate what it means to speak, and be, Buryat. The collaborative aspects of this are mitigated, however, by the performance anxiety that prevents many semispeakers from opening their mouths, as well as by tendencies to reaffirm racialized expectations and reterritorialize a Buryat minority public. These struggles over participation and performance are the subject of Part III.

Part III

PARTICIPATION AND PERFORMANCE

PERFORMANCE ANXIETY

"Why don't you know your own language?" The first time I heard this expression, it was uttered by an elderly babushka shaking her cane angrily at a young woman who stood in terrified silence, like a deer in headlights, holding a tray of meat dumplings (B. <u>buuza</u>, R. *pozy*). My friend Darima and I were in a café on the outskirts of Ulan-Ude. Two babushki, speaking Buryat, had tried repeatedly to order these buuza from the two young women behind the counter. The girls had understood the order, or at least part of it, but they answered in Russian, to which the babushki replied in Buryat, to which the girls responded in Russian . . . until the babushki began shaking their heads and "tsk"-ing with increasing frustration, whereupon the girls fell mute. Darima, sitting opposite me at a creaky little table, clearly did not want to get involved. She instinctively ducked her head, peeking over the top of her steaming mug of milky tea to watch.

As the babushki's voices grew louder, a hushed silence fell over the café, everyone's attention trained on the frozen girls. They were practically in tears, eager to please their elders and running back and forth from the kitchen, but incapable of responding in Buryat. Finally, the girl holding the buuza broke the silence by setting the tray down with a clatter, splashing some tea onto the vinyl tablecloth. The babushki began eating and chatting among themselves, and everyone returned to their own meals as though with a collective sigh of relief.

Later, I had to ask Darima about the tension in the room, and about her own apparent fear of being approached by the elderly women. This was early in my fieldwork in Buryatia in 2005; I was thoroughly an outsider, and I did not yet understand how meat dumplings could elicit such terror. Darima giggled. "*Bozhe*" (O God), she said with a dismissive wave of her hand. "It's really hard, you know, if you didn't grow up in the village and you don't speak well. Yeah, and the babushki, that's what they expect, you know. They expect that you speak Buryat." She picked some lint off her blouse and became more contemplative, frowning. "Well, and of course, we **should**," she said earnestly. "A person **should** speak their own language."

Four years later, I was sitting with a television journalist, Sayana, as she reviewed recordings of an interview in Buryat to be edited for the evening news. There were a lot of "umms" and pauses, and the man being interviewed looked uncomfortable. He switched frequently into Russian, eventually pointing to his friend and suggesting they interview him instead. Sayana sighed and tapped the screen with her pen, saying softly, "Why don't you know your own language?"

What does it mean to "not know your own language"? As noted previously, people who self-identify as Buryat often identify Buryat as their "own language" (*svoi iazyk*) based on their broader ethnic self-affiliation, regardless of their linguistic competence. Sayana extended the same expectation to someone whose self-identification she did not know, engaging in subtle racial guessing to conclude that he was Buryat and therefore *should* rightfully possess Buryat as his "own language." The positive aspect of this is that she emphasizes the would-be speaker's ownership of a powerful identity marker. But the negative consequence is that she forces that identity onto him and demands a kind of knowledge he does not share.

As for "knowing" and "not knowing," these are variable attributions that shift with context. Darima claimed that she had no knowledge of Buryat, though I had witnessed her on many occasions carrying on bilingual conversations with her relatives, they speaking Buryat and she responding in Russian. Each family member assumed the other person had at least passive knowledge of both languages and spoke with her own language of preference, a pattern common in situations of long-term bilingualism such as Ukraine, where Laada Bilaniuk (2005) describes it as "non-accommodating bilingualism." As we have seen in previous chapters, there are many people like Darima and the girls at the café, currently in their twenties and thirties, who have excellent passive competence in Buryat but cannot—or will not—speak. Others speak Buryat as a first language but are more or less illiterate in the literary standard, or (more rarely) control the literary standard but have little command of colloquial speech. There are still more who have little or no passive competence but excellent knowledge of the pragmatic uses to which Buryat, as a code, may be put. An onlooker in the café, for instance, might not understand what was being said in Buryat but understand that the babushki intensified their scolding by conducting it in Buryat, or that performing a toast in Buryat at a banquet demonstrates membership in a broader Buryat community. Such onlookers may be said to possess social or cultural knowledge of the indexical meanings of Buryat. One need not self-identify as a speaker of Buryat to have some sort of knowledge *about* Buryat—or to be taken as a speaker.

As we have seen in this book thus far, language politics are often animated by strong emotions, from joy and pride to anger and despair. This chapter delves into the shame and anxiety that would-be Buryat speakers like Darima feel when they are called on to perform Buryat and fear they either do not control Buryat or do not control the literary standard and therefore do not speak "well." Darima's fear derives from three interrelated sources of tension, explored here in turn. First, both Buryats and members of wider Russian society generally *expect* individuals racialized as Buryat to be invested in the continuation of Buryat language and culture, and one of the main ways they are supposed to demonstrate their ethnonational belonging is through the performance of good speech. These racialized expectations place a premium on knowing some Buryat, even if only a few words for symbolic use. Second, the strong opposition between the literary standard and colloquial forms leads most people to understand language mixing—such as using Buryat grammatical endings on Russian-origin terms— fundamentally as corruption, indicating a kind of misrecognition on the part of the speaker. Third, individuals feel themselves to be more or less on stage in different contexts. Their sense of potential disaster is heightened by media contexts, which are generally framed as a space for Buryat language and culture to be presented as such, cordoned off from the much more syncretic and fluid linguistic and cultural practices of daily life. Radio and television interviews in particular are, as we will see, sites of public performance in which ideas about what it means to speak Buryat "correctly" become clear. Ultimately, language shift, uneven control of the standard, and racialized expectations of "good" public performance conspire to produce a kind of performance anxiety in people—what they often call a "complex" (*kompleks*). This performance anxiety silences many would-be speakers of Buryat, excluding partial speakers or passive understanders and paradoxically furthering language loss.

Shame in (Not) Speaking

It is common for people to feel ashamed of the way they speak or of the way they do not or cannot speak. William Labov (1966) pointed this out in a classic study of the social stratification of English usage in New York City, when he observed that New Yorkers would claim that *outsiders* disliked New Yorkers' speech when what they actually meant was that they (New Yorkers) disliked their *own* speech. New Yorkers, he wrote, "show a general hostility towards New York City speech . . . The term 'linguistic self-hatred' is not too extreme to apply to the situation" (Labov 1966, 488–89).[1] Labov devised an "Index of Linguistic Insecurity" to describe the attitudes of self-consciousness, low confidence, and anxiety that he observed.

Where does linguistic insecurity come from? Labov ascribed New Yorkers' "linguistic self-hatred" to class anxiety. Speakers were aware that there was a standard American English that they did not control, and they seemed to be aware that subtle features of their own speech, such as the pronunciation of /r/, marked them both geographically and socioeconomically. Yet in and of itself, the inability to adhere to a linguistic norm does not necessitate that one feel bad about it. Concern over linguistic markedness tends to vary from person to person, just as different people are more or less concerned with their socioeconomic status. Some sociolinguistic studies on English speakers have suggested, for instance, that women exhibit greater linguistic insecurity than men (e.g., Owens and Baker 1984).

It is also common for a language to become so thoroughly conflated with a nationalized, ethnicized, or racialized group that speaking the language comes to stand in for, or index, membership. This metonymy underlies many language revitalization movements, such as Basque and Catalan language revitalization efforts in Spain. In the Basque region, speaking Basque is part of asserting political independence and indexing one's personal commitment to those efforts (Urla 2012); likewise in Catalonia, speaking Catalan has become a central way of demonstrating commitment to Catalonia's political independence (Woolard 2016). An extreme form is Tamil language devotion, which has led men to burn themselves alive in the name of their language (Ramaswamy 1997). If the social group is somehow denigrated, the same metonymy can be an additional source of shame.

In the context of language shift, the emotionality of code choice may be heightened. Public discourse about language shift draws attention to code, not only for the members of a cultural elite but for other speakers in public contexts as well. Speaking Buryat has taken on additional affective importance in public life as the political stakes of *not* speaking have risen. Now speaking Buryat is not only a matter of showing your own membership in a minority public; it concerns the future of the minority public itself. To the extent that speaking a receding language like Buryat has been conflated with investment in that *group*'s future, not speaking it looks like you do not care—or, perhaps worse, like you care but are powerless or incompetent. Thus interactions that would not normally provoke anxiety, such as ordering tea in a café, have become emotionally heightened as attention is drawn to the linguistic code—and to the speaker's inability to produce it perfectly.

Purism can also prevent semispeakers of younger generations from speaking freely. Alexandra Aikhenvald (2003, 2013) found this pattern among Tariana speakers in the Brazilian Amazon. Less fully proficient speakers who disavowed knowledge of Tariana early in her fieldwork began to reveal their competence only as her familiarity grew and as the older, more purist members of the community died. One of the consequences of enregistering a strong literary standard, as has been attempted with Buryat, is that purism has a clearer and more ideologized target. With the standardization of Hebrew in Israel, would-be speakers shifted from being proud to being insecure about their ability to uphold the standard (Kuzar 2001, 130). Yet Ron Kuzar goes on to say that people have become less insecure again over time, probably a sign that the reintroduction of Hebrew was successful—or that the status of the nation indexed by the standard is politically more secure. When Kathryn Woolard (1995) compared comedic performances of Catalan codeswitching in the late 1980s with those of a decade earlier, she found that a more secure political and public status for Catalan had paradoxically made codeswitching and syncretism more acceptable. Catalan could be more publicly profaned without threatening its status. In this light, people's personal feelings of shame about not speaking Buryat well point to the broader sociopolitical insecurity of the nation that the language is taken to represent.[2]

Feeling ashamed to speak (or not to speak) in front of others makes sense if we think of speaking as a form of performance. Most of the time the girls in the café are likely to get along just fine speaking Russian; Buryat is not often demanded in public life. And perhaps their interaction could have remained an instance of quiet, nonaccommodating bilingualism, with the babushki speaking Buryat and the girls speaking Russian. But the babushki's shouts elicit an audience. To borrow Erving Goffman's (1959, 1981) theatrical metaphor, they are forced "on stage" in front of an audience from what previously had been a public but "offstage" interaction with their customers. This effectively erects a proscenium—a separation between onstage performers and an audience—within the café, just as thrusting a microphone into an interviewee's face forces her to perform. Darima ducks her head in an attempt to stay on the audience side of the proscenium and not be called on herself to perform. But for whom are these girls on stage? Their problem is scalar. By being called on to speak their "own" language, they are being forced to account to a Buryat minority language public, a subpublic of Russian society, as opposed to the Russian-dominant mainstream public to which they usually orient by default.

Performance anxiety also rests on common language ideologies that separate public and private and denigrate the private in favor of the public. The boundaries of public and private spaces are felt with special acuteness in postsocialist spaces like Siberia, where the state has carefully directed public personhood and has demarcated spaces for its performance (Gal 2005; Gal and Kligman 2000; Lampland 1995; Lemon 2003). But we can see similar language-ideological separations elsewhere too. As Bonnie Urciuoli (1991, 1996) found in her study of working-class Puerto Rican Spanish speakers in New York City, bilingual speakers often feel a strong distinction between private and public domains of linguistic action. Urciuoli (1996, 77) described these domains as two "spheres of interaction," an inner sphere "made of relations with people most equal to one," such as family, friends, and neighbors, and an outer sphere "made of relations with people who have structural advantages over one," such as bosses, landlords, and teachers. Urciuoli found that in his or her inner sphere, a bilingual speaker felt no difficulty using English because the register of English appropriate in these contexts could incorporate resources from Spanish. But in his or her outer sphere, using English was more fraught and problematic because it needed to be "correct." Buryats similarly tend to strictly delineate public and private communicative domains, in ideology if not always in practice. While in "kitchen language," Buryat speakers accept a high degree of Russian influence and other *razgovornye* resources, in public life, they expect not only purist Russian but also purist Buryat.

Mass media are among the most important spaces demarcated for publicly performing one's good citizenship. In the Soviet period, being interviewed and photographed for the press was a key way of demonstrating your participation not only in a Buryat minority language public but also in the Soviet project writ large. So much the better for both you and the photographer if you were photographed *consuming* Buryat media, as in figure 11! Today the public performances of non-Buryats trying to speak Buryat, like former President Nagovitsyn's, demonstrate commitment to Buryatia and to the principle of a titular nationality.

The gender and racial dynamics of the café scene point to the uneven application of expectations and shame. Buryat women tend to engage more readily in self- and mutual criticism, especially in public settings. While both men and women can be accused of speaking Buryat poorly, women seldom criticize men, especially older men, due to a widely felt Buryat cultural prohibition. For a woman to publicly criticize an older man is "*nepriiatno*" (unpleasant or inappropriate), as one Buryat woman in her fifties put it to me (Graber 2017). Women, however—particularly younger women—are fair game.

ЗУРАГ ДЭЭРЭ: ВЛКСМ-ой Бурят-Монголой Областной XIV конференцид, хабаалгашад—Закаменай аймагай Карл Марксын
перэмжэтэ колхозой звеньевод Шойжонима Балданов, Закаменай аймагай Калининай перэмжэт, колхозой комсомольско эхин
организацини секретарь Долсон Очирова, Задын аймагай Сталинай нэрэмжэт, колхозой ОТФ-э дааргша Ханда Буянтуева гэгшэд
«Бурят- Монголой Унэн» газетые уншажа байна.   М. Минеевай фото.

FIGURE 11.   Workers of collective farms in Zakhaamin District and Dzhida District are photographed reading <u>Buriat-Mongoloi ünén</u>. Published in the same newspaper, 21(5692), February 1, 1949 (National Library of the Republic of Buryatia).

The interaction was also racialized in the sense that the babushki expected the girls—and not, for example, me—to speak Buryat. Racism is not widely discussed in Russia because Soviet discourse during the Cold War held that racism was a problem of the capitalist West, particularly the United States (Fikes and Lemon 2002). Nonetheless, Buryats understand themselves as racialized within Russia, without using the term. In the living room scene opening this book, Badma waved off Dorzhozhab's suggestion of using the term *rossiiskii* to describe her belonging in the Russian state. She referred to the gaps between citizenship, race, and ethnicity in contemporary Russia, according to which she felt expected to self-identify as Buryat and found a neutral Russian-citizen identity precluded to her. Xenophobia, graffiti proclaiming "Russia for the [ethnic] Russians!" (figure 7), and periodic hate crimes against Buryats in western Russian cities remind Buryats of their precarious status in Russia's racial hierarchy. Young people sometimes identify as "black" based on racialized inequality and what they see as a shared urban or working-class lifestyle.[3]

Individuals racialized as Buryat are *expected* to speak Buryat, at least a little bit. The babushki were, like Sayana, engaging in racial guessing. After all, to ask a stranger "Why don't you know your own language?" implies that the asker has some sense of what that stranger's "own" language is. Thus Darima, who phenotypically looked Buryat, feared being interpreted as a speaker of Buryat by the demanding babushki, while I sat happily with my tea and my pointy European nose, free from any expectations of linguistic competence and blissfully unaware of the danger around me. Once you have been racially interpellated as Buryat, your native language (*rodnoi iazyk*)—not the language you necessarily speak but your ancestral or heritage language—is also assumed to be Buryat by default. This is a singular category; you have only one "native language." This assumption might appear to be due to an ideology of monolingualism that is widespread, including among linguists. Dorian has argued, for instance, that linguists similarly have been "committed . . . to an ideology that recognizes only one 'native language' per speaker" (2014, 20). But the logic here is a bit different. In post-Soviet language ideologies, knowledge is separate from nativeness. Knowledge may be plural, and in fact census documents suggest that the state expects citizens of the Russian Federation to be wildly multilingual. Ancestral identity, however, is singular. On the 2010 census forms, multiple blanks were provided for the languages a respondent might have some knowledge of, but

FIGURE 12. A college student in Aginskoe is interviewed by a news team from the local television station. The journalists who approached her assumed she spoke Buryat. (Photo by author, 2009.)

only one blank was provided for *rodnoi iazyk* (Rosstat 2012–13). Expectations of knowledge nonetheless follow closely behind ascriptions of nativeness, based on race.

Racial guessing was by far the most common way radio and television reporters identified potential interviewees while out in the field collecting material, though it did not always result in a good story (figure 12). Even if the news team managed to record an interview with a person they identified phenotypically as Buryat, it might not yield sufficient usable material. Sayana, for instance, had made this mistake with the man of whom she asked, "Why don't you know your own language?" She had interpellated her subject as a potential Buryat speaker, and then as a *failed* one. Her interviewee, in the midst of his stuttering, seemed to know it and suffer from it.

Kinds of Knowing

What, then, does it mean to "know" a language? Darima, the café girls, the babushki, and I all demonstrated wide-ranging levels and types of competence as speakers of Buryat. I have been referring in this book to anyone who is not taken to be a fully competent speaker of Buryat as a "semispeaker," but this term is insufficient in some important ways. Dorian (2014, 148) describes semispeakers as "individuals whose mastery of the language which is gradually being given up is incomplete, so that they are imperfect speakers whose performances are riddled with what an older, more competent generation could only consider mistakes" (see also Dorian 1973, 1977). The term suggests that there are older elites—perhaps the babushki, or perhaps journalists like Sayana—who "know" the language fully in contradistinction to large numbers of speakers who simply do not. Sometimes speakers very much feel that way. For instance, Masha concluded that she had a "low-level knowledge" of her native language based on her difficulty understanding the newspaper. It is also certainly true that some speakers, especially from among the aforementioned elite, judge others' speech as riddled with "mistakes." Yet in the context of everyday life, the relevant distinction is not usually that between "full" and "partial" speakers. The babushki command colloquial Buryat, while Sayana is in her position because she is an expert in the standard literary language; similarly, I can recite poems but do not share Masha's native command of colloquial, spoken Buryat or Darima's excellent passive knowledge of her family's dialect. Sociolinguists and linguistic anthropologists have often noted the difficulty of determining who counts as a speaker during language attrition, but the role of semispeaking and the contradictions generated by degrees of knowledge in language shift have rarely been thematized as such.[4] So we end up with "semispeaking" as a catch-all term for what is, in practice, a wide array of abilities that are more or less salient depending on context. We might better think of these abilities as kinds of knowing. To do so brings us closer to understanding where shame in linguistic performance comes from. By the definition above, *most* speakers of Buryat are semispeakers. Thus the more relevant questions are: What sort of knowledge does the interaction demand? What will serve as sufficient evidence of belonging to the Buryat public?

At a basic level, performance of Buryat is about meeting basic expectations of adherence to code. When acquaintances implored me (usually in Russian) to "say something—anything—in Buryat," they wanted to witness the novelty of a European-faced foreigner speaking the language. Russian speakers—including ethnic Russians—can mark their regional identity by using a few words of Buryat, usually greetings and daily expressions such as <u>Sain baina!</u> (Hello!), <u>Sagaalga-naar!</u> (Happy Sagaalgan!), or <u>hain daa</u> (thank you). But the sentiment that any bit of Buryat will do was often not far off the mark for ethnic Buryats either. The romantically challenged Vasilii, for instance, was advised by his friends that he would need no more than a few words of ceremonial Buryat to appease potential in-laws. Television journalists often displayed a similar attitude when they went in search of Buryat-language interviewees. In these contexts, the potential content of the interview and the length and quality of the interviewee's speech were not nearly as important as her ability to produce even a few words in Buryat, particularly because the television crew could fill in missing content through a voiceover or editing in the production room.

The multiplicity of degrees and ways of knowing Buryat, and the multiplicity of *expectations* for knowing Buryat, are on clear display in Buryat-language television interviews. As an example, let us look at the production of a news story about a syphilis outbreak that aired on state television.[5]

News coverage of the syphilis outbreak was not particularly extended or extreme; the events were approached with an air of daily journalistic routine and were reported mainly as a public service. It happened to be the story I was assigned one morning as an observer "intern" at BGTRK. *Inform polis* had recently run a story about cases of syphilis showing up in a local kindergarten, and one of the news department heads felt that it was the news team's public duty to cover the syphilis outbreak immediately, to help prevent an epidemic. I accompanied a lead correspondent, Zhargalma, who was responsible for the Russian-language story, and a second correspondent, Dashi, who was responsible for the Buryat-language story.

Zhargalma was not pleased with this assignment. She was, in general, less enthusiastic about the public service dimension of her job and preferred to cover concerts, theatrical performances, and other cultural events. Today her boss had given her no choice of topic. She looked embarrassed as she told me where we were going: the dermatological and venereological clinic. The film crew cracked jokes about venereal diseases as they packed their equipment and themselves into a tiny eggplant-colored Lada sedan, everyone professing to have *no idea* where the clinic was located and Zhargalma silently suffering.

When we arrived at the clinic, however, and saw how delightfully gross everything was, Zhargalma's spirits lifted. The cameraman insisted that it was illegal for him to film the patients in the clinic.[6] As a result, the crew had to settle for filming posters and the pages of a giant medical textbook depicting oozing sores, blistering rashes, and festering open wounds. These images were sufficient to elicit cries of titillated horror and "oh my god!" (*bozhe moi!*) from all of the editors and production crew members who worked on the footage over the course of the day, and Zhargalma would end the day satisfied that she had made a compelling story for the evening news.

Where Zhargalma had it easy, however, Dashi—who seemed to have accepted the assignment in stride—struggled. Narrative conventions of news storytelling demand that there be a hero (*geroi*) and preferably at least one supporting character, so the goal for an assignment like the syphilis story is two interviews. This is not an easy task. The senior male doctor who produced the main statistics and information about the syphilis epidemic gave a fine interview in Russian but would not give an interview in Buryat. Like his colleague Sayana, Dashi was using racial guessing; he assumed that the doctor might speak Buryat because phenotypically he *looked* Buryat. In this case, however, the doctor summarily avoided the fate of the floundering interviewee. He would not say that he did *not* speak Buryat, simply that an interview in Buryat "won't work out" (*ne poluchitsia*). Dashi, who was usually quite persuasive in these situations, tried a couple of times before giving up.

At our next location, a laboratory on the outskirts of town, Dashi succeeded in convincing two middle-aged women, a doctor and a laboratory technician, to give interviews in Buryat, though only after extensive cajoling. They never spoke Buryat at work, they said. They feared their Buryat was too colloquial, and that they would forget the "right words." I had witnessed hesitation with other potential interviewees—there is, after all, some element of nervousness with most interview situations, regardless of the language spoken—but here the requirement to speak *Buryat* on camera clearly occasioned special fear.

Dashi began by speaking Buryat, like a warmup to ease the transition. But the doctor resisted this frame, instead speaking Buryat only while the camera was trained on her and frequently switching back into Russian. When she hesitated or switched, Dashi would patiently lead her back into Buryat, suggesting the words or phrases she might be looking for. He stopped short of providing medical terminology and did not correct her on her use of Russian-origin terms like *vrach* (doctor) and *gazet* (newspaper), which have common Buryat-native alternatives but are widely used in Buryat. Sometimes journalists do provide these kinds of corrections, but things were difficult enough for this interviewee, and any correction would have risked further embarrassing her and shutting down the interview entirely. At one point she broke off in exasperation, switching into Russian: "It's very difficult to translate '*sifilis*'!" (*Perevesti sifilis ochen' tiazhelo!*) "Ti:mé" (Yes), Dashi agreed, switching pointedly back into Buryat to complete the interview. When the doctor appeared thoroughly exhausted and Dashi thought he might have enough material to piece together a story, he thanked her and ended the interview. She looked both relieved and distraught. "Oy, I spoke so poorly!" she cried, in Russian. And Dashi relented and switched into Russian, assuring her that she had given him "very good material."

Back in the editing studio in the afternoon, Dashi recorded a voiceover script and pieced together bits of the women's interviews to produce his evening broadcast, a portion of which I reproduce here. The broadcast began with images from the dermatological-venereological diseases clinic and the clinic where testing for syphilis is done, over which was layered a voiceover from our correspondent, Dashi (table 6.1).

TABLE 6.1

	SPEECH AS BROADCAST	ENGLISH TRANSLATION	ACCOMPANYING IMAGE IN BROADCAST
1	Arhanai bolon *venericheskẹ*	On the walls at the Ulan-Ude	/front door and sign
2	übshẹngüüdye argaldag	municipal medical clinics	of dermatological-
3	Ulaan-Üdẹ khotodokhi	treating skin and *venereal*	venereological clinic/
4	ẹmnẹlgẹnüüdtẹ khananuud	diseases are informational	
5	dẹẹrẹ mẹdẹẹsẹlẹi	posters.	/poster entitled "the price
6	sambarnuud baina.		of carelessness"/
7	Tẹndẹn' hain azha huugty,	Written there are slogans	
8	khünüüdtẹ haalta bü khẹgty	telling people to live well,	/hand-drawn
9	gẹhẹn uriaa bẹshẹẹtẹi.	[and] what they should not	informational posters and
		do.	photographs of syphilis

	SPEECH AS BROADCAST	ENGLISH TRANSLATION	ACCOMPANYING IMAGE IN BROADCAST
10	Saashan' unshakhada	In reading further, it is	sores/
11	veneri:cheskė aiaar khori	explained that there are as	
12	garan übshėngüüd baigaalida	many as twenty-some	
13	bii ium baina gėzhė ėlirnė.	venereal diseases occurring in nature.	
14	Tėdėnhėė bėeė khamgaalzha,	There are slogans about	/flipping the pages of
15	bėe bėedėė ankharaltaigaar,	protecting one's body from	an "atlas" of infectious
16	narin niagta iabakha tukhai	these by being careful and	diseases, with the title
17	uriaanuud baina.	treating each other with care.	page "sifilis" opening the book/
18	Mai hara khakhadlaba, gazaa	As we reach mid-May, with	
19	huraggüi dulaarba, iimė	it getting somewhat warmer	
20	orshon baidalda arhanai	outside, doctors working at	/photograph in book of a
21	bolon veneri:cheskė	the Ulan-Ude municipal	blistered nose/
22	übshėngüüdye argaldag	medical clinics treating skin	/photograph in book of an
23	Ulaan-Üdė khotodokhi	and venereal diseases are	infant covered in sores/
24	ėmnėlgėnüüdtė khüdėldėg	getting this nearing situation	/cut to lab technician in
25	ėmshėd arad zondo garazha,	out to the people,	scrubs filling test tubes/
26	oilguulamzhyn khüdėlmėri	it not being possible to	/lab tech with test tubes/
27	iabuulaagüidėn' iaakha	launch an informational	
28	argagüi.	campaign.	

Dashi speaks fluently with complex grammatical constructions, characteristic of the literary language. Note how few Russian-origin terms he uses: only *Mai* (May) in line 18 and *venericheskė* (venereal, from R. *venericheskii*) in lines 1, 11, and 21. He nativizes Russian *venericheskii* phonologically by ending with Buryat *ė* rather than Russian *ii*, and by applying Buryat vowel length to the stressed Russian [i] in lines 11 and 21 (*veneri:cheskė*).

By contrast, his two interviewees produce short sentences with syntactic repetition and avoid complex constructions. The doctor's interview as aired was cobbled together from the short stretches of her discourse that Dashi found acceptable in the editing process, resulting in a series of film breaks and a disjointed feel in the broadcast. She stands in the lab area and blinks into the camera, clearly searching for words. Notice the number of pauses (.) and film breaks in her speech (table 6.2).

The doctor uses more Russian borrowings than Dashi, including some that have Buryat equivalents. Some, such as *televizor* (television), have Buryat options

TABLE 6.2

SPEECH AS BROADCAST	ENGLISH TRANSLATION	ACCOMPANYING IMAGE IN BROADCAST
29 Zaluushuulai (.) dunda ekhè	Really, this *infectious* disease is	*title on screen:* Ulaan-Üdė
30 taradag ėnė (.) *infektsionno*	very widespread among youth.	khotyn
31 übshėn bii gèėshè aab daa.		*kozhvendispantser* èi
32 Dėlkhėi dèėrė khorëod	On the earth there number	*vrach* [Ulan-Ude
33 übshėn gėzhė toosodog.	about twenty diseases so called.	Municipal *Derm-Ven*
34 Tiigėėd tėdèėnėi khoorondo	And among these, *syphilis* is	*Dispensary Doctor*]
35 ekhė aiuultainiin' (.) si:*filis*	particularly dangerous.	/doctor stands in white
36 bolono.		lab coat in front of glass
37 Tiigėėd ėnė harada manai	Then [uh], I think that this	cabinet containing paper
38 khėhėn azhal ekhė gėzhė bi	month our work will be great.	files/
39 hananabi.		
[/film break/]	[/film break/]	/film break/
40 Erèhėn zaluushuulsh'e,	We will probably be examining,	
41 iamarsh'e erèhėn khünüüdye	looking at youth who've arrived	
42 üzėzhė kharazha, abakha	[from elsewhere], other people	/looks to side of camera
43 *analiz*uudyn' abazha, (.)	who've arrived [from	with eyes moving around
44 übshėntėi baigaa haan'	elsewhere], receiving *analyses*	room, apparently
45 übshėniien' argalzha, zaazha	to do, treating the illnesses of	thinking/
46 kharazha, kharuulzha khėlėnė	the diseased, looking at—	
47 gėėshė aabzabdi daa.	demonstrating—examination(s).	
[/film break/]	[/film break/]	/film break/
48 Bėeė dèėgüür tatazha abazha	(If) your body starts intensely	
49 hainaar iabakhyn tülöö, gèntė	dragging, declining, after	
50 bolohon uulzalganuudhaa	"chance encounters,"[1] to the	
51 hüüldė *vrach*uudta . . .	doctors . . .	
52 ėnė tėrė iuumėnėi boloo haa,	if something like this happens,	
53 *vrach*uudta erėzhė üzüülėgty	we are advising that you go to	
54 gėzhė khėlėdėg gėėshėbdi.	the *doctors*.	
55 *Televizor*èėrsh khėlėnė	We are probably speaking on	
56 gėėshė aabzabdi daa, *gazet*	your *television*, we have had	
57 iuumėdėsh'e	some *newspaper* items	
58 bėshėgdėdėgbdi.	published.	

[1] This is an example of a more subtle type of Russian influence. The expression here, gèntė bolohon uulzalganuud (lit. suddenly happening meetings), is a euphemism for casual sexual relations, calqued from R. *sluchainye sviazi* ('chance encounters').

that only language elites and a limited number of other speakers know, such as the semi-neologism sènkhir *èkran* (lit. light blue screen). Others, however, such as *vrach* (doctor) and *gazet* (newspaper, from R. *gazeta*), have widely used Buryat-origin equivalents.

Dashi himself uses terms that have been borrowed into Buryat from Russian when they might be considered "internationalisms"—namely, words from Greek and Latin. An example appears in his transition to the second interviewee within his story. Notice how he nativizes *klini:cheskė* (clinical) in line 60 in the same ways he nativized *veneri:cheskė* (table 6.3).

Like the doctor and Dashi, the laboratory technician uses Russian medical terminology. Like the doctor, she also uses simple grammatical constructions and searches for words. But while the doctor struggles, the laboratory technician speaks fluidly; she is at much greater ease (table 6.4).

TABLE 6.3

	SPEECH AS BROADCAST	ENGLISH TRANSLATION	ACCOMPANYING IMAGE IN BROADCAST
59	*Steklozavod* huurinda	Studies are based at the	/lab interior and
60	klini:cheskė serologiin	clinical serological place	exterior/
61	talaar shėnzhėlgėnüüd	in the neighborhood of	/close-up of samples
62	iabuulagdana.	*Steklozavod.*	and testing equipment/

TABLE 6.4

	SPEECH AS BROADCAST	ENGLISH TRANSLATION	ACCOMPANYING IMAGE IN BROADCAST
63	*Serologicheska*	We have a serological	title on screen: Ėmshėn
64	*laboratoritoibdi.*	laboratory.	[Doctor]
65	Khoёr vrach, khoёr *laborant*	Now working are two doctors	/lab tech sits behind
66	khüdėlzhė bainabdi.	(and) two laboratory technicians.	tray of samples in test
67	Nėgė *registraator* i . . . khoёr	One receptionist and . . . two	tubes, in white lab coat,
68	*sant-, sanitar-*(.)	ai-, aid-, aides.	addresses journalist off
69	*sanitar*kanuud.		to side/
70	Tiigėėd . . . (.)	And . . . (.)	
71	iuun . . . (.)	what . . . (.)	/looks to side, thinking
72	teė üdėr bükhėndė bi ėnė	well, every day I [do] this	of what to say next/
73	*serologicheska* [???] nöökhi	serological [???] that very	
74	tėrė *venicheskė* übshėn–	venereal disease–	
75	tėrė *sifilis* gėzhė übshėnėi	I have to do a lot of the	
76	*reaktsiia Vassermana*	Wassermann reaction of the	
77	gėėshyen' olodogbi.	disease called syphilis.	
78	Tiigėėd *IFA* gėzhė *analiz* . . .	Then the analysis called IFA . . .	
79	*imunno-fermentnyi analiz*	we do the immunological	

(Continued)

TABLE 6.4 (Continued)

SPEECH AS BROADCAST	ENGLISH TRANSLATION	ACCOMPANYING IMAGE IN BROADCAST
80 gėzhė khėdėgbdi.	fermentation analysis.	
81 Tiigėėd üdėr bükhėndė	Then every day, of course,	/looks to samples and
82 khamag gorodhoo asardag lė	everything from the city is	rushes forward,
83 daa.	brought in.	speaking quickly/
84 Dürbė-taban zuun analiz	We do four to five hundred	/cut to gloved hands
85 khėdėgbdi üdėrtė.	analyses in a day.	dealing with samples/
86 Tiigėėd khoėr raion erėdėg.	So, two districts arrive [daily].	
87 Tarbagatai, Ivolga gėėd	Tarbagatai, Ivolga—er, Ivolginskii	
88 Ivolgiinska raion.	district.	/cut back to lab tech/

This interviewee does not nativize many of her Russian borrowings, and she begins to codeswitch fully into Russian in line 67. Like the doctor before her, the laboratory technician uses Russian borrowings even outside the domain of medicine, and even when there are clear Buryat-origin equivalents in wide use. Her terminology for geographic units, for instance, is Russian. In line 82, she uses *gorod* for 'city,' versus the Buryat khoto that Dashi uses in lines 3 and 23; and in line 88, she uses *raion* for 'district,' versus Buryat aimag. To be fair, this ambivalence was present in the editorial room as well. Notice that in the doctor's title, the television team used the Russian of her official title—*vrach* (doctor)—as opposed to the Buryat ėmshėn they employed for the laboratory technician. Ėmshėn here is 'general medical practitioner,' contrasting with Russian-origin *vrach*. Ėmshėn could have been used in both cases; note that in lines 25 and 63, for instance, doctors are referred to as "ėmshėd." In lines 29–58, the use of Russian *vrach* emphasizes that this is the doctor's official title, as opposed to a general description of her occupation. In small ways like this, journalists subtly reinforce a division of labor between Russian, as the language of official titles and public life, and Buryat, as a more general, vernacular code.

Despite the formal similarity of their speech, the laboratory technician contrasted starkly with the doctor in that she appeared to suffer little performance anxiety on camera. While initially hesitant to be interviewed in Buryat, in fact she produced her interview clip in a single take. From the perspective of the journalists editing these stories, someone like the laboratory technician is a good interviewee, while the doctor is barely passable.

This points to another material outcome of an interviewee's discomfort, in addition to disjointedness like that found in the doctor's interview as broadcast.

In most broadcast production contexts, crews collect more footage than the broadcast will require, and a radio or television editor does not need to use more than a small percentage of the original footage collected in a final cut. But the situation is different in minority-language journalism in situations of extreme language shift, where fluent speakers are hard to find and where deeply felt shame and embarrassment over not producing the language correctly make it difficult to procure interviews. The inefficiency of Buryat-language interviewing is in tracking down the interviewee in the first place and then easing her into the minority-language news frame; once the interview is secured, most of the material recorded will end up on the air. In the dual-language radio and television broadcasts that I observed being produced, a much higher percentage of Buryat-language interview material made it to broadcast than was true of Russian-language interview material.

The syphilis story's production also reveals much about how and why so much Russian linguistic influence makes its way into mass media that are otherwise framed as Buryat. Both Dashi and his head editor, Bator, acknowledged and ultimately broadcast kinds of knowing Buryat that included codeswitching, Russian borrowings, and "internationalisms" that have been borrowed from Russian into Buryat, such as references to *imunno-fermentnyi analiz* (line 79), *reaktsiia Vassermana* (line 76), and *sifilis*. Dashi was not surprised by the doctor's difficulties. He expected his interviewees not only *not* to control the literary standard that he himself employed, but also to possess different degrees and kinds of knowledge depending on the context of their interactions. Workers in Russian-language-dominant technological fields were among the least likely, in his view, to control the spoken language actively and without frequent borrowing or codeswitches, so he considered the story a success in the sense that the doctor and lab technician had both been able to produce anything recognizably Buryat.

In addition to these flexible interpretations of interviewees' knowledge, Bator recognized the importance of allowing some *razgovornye* resources into SLB for their audience. Writing up his story script later in the newsroom, Dashi tried to do exactly what the doctor he interviewed had noted was so difficult—to translate *sifilis*. In his first script, he produced inventive Buryat neologisms for 'syphilis' and 'venereal disease.' Bator flatly rejected them. This was the same journalist whom we met in the preceding chapter, who was praised by viewers for using purist, literary Buryat on screen. Those viewers were over-ascribing a purist ideology and purist practices to Bator, based on his personal authority; in fact, he acted on different principles when he worked in different media platforms. When I spoke with Bator in the evening, he explained that the neologisms felt "twisted" and unnecessarily difficult. While Bator believed strongly in the preservationist role of Buryat-language media, he did not believe that their audience would be able to understand these terms instantaneously—which was, in his view, a primary requirement in the television medium. Thus while a newspaper editor might have included a Buryat neologism for 'venereal disease,' perhaps glossing it in Russian or Buryat or leaving it to the reader to decipher at her leisure, Bator returned Dashi's draft script with it excised.

"The Single Most Important Mistake"

While journalists like Bator and Dashi acknowledge different types of linguistic knowledge among their interviewees as "Buryat," viewers can be hard on interviewees like the doctor and laboratory technician. In focus groups and interviews in which I tested the relative intelligibility of different media, participants often chortled or shook their heads, bemoaning interviewees' use of dialectal forms and colloquialisms. They leveled their harshest criticism against the use of "mixed" language, which they took to be a kind of misrecognition on the part of the speaker.

For example, another medical interviewee gave the following informational overview of a new department in her hospital (table 6.5).[7]

TABLE 6.5

	SPEECH AS BROADCAST	ENGLISH TRANSLATION	ACCOMPANYING IMAGE IN BROADCAST
1	Manii peérvé gorodskoi	In our Municipal Hospital No. 1	/interviewee, in white lab
2	bol'nitsada reanimatsionno	a reanimation department has	coat, standing in hallway of
3	otdeleni neégdébé.	been opened.	clinic/
4	Zhorgoon koikomestétéi. (.)	With six [hospital] beds.	title on screen: Larisa
5	Go:rodoor vtornik, sreda,	We work in the city on Tuesday,	Khaltanova, Ulaan-Udyn 1-
6	chetverg azhallanabdi.	Wednesday, [and] Thursday.	dékhi bol'nitsyn
7	Aa, zh—Zheleznodorozhnyi,	Uh, the Zh—Zheleznodorozhnyi	terapevticheské tahagye
8	sovetskii raion . . .	[and] Soviet Districts . . .[1]	daagsha [Director of the
9	Manii otdelenidé shéné	In our department there is new	Therapeutic Department at
10	apparatura bii.	equipment.[2]	Ulan-Ude's Hospital No. 1]

[1] The interviewee refers here to two of the three administrative districts of the city of Ulan-Ude, without Buryat phonological or morphological nativization. Both district names can be translated into Buryat, though this is rare.

[2] There is no widely used alternative to Russian-origin apparatura.

Larisa Khaltanova uses many resources that fellow speakers might identify as *razgovornyi*. To a linguist or a viewer knowledgeable about western dialects, she reveals herself quickly in these few lines to be a speaker of the Tunka dialect, spoken west of Baikal.[8] But that is not what most viewers I interviewed seized on. This interview, like that of the medical personnel above, shows extensive Russian influence in the form of some nativized borrowings and at least one full codeswitch into Russian (in lines 7–8).[9] Her numbers, pronouns, verbs, and word order are recognizably Buryat, but her adjectives and nouns are almost exclusively Russian and Russian-origin. She regularly uses Russian-origin variants even when the concepts she names have widespread Buryat-origin variants. For example, like the laboratory technician, she uses the more Russian resource for 'city,' *gorod*, in lines 1 and 5, as opposed to Buryat-origin khoto. Similarly, she uses Russian-origin *otdeleni* (department, from R. *otdelenie*) in lines 3 and 9 instead of tahag, the Buryat-origin term favored by journalists and used throughout the longer broadcast, including in the interviewee's on-screen title.[10]

Viewers interpreted Larisa Khaltanova's speech as evidence that she was like many Buryat heritage speakers in understanding well but "speaking poorly" (*plokho razgovarivaet*) due to little practice. She was, according to one focus group participant, a "brilliant example" (*iarkii primer*) of this phenomenon because she made the "single most important mistake" (*samuiu glavnuiu oshibku*) of speaking in two languages, using both Russian and Buryat words, at once.

Why is language mixing the cardinal sin of Buryat linguistic performance? Why is this particular *razgovornyi* way of speaking, as opposed to, for example, dialect use, to be so strenuously avoided when on stage? Speakers' criticisms of one another's speech show that ideologies of purism extend beyond Standard Literary Buryat to Russian as well, and that there is more at stake here than words. Sometimes language mixing evokes strong negative emotions, even disgust and repugnance, such as Aikhenvald (2001) found among Tariana speakers. Many Buryats argue, or assume, that to speak Buryat with much of the lexicon borrowed from Russian is tantamount to destroying *both* languages, and thus should be avoided, even if it means speaking only in Russian. As one middle-aged Buryat man, Maksar, explained it to me, above all, a person should know the difference between Buryat and Russian and should keep them separate, even if doing so entails not teaching his own children Buryat. He himself had consciously decided not to speak Buryat with his children for this reason, although he reported that his wife sometimes "forgot" and spoke a sentence or two, especially when she was angry. The two of them had grown up with different dialects and were unaccustomed to speaking Buryat with one another anyway, so it had been an easy decision to make. Many people in my research, including some

Buryat-language journalists, reported having consciously decided not to speak Buryat with their children. Often they explained that they thought this would make them better Russian speakers. But at least as often, they repeated Maksar's logic, saying that they did not want their children to speak both languages *poorly* or to "not know the difference" between them. What these parents hope to secure is not only their children's socioeconomic success but also their emotional and psychological health, as they try to avoid the "complex" from which so many Buryats already suffer.

Notably, no one in my focus groups or interviews argued that interviewees should give up speaking impure Buryat in favor of just speaking Russian, even when they evinced embarrassment or pity for the interviewees. They instead were inclined to criticize interviewees like Larisa Khaltanova for not practicing Buryat enough or for being lazy or apathetic, implying that purist—or pur*er*—Buryat was potentially within the grasp of any heritage speaker. The interviewees' speech prompted some viewers to give some locally famous examples of what is often humorously called a "pidgin," in which the lexicon is Russian and the grammar is Buryat (Graber 2017).

From a linguistic standpoint, codeswitching, borrowing lexical and grammatical material, nativizing Russian-origin terms in Buryat, and otherwise incorporating more Russian into Buryat are natural outcomes of long-term language contact where Russian enjoys greater socioeconomic status. Yet that is not at all how speakers themselves discuss and react to such language contact phenomena. Far from being considered natural language change, incorporating more Russian into Buryat looks to most onlookers like an impurity in Buryat, a malign mistake, and an admission of more thoroughgoing Russification, while also indexing, in many listeners' and viewers' minds, stupidity or ignorance.

The Disappearing Interviewee

If ordering dumplings can evoke performance anxiety, mass-mediated performances bring it even more to the fore. Media interviews like those above are a particularly good place to witness emotional responses to speaking Buryat in public life because they are very much "on stage." Shoving a television camera or microphone into a person's face achieves the same effect as babushki publicly interpellating girls as people who should control Buryat. It forces a person into the role of speaker and foists her into a position of public scrutiny.

Television interviewees like the doctor often already suffer from some of the same performance anxiety that afflicted the girls in the Buryat café, who could not produce Buryat on demand. They may avoid functions at which they might have to offer Buryat toasts, for instance, or preemptively claim to not speak Buryat. Most ethnic Buryats with whom I have been acquainted in Ulan-Ude delimited our conversation to Russian as soon as I was introduced, in Russian, as a researcher of Buryat-language media. There was a common pattern of avoidance. "Oh," they would say. "It's nice to meet you. I don't speak Buryat" (or, sometimes, "I understand but can't speak," or "I don't know literary Buryat," "I didn't study Buryat in school," "I can't read the newspaper," etc.).

Introducing a video camera or microphone only heightens this anxiety. The interviewee is highly aware that strangers well beyond the immediate context of performance will see or hear the broadcast. Additionally, media workers like radio and television journalists have been specifically selected for qualities of "face" and "voice" and are trained in performance, while their interviewees most often are not. These media workers are revered as standard-bearers and are much more likely than average speakers to be able to pass judgment on you. For all of these reasons, it is difficult for journalists like Dashi to find willing interviewees.

There is a tendency among contemporary journalists to ascribe their difficulties in finding willing interviewees to the present moment and to remember Buryat media's past as a time when all Buryats were fully literate in the standard literary language and fluent in spoken varieties and were actively consuming Buryat-language media, so that the audience for Buryat-language media was coextensive with Buryats. But in fact, the gap between journalistic expectations and the audience's competence—or willingness—to perform Buryat began as early as the late 1950s. Archival records from Buryatia's media institutions show that minority-language journalists have spent the last fifty years increasingly plagued by the problem of getting their audience to talk back.

We see an early indication of this in 1959, when an editor at the Buryat radio and television company defended himself against the constant criticism that he was not producing enough original materials in Buryat. Fulfilling work quotas was very important at this point in the Soviet Union, and in this case his superiors wanted him to produce 50 percent of Buryat-language broadcasts based on original material, not the translations from Russian that were overwhelming the broadcasts: "They say that I work poorly. But what interests me is why 50 percent of *Poslednie izvestiia* [The latest news] should consist of original materials in the Buryat language. Really not one of our correspondents gives materials, and I am not in any condition to support it alone. What's more, in the institutions of Ulan-Ude many Buryats are not able to say [anything] in the native language."[11] He goes on to emphasize differences between news production and the production of cultural programming. Because it is so difficult to find material in Buryat in Ulan-Ude, the news correspondents would need to go out into villages and outlying areas where Buryat is more widely spoken to gather materials, but on a tight schedule with fast news production this is not feasible. The same urban/ rural split was at issue for an editor in 1962, when he emphasized the need to increase the number of broadcasts in Buryat on agriculture. This will bring broadcasts, he said, "closer to life" (*blizhe k zhizni*)—that is, closer to the life of the people who actually speak Buryat. In children's programming, he said, we should "orient to the rural children, who know the language well" and can therefore produce original materials.[12]

"The difficulty for us," a Buryat editor would say again in 1980, "is that few people present in Buryat."[13] By this point, radio and television broadcasters were making more use of rural speakers and covering more localized Buryat topics like animal husbandry that were popular among rural viewers and listeners. But they continued to aspire to motivate an urban audience and to link rural Buryat life with centers of political and economic power in Ulan-Ude. This editor went on to suggest that it would be good if people in leadership positions of the republic would come to the microphone more often "in the native language" (*na rodnom iazyke*).[14]

When journalists did find interviewees in the institutions of Ulan-Ude, they lamented the poor quality of many of these interviews. In an internal report produced for party higher-ups in 1973, we see this criticism of the Buryat-language editorial process:

> You all remember well the performance of the Candidate of Sciences Bazarov, who sadly has become famous for when he went on air, with the permission of the editor in chief, without any preparation and could not properly pronounce even one word. What the presenter wanted to say, even the production team couldn't tell. Everyone thought that from the scandalous case with Bazarov, the editorial board would draw the necessary conclusions and nothing like this would be repeated for at least the next hundred years.[15]

But then, the report goes on to say, they have done something equally stupid and allowed a Buryat theatre director to go on air and codeswitch into poorly produced Russian. In part, this is a matter of ritualistically denigrating the editorial staff, as was required during this period in Soviet organizational culture. But the Russian-language editorial board was not subjected to this particular kind of criticism; there the linguistic criticisms tended to focus more on shortcomings in political ideology as manifested in linguistic style, probably because the broadcasts were more referentially transparent to party higher-ups who controlled these styles in Russian and tended to be Russian-language-dominant.

Buryat-language media was constantly criticized from both within and without instead on the basis of code. Judgments regarding style, accent, and register crept in sideways in the guise of statements about the quality of material, such as this indication that Buryatia's public intellectuals were producing embarrassing Buryat interviews.

The ascription of responsibility for poor Bazarov's communicative failure reveals another function of journalists in managing a Buryat language public. For the author of this report, it is the fault not of Bazarov for being a shoddy speaker of Buryat, but rather of the editorial leadership for not having shielded Bazarov from making his infelicities public. This suggests a subtle collusion, in which everyone agrees not to make public the private understanding that few people control Buryat adequately for the purposes of broadcast.

Silence

This chapter has explored shame, insecurity, and emotional responses in interactions in which a speaker (or would-be speaker) feels called on to perform. In the performance anxiety that would-be Buryat speakers evince in public life, we see how cultural expectations shape linguistic production and processes. While performance anxiety suggests that speaking well is of paramount cultural value, paradoxically it also motivates minority-language speakers' silence.

Of course, plenty of Russian speakers also decline interviews. Russian-speaking interviewees are also often nervous and might also want to speak "well" on camera. But their concern is more often with socioeconomic class differentiation, such as is indexed by not having learned academic Muscovite Russian. For Buryats, performance expectations are instead tied very closely to race and ethnicity. You may be taken at any moment as a potential performer of the language by virtue of *looking ethnically* Buryat, and if you fail, you have failed not just at being an accomplished, polished, and possibly erudite stage performer but also at being Buryat.

Silence in public performative contexts becomes, in its own micro-interactional way over time, language shift. As Kulick points out in his study of language shift in Gapun, focusing exclusively on macrosociological pressures can "obscure the perspective" from which individuals actually act (1992, 249; see also Tsitsipis 1998). Buryat-Russian language shift can be partially explained by macrosociological factors, but there are other, subtler reasons for the increasing incorporation of Russian into daily life in Buryatia. The small ways in which semispeakers of Buryat further avoid speaking are just such factors.

Interviews are also a powerful reminder of the regimenting role that journalists play in linguistic participation and performance. Like letters to the editor in newspapers, interviews in audio and audiovisual formats constitute a crucial way in which nonjournalists' voices are incorporated into news journalism and made available to media audiences. There are limits, however, to what ultimately enters mass-mediated linguistic practices. It may be tempting to think of media producers and their audiences as linguistic co-producers, but this risks downplaying the unequal role of journalists as authoritative arbiters of language. While minority-language journalists do not simply model linguistic standards for acquiescent audiences, neither do audiences control *what* of their linguistic production will be subjected to scrutiny and ultimately considered fit to air—other than by refusing the interview.

EMERGENT MINORITY PUBLICS

piliat', muzhik zhret mlaso, a vot kto burlat oblzhat' budet tomu samollchno plzdiulel vstavliu. Llubllu étu natsllu, oni nashi.

fudge, the man gobbles meat, and whoever offends the Buryat I will personally punch the bloody hell out. I love this nation, they're our people.

—*Andronav*

davno burlat to vldel v zhlvulu?

has it been a long time since you saw [a] Buryat in real life?

—*marjunka*

kto nazhal "ne nravitsla"—<u>tugélséguud!</u>

whoever clicked "dislike" is <u>assholes!</u>

—*KhoitoGol*

There is little question that the movement of discourse into online fora has changed its tenor and its sociocultural and political impact. A number of large-scale studies of Russian online media have found notable discrepancies between the "news diets" and political leanings of Russians who use the internet versus those who do not (e.g., Gorham, Lunde, and Paulsen 2014). In contrast to more mainstream institutionalized media, such as state-controlled television stations, the Russian blogosphere hosts diverse political viewpoints that often run counter to mainstream politics. Less clear is what this lively context means for ethnic minority politics. What happens when national, international, and local scales of political activity are collapsed online? What voices have become more prominent, and who is excluded?

Scholarship of digital connectivity is plagued by assumptions that the increased density and speed of interactions on, say, social media platforms makes possible radically new publics. But online publics rely on modes of communication and genres of discourse that have their roots in earlier times. Soviet efforts effectively reverse-indigenized media institutions: rather than giving institutions the characteristics of indigeneity (whatever those might have been), *korenizatsiia* assimilated cadres of young language workers and journalists into what rapidly became mainstream Soviet values. By the end of the Soviet period, most media produced by and for ethnic minorities in Russia was looking like it addressed what Warner (2002) calls "subpublics"—subsets of a larger, mainstream Soviet public. Buryat- and Tatar-language television broadcasts paralleled Russian-language broadcasts, for instance, but in a more limited form, and neither journalists nor viewers were under the illusion that Buryat- or Tatar-language media served a public that was "equal" in sociopolitical power. Buryat-language media served a subset of the Soviet public, unified around shared interests—just as such media now serve a subset of the *rossiiskii* public. Historical legacies are visible in form and genre, too. The Russian blogosphere depends on speech genres from unmediated space or prior media, such as letters to the editor and family debates in response to co-viewed television broadcasts. What might a minority public that posed a genuine alternative to and truly *countered* a mainstream Russian public— what Warner terms a "counterpublic"—look like? To understand whether there is anything subversive or "counter" in new media, we must attend more carefully to the ways digital media are developing, particularly in how political discourse is moving from living rooms to digital platforms.

This chapter considers what kinds of counterpublics are possible in contemporary Russian digital media by looking at one corner of the Russian internet: websites, blogs, chatrooms, and networked social media posts concerned with Buryatia and Buryat politics. I focus on the ongoing movement of political discussions from living rooms into digital media and on the relationships between these different spheres of interaction. My analysis is based on a systematic review of—and occasional participation in—digital media about Buryatia, from 2008 to the present. Integrating this digital ethnography with the long-term ethnographic field research informing the rest of this book, I rely on my familiarity with Buryat living rooms and newsrooms to trace the movement of discourse between offline and online contexts. This chapter addresses emerging patterns of media participation in digital contexts, chiefly (1) the increasing production of media by individuals working outside of traditional media institutions, such as bloggers and social media users, and (2) the Buryat diaspora's increasing participation in internet-based discussion boards and social media. These trends offer the possibility of democratizing engagement and expanding the Buryat public to include new members outside of traditional institutions and beyond the region. At the same time, forms of digital media are easily used to transgress strongly felt divisions between public and private interactional spheres and between conversations of different scales and temporalities. Paradoxically, the perceived *de*territorializing effects of digital communication inspire internet commenters to police language use according to a purist language ideology, reassert the importance of language as the key criterion of Buryat belonging, and reterritorialize Buryat belonging within the geographic boundaries of Buryatia.

Living Room Politics

Domestic contexts are central to local media consumption practices. The domestic scene is not, however, that of the lonely television viewer or the solitary reader, silently glancing over stock market indices while he sips his morning coffee.[1] I observed a great deal of print exchange and discussion, mainly around newspaper kiosks and in homes, and less often in workplaces, and I was part of various informal exchange networks (due in part to the unusual quantity of newspapers, magazines, and other print material that I purchased and read during research). Most households had multiple televisions, and most families gathered around one in their living room in the evening to watch the evening news. BGTRK radio was on in the background in some homes, usually playing in the kitchen on a Soviet-era wall "radio point" (*radio tochka*)—now a relic—that was designed to broadcast a single government station (figure 13). Interviewees and focus group participants also reported discussing Buryat-language newspapers with their parents, cousins, aunts, uncles, or other Buryat-speaking members of their households—less, it seems, as an overt attempt at language maintenance and revitalization than because Buryat-language newspapers are taken to instantiate broader Buryat ethnonational interests. Consider, for example, this comment from Aidar, a Buryat man from Iaruuna in his early twenties:

> We have, like, in [our] family, yeah? (..) Well (..) every week, we [talk about] these weekly newspapers, basically in Buryat, like this [gestures toward <u>Buriaad ünèn</u>] (.) And everyone gathers, some after work, some after study, someone else after something-or-other, (.) we all gather as a **family**. (.) After dinner we sit down, we read, and we discuss—we have these, well let's say, **debates**, or **discussions**. That is—what's written, but [also] what is not—(.) **finished** being written, we could say.

Later in the same conversation, Aidar picked up a copy of <u>Buriaad ünèn</u> that was lying in front of him, pointing out interesting bits to me. One article reminded him of his aunt, another of his grandfather. Different items reminded him of conversations that he had had, which he began to recollect for me. It was clear that for Aidar, the newspaper was neither the carrier of a message shipped from producer to receiver, nor a sphere for debate in and of itself. It was rather one text among many fully integrated into his daily life, and the evocative medium through which he intertextually linked our conversation and its context to conversations and debates over politics and society that he had had in other contexts—namely, after-dinner gatherings at home.

In this very common scenario, mass media are not the site of the most politically meaningful interactions. Rather mass media, especially news media, provide

FIGURE 13. A kitchen in Ulan-Ude with a typical *radio tochka*. (Photo by author, 2009.)

means or context for sussing out private political positions in the family apartment. In the living room or the kitchen, you may try out your membership in different overlapping social groups of different scales—the family, the Russian nation-state, the Buryat ethnonation.

Notably, living room politics maintain a clear separation of public and private space. Aidar, for instance, distinguishes between the public newspaper or television broadcast and the private discussion that his family will have about it. This separation of interactional spheres and performative contexts is being challenged with the movement of Buryat living room politics into digital media platforms.

Buryatia in the Blogosphere

The Russian blogosphere is a large and rapidly expanding part of the Russian-language internet. The Buryat-*language* blogosphere is too small to have a very distinctive identity; the same few individuals comment on one another's posts.

But because Buryat-speaking internet users are at least bilingual in Russian (and sometimes semi-trilingual with English or Chinese), they often tack back and forth between Russian- and Buryat-language sites or use both within a single site. Within the Russian blogosphere, there is a densely intertextually linked set of social media networks, blogs, and websites that constitute what might be considered a discrete Buryat blogosphere.

Sites and social media platforms dealing with Buryats, Buryatia, and the Buryat language include blogs on LiveJournal and rambler.ru, several active groups on Facebook and VKontakte, and some popular YouTube channels, where commentary on individually posted videos is especially rich. There are also some independent web platforms that host both editorially curated content and chat rooms or web forums. Most notable among these is Buryatia.org, a nonprofit website dedicated to "the Buryat people" and frequented by political activists, Buryat nationalists, and people generally interested in Buryat cultural and linguistic heritage.

The Buryat audience that is being reached, interlinked, and created by digital media overlaps unevenly with the audiences of print journalism and traditional radio and television broadcasting. Until the 2010s, internet access within the territory of the Republic of Buryatia and Buryat autonomous regions was limited to well-heeled offices and internet cafés in urban areas. In 2005 during my initial fieldwork, most of my research participants did not have email addresses, and those who did would check their email and surf the internet in cafés frequented mainly by gamers. In 2012, Wifi was available in some upscale coffeehouses and it was possible to get a domestic DSL line in the city, but these options were still prohibitively expensive for most residents. Thus for much of the twenty-first century to this point, the Buryat blogosphere has been populated largely by urban elites and by people *outside* the Buryat territories, living in diaspora in Moscow, St. Petersburg, Europe, China, Mongolia, and the United States. Currently, however, a combination of telecommunications development, the growth of the Russian credit market, and steadily (if slowly) rising incomes mean that hi-speed domestic internet access is booming, and direct cellphone access to the internet is available even in some of the poorest and most rural areas of Buryatia. Increasingly, then, websites, forums, and networks geared toward Buryat- and Russian-speaking co-affiliates interlink internet users in disparate parts of the Russian Federation and the world, with an expanding contingent within the Buryat territories.

Crucially, the overwhelming majority of what is stated about Buryatia and Buryats online falls well outside what we might call "mainstream," institutionalized media. The state institutions that have traditionally supported minority-language media in Soviet and post-Soviet Russia are not yet putting significant resources into the development of online media. Core Buryat media institutions like <u>Buriaad ünėn</u> and BGTRK have a limited online presence that mostly recapitulates what is printed and broadcasted. Instead what is being produced online might be less comparable in their linguistic form and social significance to newspapers or broadcasts than to the "small media" of daily life—street signs, for instance, or personal love letters (Ahearn 2001).

To be sure, audiences have long participated in "traditional" media production by serving as interviewees, writing letters to the editor, and informally interacting with journalists and other media workers. Writing letters to the editor in particular was a key way of performing good citizenship in the Soviet era, when editorial boards paid close attention to the number of letters they received. Call-in radio and television shows performed a similar function. More subtly, *consuming* media has been a way of demonstrating political participation. In the middle of the twentieth century, reading the Buryat newspaper was part of demonstrating proper citizenship in the Soviet project, not only as a Soviet person reading the newspaper but also as a Buryat citizen participating actively in the fight against backwardness (Graber 2012). Subscribing to Buryatia's flagship Buryat-language newspaper continues to be a way of showing membership in, and support for, the project of maintaining and continuing to build the Buryat (ethno)nation, even if you cannot read Buryat.

What is new is the scale on which nonprofessionalized, noninstitutionalized media makers are producing original content without the explicit editing or guidance of professionals. (The same thing is true elsewhere; the so-called "citizen journalist" phenomenon is a major component of what has been called the "crisis of journalism.") What is moving online is not the heavily edited, collectively authored discourse of professional journalists working under the imprimatur of institutions but rather the more informal, ad hoc discourse of individuals who may be tightly and densely networked with one another but who nonetheless work outside of institutions. In essence, living room politics have been moving online.

Discussions of Buryat cultural politics within online spaces differ from discourse in living rooms in some consequential ways, explored in the remainder of this chapter. Arguably discourse online is more disputatious, marked by speech genres that have become associated with internet communication more broadly, including trolling (R. *trolling*) and *kholivar* (after English "holy war," meaning a rancorous dispute, usually in a chatroom, blog, or other semi-open digital forum). Insofar as such speech genres run counter to the rational, critical-thinking-based, consensus-driven discourse that many postsocialist states have pursued

(Larson 2013), they may provide means for imagining a counterpublic that subverts dominant Russian narratives, at least in interactional style—a possibility due in equal parts to Soviet-Russian discursive history and to the particular technological affordances of online communication. Habermas's notion of rational public discourse was based on the face-to-face conversation more likely to happen in a living room (or café) than in a chatroom in which the participants are rarely fully sure of one another's identities or reactions. Yet the internet is not quite (or only) a post-Habermasian dystopia of screaming strangers engaged in endless *kholivar*. Online anonymity is uneven, and the Buryat corners of the Russian blogosphere are frequented by a relatively small group of users who *do* often know each other offline, or who interact so frequently across multiple sites and platforms that they can predict one another's reactions. Broadly speaking, however, due to anonymity and to other reasons, discourse in the Buryat corners of the Russian blogosphere is more politicized than talk offline, and it is very lively on the topic of ethnic minority politics.

Ethnicization Online

The population of the Republic of Buryatia is mostly ethnically Russian, with self-identified ethnic Buryats making up only 30 percent of the population. Yet very little about Buryatia appears in the Russian blogosphere that is not specifically about Buryat ethnicity, culture, or language. Thus the interests of a statistical minority are overrepresented online as constitutive of the polity of Buryatia. This is an odd echo of Leninist nationalities policy or what Terry Martin (2001) called the early Soviet Union's "affirmative action" policy: in online discourse, the titular nationality performatively becomes the de facto majority.

One of the reasons for this is the legal requirement to produce media in the titular nationality's language. Government sites must be in multiple languages. Buryat appears alongside Russian as a symbolic nod to equal representation, visually creating an equivalence that appears false in the face of Russian's overwhelming dominance in education, restaurants, stores and markets, most workplaces, and other domains of public life.

Another reason for online ethnicization is that digital media have become a key site of language revitalization efforts. While VKontakte and other social media networks include a growing number of senior journalists, lamas, and other authoritative elders, online forums about Buryatia remain dominated by a younger contingent of Buryat speakers, who are less likely to control Buryat, at least in its standard literary form. This directs the focus of such forums onto language learning and metalinguistic discussion in Russian. Indeed, one of the most popular places to learn the Buryat language today is not in the Siberian villages where it is mostly spoken but on YouTube, Facebook, and VKontakte. A wealth of youth-oriented music videos and social networking in Buryat has organically populated the internet. Also, some dedicated schoolteachers, journalists, and language activists in the territory of Buryatia are making a concerted effort to use digital platforms as new pedagogical tools to teach (or, as they often see it, to *re*teach) Buryat to generations that have grown up in a Russian-dominant society. Journalists have begun producing language lessons for television and posting them on YouTube, activists run conversation groups on web forums, and there is a small but significant stream of projects to subtitle American films in Buryat (which get shared on piracy networks) and to dub Russian-language cartoons into Buryat for YouTube.

By moving this native Mongolic language that generally has low socioeconomic prestige and indexes tradition and rurality into digital media platforms that have been dominated by English and Russian, activists hope to capitalize not only on the dissemination potential of the internet but also on the hipness and newness of digital media. Buryat "needs to be updated," as one of my research participants put it, and moving the language "into the internet" is an obvious way to do it. In the absence of major state-driven funding, activists increasingly welcome internet-based language practices as a language revitalization opportunity external to—or at times parallel to—native-language education, radio programming, and other institutional projects to raise the profile and increase the use of Buryat.

Political discussions online often appear more ferocious and polarized due to certain material affordances of digital media platforms. Zombie threads—that is, comment threads that lie dormant for a long time before they are revived by a new comment—and the ways that text is archived online can give the impression that something written several years ago is the natural first part of a fresh new conversational dyad, prompting new commentators to respond to old comments and visually compressing the timespan of "an" interaction. This material technological affordance of platforms like YouTube, in the context of the hyperpoliticization of the Russian blogosphere, has another important consequence in digital discourse: events and topics that are barely discussed in offline public discourse may have extensive lives online. For instance, pages and pages of commentary were generated when a public talk that I gave in Washington, DC, in 2012 was liberally reinterpreted by a journalist on Voice of America's Russian-language website and subsequently recirculated within Buryatia and the Buryat blogosphere. This occasion afforded an unusual opportunity to trace the reporting, recitation, and general circulation of a bit of discourse—a speech event—across online and offline contexts and over a wide geographic territory (Graber 2013). What began as a rather dry talk became hyperpoliticized online, with stakes worthy of a Cold War spy novel. To judge by the quantity and passion of the hyperbolic rhetoric cast in my direction online, I was either a powerful agent of anti-Russian US interests or the savior of an oppressed Buryat minority, or both. Yet when I returned to Russia shortly after these events unfolded online, it was clear that the blogosphere-based discussion had barely affected discourse offline. The only people who even seemed aware of the kerfuffle were a few particularly active participants in the Buryat blogosphere.

Thus the fervor and extent of discourse about an event online may be entirely disproportional to how it is discussed in Buryatia. This observation should caution against relying exclusively on digital ethnography to draw conclusions about political climate. It also points to the difficulty, and the importance, of pinpointing who is participating in a given political discussion.

Stranger Danger

This brings us back to perhaps the most significant difference in shifting informal political discourse online: who can participate in mediated discussion about Buryatia. Preliminarily, we might note that the blogosphere opens discourse up to commentary by strangers. It is almost definitionally true that publics are composed of strangers, and the sociopolitical power of media has always been in interlinking strangers (e.g., Anderson 1991). Yet the anxiety often accompanying online discourse—whether about threatening American anthropologists or YouTube commentators—suggests that there is something particularly unsettling about strangers online. While living room politics maintain a clear separation of public and private space, anonymity in digital politics troubles the boundary between public and private. It is not always possible to identify your interlocutor.

More specifically in the Buryat case, there is suddenly a great deal of input from the diaspora. Different players can suddenly participate in discussions about Buryat politics and ethnonational belonging. Voices in Moscow, St. Petersburg, Germany, Poland, China, and elsewhere have become more prominent—at least online.

One potentially potent political consequence of interlinking internet users across Russia's territories is that it has reenergized pan-Mongolian sentiment.

Digital connectivity subtly undoes centuries of what were sometimes implicit and sometimes explicit efforts, on the part especially of Russian, Chinese, and Soviet authorities, to separate Mongolic-speaking and Mongolic-identifying peoples by means of borders and geographic distance. On Buryatia.org, this is visible in the way people advertise products and services to one another. A distributor based in Moscow, for instance, sells "ecologically pure" mutton from Kalmykia, another Mongolic territory of the Russian Federation geographically distant from Buryatia and Mongolia. The advertisement is for residents of Moscow, but the people who write in queries about ads like this are often in the Buryat territories trying to supply family and friends with (what they see as) traditional, high-quality meat for feasts and café business ventures in Moscow. Such advertisers capitalize on—and reinforce—deeply felt connections between Moscow, Kalmykia, Buryatia, and Mongolia as part of a continuous Eurasian Mongolian space. The same digital pan-Mongolism is evident in the forums on Buryatia.org, in which contributors from all over the world ask each other not only about where to get good mutton, but also about where to find Buryat conversation groups and how to configure their laptops to display Mongolian script. This use of digital media, for individual-level language revitalization, points to the broader possibility of reconfiguring the minority language public that provides the basis of Buryat ethnonational belonging.

The fact that the internet is largely a visual medium helps, in that people with no knowledge of the Buryat language can participate in representing Buryatia and in adjudicating what "counts" as Buryat within cultural politics. Language practices are being diversified as semispeakers and semiliterate writers contribute, venturing to produce nonstandard forms within print contexts. And the language community is expanded in some politically consequential ways. But at the same time, participants make in their metalinguistic commentary very strong claims about who counts as a speaker of Buryat, and who counts as an authoritative speaker, not just of Buryat but about and on behalf of ethnic Buryats.

Reterritorializing a Buryat Minority Public

We can see this ongoing expansion-restriction dynamic in the digital mediation of Buryat social boundaries by examining online interactions and YouTube comment threads in which contributors assess speakers' (and fellow commenters') language use and cultural expertise. Apparently (but not actually) untethered from institutional sites of expertise, commentators nonetheless employ language ideologies that will already be familiar: pursuing a purist code of SLB with neologisms, for instance, and investing authority and responsibility for intergenerational language transmission in Buryat babushki.

Present in such discussions are two distinct types of metalinguistic commentary characteristic of the Buryat blogosphere. The first is between language experts and elites, usually prescribing or proscribing specific linguistic forms for the standard literary language. In the post-Soviet period, SLB has been actively renegotiated in a number of venues, including new media platforms such as online native-language forums and social networking sites, as well as crossover activist projects in more traditional state institutions. Digital media in Buryat include the same range you might expect to find in any language, from very colloquial text messaging and YouTube comments to official websites written in the literary standard. Sometimes these become important sites for contesting Buryat written standards.

A project from buryadxelen.org, for instance, included a list of recommended new Buryat neologisms to prevent the use of Russian borrowings (though not necessarily internationalisms) in twenty-first-century domains. A keyboard driver should now be denoted not as *klaviaturnyi draiver* but as tobsholuurai draiver, anything that was previously *èlektronnyi* (electronic) should be sakhim, and *sponsor* (sponsor, advertiser) should now be èbèèntèdkhègshè. The new standards released by buryadxelen.org had been hashed out in forums like these on Buryatia.org, one of a limited range of important online sites in which the standard literary language is renegotiated—and subjected to ongoing standardization. While such projects do not approach the grandeur of language standardization efforts in the Soviet 1920s, they represent ongoing efforts to standardize Buryat in the face of new influences.

In this type of commentary, there is a great deal of intertextual movement between the online forums, traditional published print sources like books and academic journals, and offline debates that have occurred in the hallways of the Ministry of Education, local universities, and the local branch of the Russian Academy of Sciences. It is fair to say that expertise and authority have been established in these other offline domains and are drawn upon online. But at the same time, there is movement from the forums into offline domains, such as when the neologism tobsholuurai draiver, proposed by a Mongolian-speaking computer programmer, is taken up by a Buryat lexicographer at the Russian Academy of Sciences. So influence is multidirectional or reciprocal, and yet it is not broad. Ultimately it is the same relatively constrained group of people who are circulating linguistic material online and offline.

The larger indexical meanings of using one linguistic form or another are worked out not among these language elites but in a second type of online metalinguistic commentary. This is commentary that is about language only in passing—that is, not between linguists but between people who are trying to make some other kind of point. This kind of metalinguistic commentary is undertaken by a much wider group of commentators, many of whom are not physically located within Buryatia and most of whom do not have firm knowledge of the Buryat literary standard (which they often reveal by spelling phonetically in Cyrillic instead of following standard orthography, and occasionally by using dialect forms). It is here that we see contributors confronting the peculiar possibilities and challenges that digital media present for bounding speech communities—and language communities—online.

A case in point is commentary on a home video that was posted to YouTube in 2010 and is still generating commentary. The video features a small boy, perhaps two years old, gnawing the meat and fat off a large animal bone with great gusto. Off screen an older woman, apparently his grandmother, giggles with delight, asking him repeatedly in Russian whether the meat is tasty (*Vkusno?*). The video is titled "a genuine Buryat" (*istinnyi buriat*). When the video was first posted, commenters gushed about the boy's zest for meat (table 7.1).

TABLE 7.1

1	ResegVeandar:	Nastoiashchii BURIAT!!!!!! Krasavcheg))))[1]	A real BURYAT!!!!!! A handsome guy ☺)))[2]
2	GLEBAN1000:	éto zhe buriat, daite emu byka on byka s"est-sila!	that's really a Buryat, give him a bull and he'll eat it all up!
3	vorobeyization:	Khar tolgé! Uragsha!	[A good] black head! Tally-ho!
4	Horchiuzon:	On ne buriat i babushka ego ne buriatka esli oni buriaty to pochemu oni govoriat po russki AAAA oni obrusevshie mongoly kotorye zabyli svoi iazyk i dumaiut chto oni zhivut v Evrope i sovsem ne mongoly pochti ili nemnozhko russkie to est' evropeitsy	He's not a Buryat and his babushka's not a Buryat if they're Buryats then why do they speak Russian AAAA they're Russified Mongols who forgot their language and think they live in Europe and are totally not Mongols almost or a little bit [ethnic] Russians that is Europeans
5	Tsebeen:	Üri khüügédtéeé buriaadaaraa duugarbal hain baigaa.	It would have been good if [she] had spoken to her children in their own Buryat.
6	Larkvlad:	Mozhet i govorit ona po russki, no aktsent zhestko Buriatskii—éto znachit chto po Buriatski govorit khorosho	Maybe she does speak Russian, but the accent is strongly Buryat— it means that she speaks Buryat well

(Continued)

TABLE 7.1   (Continued)

| 7 | Andronav: | piliat', muzhik zhret miaso, a vot kto buriat obizhat' budet tomu samolichno pizdiulei vstavliu.[3] Liubliu étu natsiiu, oni nashi. | fudge, the man gobbles meat, and whoever offends the Buryat I will personally punch the bloody hell out. I love this nation,[4] they're our people. |
| 8 | KhoitoGol: | kto nazhal "ne nravitsia"—tugėlsėguud![5] krasavchik! Budushchii "Avarga Bukhė") Let cherez 15 budet vsekh rvat'!kak obez'iana gazetu!) | whoever clicked "dislike" is assholes! a handsome guy! A future "[Wrestling Champion]"☺ In about 15 years he'll tear everyone up!like a monkey [does] a newspaper!☺ |

[1] The comments transliterated here originally appeared in Cyrillic.

[2] Russian texting style is to represent a smile with a single parenthesis, as opposed to the English style of colon or semicolon plus parenthesis.

[3] This writer uses Russian slang cleaned up for Internet presentation, including *piliat'*, a homophonous euphemism for a much stronger word for 'whore' used as an interjection like English "fuck!" and *pizdiulei*, a crude term for 'a punch.'

[4] Meaning the Buryat nation, not the Russian nation-state.

[5] The Cyrillic y (u) letter in this commenter's Buryat use should be the letter γ (ū) to reflect vowel harmony. It's likely that the writer simply does not have a keyboard driver with the "extra letters" of the Cyrillic Buryat alphabet and is typing with a Cyrillic Russian keyboard.

Early comments were along the lines of "What a man!" (comments 1, 2, and 3). Then, however, the comments turned negative (comments 4 and 5). Other commenters then came to the defense of the little boy and his grandmother, arguing either that they might possess Buryat knowledge and are just not displaying it in this video (comment 6), or that any doubt as to their Buryatness based on the criterion of linguistic knowledge is unwelcome and offensive (comments 7 and 8).

This commentary shows how language choice and linguistic knowledge index the Russian-Mongolian and European-Asian borders—and, conversely, how these borders provide the discursive means by which language choice can become meaningfully indexical of social position. It also shows how easily discussions about Buryat-Russian language contact phenomena in a single family and in a single interaction can be "scaled up" to index these larger borders. In the longer stream of commentary, contributors wrote in Russian, Mongolian, Kalmyk, and Buryat. This is typical of the Buryat blogosphere and remarkable because Kalmyk, Buryat, and Mongolian are not uniformly mutually intelligible. In the territorial space that is Buryatia-Mongolia, we might think of the Mongolic languages as a dialect continuum, with the dialect basis for standard Mongolian (Khalkh) at the southern end and the dialect basis for standard Buryat (Khori) at the northern end. Yet the spatial compression for which internet-based communication is famous brings disparate speech varieties together into the same discursive frame. Within this frame, all of the Mongolic languages are sufficiently mutually intelligible that users in chats and public forums like YouTube often comment on one another's posts. The famous "space-time compression" of digital media is thus incredibly meaningful for speakers of a contracting language like Buryat, in a perhaps surprising way. Speakers are not just linked up with existing other speakers of Buryat; when multiple almost mutually intelligible dialects and languages from different parts of a dialect continuum are brought side-by-side, speakers of one of those languages or dialects suddenly gain a sense of greater unity between Mongolic languages and an expanded notion of the language community.

Language is not the only semiotic mode that encourages this expansion. YouTube is rife with music videos in Buryat and Mongolian that encourage viewers to identify as Mongolic, or rather pan-Mongolian. Viewers frequently write in these spaces in multiple languages about the glorious Mongolian peoples and their future territorial unification—references to a political movement that has otherwise not seen serious public expression since its Soviet repression in the 1930s.[2]

These commentators are usually among the many self-identifying Buryats interested in Buryat linguistic and cultural preservation who are located outside the territory of Buryatia. The blogosphere—including single-authored blogs as well as forums and YouTube comment threads—gives these people a chance not only to monitor what is going on in Buryatia but to contribute to it. For the Buryat diaspora, the rapidly expanding Buryat blogosphere grants many of the same possibilities and conundrums as online communication for communities living in exile or diaspora, or any dispersed group of co-affiliates. As much scholarship on digital media has shown, internet-based communication invites greater fellow-feeling and political participation from people who are geographically widely dispersed but nonetheless self-identify with a home community (Bernal 2005; Eriksen 2007; Karim 2003; Panagakos and Horst 2006; Parham 2004; Whitaker 2004). At the same time, this digital connection can foreground and exacerbate conflicts, particularly over who has the right to speak for whom (Coleman 2010; Kendzior 2011).

A poignant example came in the reportage and recirculation of the author-anthropologist's aforementioned talk. In the comments forum of an online newspaper, readers disputed in a torrent of comments whether this "agent of the US government" had been to Buryatia and, if I had, what would constitute authentic engagement with "the people"—in the course of which they jockeyed for authority among themselves based on their familiarity with the local spatial and social landscape. Commenters referred frequently to town squares, monuments, city neighborhoods, and other local landmarks to establish expertise. The many commenters who came from elsewhere were carefully policed and often excluded.

One of the first comments to appear online was from "Bambi Bambi," who cited and responded to a line in the article reporting on "two periods of linguistic transformation: from Buryat monolingualism to Buryat-Russian bilingualism and then to Russian monolingualism" (which, incidentally, I *had* said), in comment 1 (table 7.2).

In a thread interspersed with pages of other commentary, other commenters responded to Bambi Bambi's remark (comments 2, 3, and 4).

TABLE 7.2

1	Bambi Bambi [Bémbi Bémbi]:	Tsitata: "dva perioda iazykovoi transformattsii: ot monolingvisticheskoi— buriatskoi, k bilingvisticheskoi— buriatsko-russkoi i snova k monolingvisticheskoi—russkoi."	Citation: "two periods of linguistic transformation: from Buryat monolingualism to Buryat-Russian bilingualism and then to Russian monolingualism."
		nu éto zhe bred, vse buriaty znaiut buriatskoi iazyk, khotia by na nachaľnom urovne.	well that's just nonsense, all Buryats know the Buryat language, although at the beginner's level.
2	Calculating [Vychisliaiushchii]:	da uzh bémbi. ty vidimo i vpravdu eshche toľko bémbi ili slishkom daleko otorvalsia ot naroda. mnogie iz buriat ne znaiut svoego iazyka i éto fakt ne trebuiushchii dokazateľstv.	really bambi. you evidently truly are still just a bambi[1] or you've gotten too far out of touch with the people. many Buryats don't know their language and it's a fact that doesn't require proof.
3	marjunka:	"vse buriaty znaiut buriatskoi iazyk, khotia by na nachaľnom urovne"—nu éto zhe bred! davno buriat to videl v zhivuiu?	"all Buryats know the Buryat language, although at the beginner's level"—well **that's** just nonsense! has it been a long time since you saw [a] Buryat in real life?
4	Andrei Arlovskii:	Buriaty, kotorye rodilis' i vyrosli v Ulan-Udé v boľshinstve svoem ne znaiut rodnoi iazyk, i éto ne ikh vina.	Buryats who were born and raised in Ulan-Ude in the majority don't know their native language, and it's not their fault.

[1] That is, 'a naïve young thing.' Through grammatical endings in Russian, Bambi Bambi revealed himself to be male gendered.

It does not take a specialist to recognize that language shift to Russian in Buryatia has been extensive, and that many residents who self-identify as Buryat or are racially interpreted as Buryat do not speak Buryat. In this context, Bambi Bambi's comment revealed that he was likely not familiar with the contemporary situation in Buryatia. Subsequent commenters seized on this not only to correct the mistaken view but also to question Bambi Bambi's more general competence about Buryatia and right to speak to the issues at hand. They were reacting to the threat of digital deterritorialization, in which national, international, and local scales of discourse are collapsed, with participants potentially entering a discussion from any scale.

Police work like this shows that the context of the internet does not necessarily deterritorialize or democratize discussion. Rather, commenters online are often preoccupied with tethering comments to specific, embodied authors living in offline space and with rebounding and respecifying a Buryat territory. While the public assessment displayed by commenters like Larkvlad and marjunka might democratize language use, these practices also reterritorialize the linguistic community by emplacing the "real" language and its authoritative speakers in offline contexts within Buryatia. And because internet commentators continue to insist on language as the main criterion of Buryatness, they narrowly circumscribe a Buryat public that might act politically.

Mediating Belonging Online

In sum, Buryat belonging in the digital age is characterized by anxiety over who can speak for whom and how. Might there be something different about the *digital* mediation of publics, as opposed to any other such mediation? While the metalinguistic commentary in online forums is in intertextual conversation with such commentary in other offline domains, there are some peculiarities of internet-based communication that bring the negotiation of borders and boundaries to the fore. Space-time compression brings together otherwise geographically and temporally disparate speech varieties. The expanded speech community ultimately creates a sense of an expanded *language* community that exists primarily online, and only secondarily offline. At the same time, some of the same commentators draw on familiar language ideologies linking Buryat to Buryatia, working very hard to locate that speech in physical space, and tying the authority to speak to specific territories.

This is all especially clear in the Buryat case because heightened anxiety about linguistic and cultural loss has made linguistic metacommentary a whole genre of online interaction. But what is being accomplished via linguistic metacommentary has to do with personhood and politics more broadly, as commenting on one another's language allows participants to comment indirectly on other aspects of personhood that might be risky to make explicit. It allows them effectively to police the boundaries of belonging. This push-pull or expansion-restriction dynamic, in which internet-based communication feels to users more *de*territorialized than other forms of communication, and therefore prompts discursive *re*territorialization, is likely at work in other language and speech communities whose borders are in flux.

On the whole, when presented with the possibility of radically expanding a Buryat public online, digital media users insist on realigning a Buryat minority public with the existing Buryat ethnonation as they understand it—territorialized within the political boundaries of a semi-independent Buryat state. In the absence of other criteria of belonging, they continue to draw on tried and true linguistic, spiritual, and racial characteristics. This might in fact be the most subversive possibility of emergent minority publics online: more strongly and forcefully rearticulating ethnonational identity in a supposedly postnational world.

Conclusion

In March 2016, Vladimir Zhirinovsky, a fiercely nationalist Russian politician and leader of the Liberal Democratic Party of Russia, declared that Buryats, as a discrete ethnicity, did not exist. Bolsheviks, he claimed, had essentially invented the Buryats (and Tuvans) to prevent Mongols from taking what he called "northern Mongolia." Thus "Buryatia," he concluded, "is Mongolia!" (Sagan 2016).

There is a grain of truth in this, in the sense that Soviet leaders appear to have emphasized the distinctions between Buryats and other Mongolic-speaking peoples to reinforce the territorial border, just as tsarist leaders and Orthodox missionaries had done before them to claim Buryat land and souls for their own (Graber and Murray 2015). Zhirinovsky, however, was taking the socially constructed nature of ethnolinguistic categories to mean that they were insignificant or *unreal*, an all too common but misguided perversion of social theory. It might not be immediately clear why a Russian politician would want to claim that part of the federation's territory rightfully belongs to a neighboring nation-state. The claim seems to play into fantasies of pan-Mongolian political reunification. Onlookers in Buryatia immediately understood, however, that his comment could serve to undermine the territorial integrity of Buryatia within Russia. If there are not meaningfully unique ethnicities in Asian Russia, why should territory be divided with their self-determination in mind? The context of Zhirinovsky's comment was his proposal to change the Constitution of the Russian Federation from describing the federation as a "multinational country" (*mnogonatsional'naia strana*) to one consisting of "the Russian and other peoples" (*russkii i drugie narody*), downgrading "nations" to "peoples" and privileging ethnic Russians. At stake is the future of Russia as a federation and the future of Buryatia within it.

Buryatia's marginality presents political problems as well as opportunities, depending on one's position. In her study of a marginalized group in the rainforest of Indonesia, Anna Lowenhaupt Tsing observes that "turning to state peripheries shed[s] light on both the limitations and the strengths of state agendas." In an "out-of-the-way place," she notes, "the instability of political meanings is easy to see. . . . The cultural difference of the margins is a sign of exclusion from the center; it is also a tool for destabilizing central authority" (Tsing 1993, 27). Tsing describes people far more loosely organized and politically marginalized than the Buryats within Russia. Yet the key tension for state power is the same: cultural difference, sustained in Buryatia through daily linguistic and media practices, represents both exclusion and independence. It is both an impediment to federative integration and a potential source for political action, including separatism. Badma, watching gymnastics in her living room, calls herself a Buryat but not a Russian. She wants to identify positively as a Russian citizen but feels that this is denied to her by a social system that recognizes her cultural difference as either totalizing or only begrudgingly as part of a multicultural federation. Sayan, an activist who supports reunification of Buryat territories but not separation from Russia, put the point more angrily, directing his ire toward "them," meaning central authorities in Moscow and local politicians whom he sees as kowtowing to them: "Of course, they want me to be a Buryat, but, please, not **too** Buryat."

The conflict Sayan and Badma express is but one of the many ways in which the people populating the pages of this book receive mixed messages and encounter impossible expectations, leveled by both themselves and others. On one hand, they are expected to play the role of Russia's exotic, eastern "Other"; on the other hand, they are supposed to be "model minorities" and exemplars of the triumph of modernity. On one hand, they share an ideal of linguistic (and thereby cultural) purity; on the other hand, the language and media that they produce, read, hear, watch, and share is always to some degree mixed. In large part, these competing expectations result from disjunctures between the scales that people traverse on a daily basis—and even within single interactions. The same practices that are correct, prestigious, or progressive at one scale of belonging (such as speaking standard Buryat among Buryat elites) may be denigrated as backward, rural, or nationalistic at another (such as speaking Buryat at all among Russian colleagues). Individual speakers actively negotiate multiple, sometimes competing affiliations at once.

As we have seen throughout this book, mass media are key resources for renegotiating belonging. Media offer opportunities (and expectations) for exercising one's "voice," contributing to public discussion, and participating in the Buryat minority public. Democratic ideals of media participation might seem anathema to contemporary Russian media, as censorship increases and the ideal of a "free press" remains tenuous at best. But Russian media institutions continue to provide a platform for demonstrating political participation, even if the state delimits the acceptable bounds of such participation. Circulations of native-language media create and maintain a Buryat minority language public that is politically important in its ability to symbolize Buryat cultural vitality, including (and perhaps especially) for members of the Buryat ethnonational community who do not control Buryat. In this historical moment in Russia, when reasserting a distinctive cultural identity has become a political strategy that can serve many, cross-purposed ends, minority-language media have taken on special meaning. For ideological and historical reasons, language has been central to determining who counts as a member of the ethnonational community, who represents it, and who has the right to speak on its behalf. As we have seen, it is media, from carefully crafted television broadcasts to offhand remarks in internet forums, that largely answer the linguistic questions that follow from this: who counts as a speaker, who counts as a speaker worth listening to, and who has the right to ask?

On these points, minority-language media present mixed messages in more ways than one. Both the producers and consumers of Buryat media orient toward a standard that is not really anwhere to be found in practice. Buryat-language media are always to some degree multilingual; whether in their framing, lexical choices, or grammatical influences, they are always "mixed" in some way, rarely meeting purist expectations. Such media also present mixed messages regarding the social location of expertise and authority for deciding what counts as "speaking" or "knowing" Buryat. Outside of mass media, what counts as linguistic knowledge is fractured, unclear, and highly dependent on immediate social context. By contrast, journalists hold themselves to be standard-bearers, but they also showcase lamas, shamanic elders, and grandmothers, making plausible a range of opinions about where (and in whom) linguistic competence is located. Moreover, although media institutions position themselves—and are locally interpreted—as monolithic arbiters of linguistic authority, encapsulated in a strong Buryat literary standard, they in fact manifest great diversity in ideology and praxis, shaped by the material demands of specific mediums. This situation presents an indexical disjuncture between the authority granted to individuals and their actual linguistic practices, unevenly extending the imprimatur of institutional authority over practices that would not otherwise be interpreted as "standard" and further confusing the issue of what counts as "Buryat," and for whom.

Neither are the goals of minority-language media always clear. Observing minority-language production at Radio Zambia circa 1990, Spitulnik (1998, 182) described an institution rationalizing both an ambitious state ideology of "ethnolinguistic egalitarianism" and its "opposite," a sociolinguistic hierarchy. She found hierarchy in the relative amount of broadcasting time allotted to Zambia's languages. While it is significant that the number of minutes and pages of Buryat vis-à-vis Russian in mass media has declined over the past several decades, the ways in which media institutions reinforce a sociolinguistic hierarchy are far more subtle and thoroughgoing—and harder to disrupt—than relative time and page allotments. Media institutions are supposed to have been "indigenized" as Buryat, but the forms they take are also assimilatory and hyper-institutional. Indeed, the production of minority media is itself Janus-faced, in the sense that it both empowers indigenous self-determination and assimilates indigenous difference into a mainstream institutional project.

Some of the subtlest but most significant disjunctures are to be found within the minority language elite itself. Throughout this book, we have seen diverse ideological positions taken by Buryats working for cultural and linguistic revitalization, with different strategies for mobilizing mass media to encourage the use of Buryat. The differences often come down to the extent to which a person believes the language can be re-indexed—that is, the extent to which a person sees Buryat's evocation of and connections to premodern lifeways as changeable or unchangeable. The Tolon founder Dorzh articulated a common view when he described Buryat as an "ancient language" inextricably linked to a bygone era. In Dorzh's view, Buryat so strongly indexes a premodern, pre-Soviet past that it cannot be remade; perhaps, he suggests, it could have been "updated" during the Soviet period for modern life, but because it was not, it is now practically unusable in many domains of social life. Dorzh sees it as only natural that ethnic Buryats therefore abandon the Buryat language in favor of Russian. One possible response to this problem—the response undertaken by Tolon and by other editorial boards of formerly Buryat-only publications—is to adopt Russian material alongside Buryat. Similarly, many television journalists in need of interviewees are willing to relax purist expectations and open Buryat to Russian influence, albeit somewhat begrudgingly. Drawing in an audience of passive understanders and semispeakers will, they hope, allow them to reacquaint people who *should* speak Buryat with at least some aspects of Buryat culture and language. Another possible response to the same problem is to embrace Buryat's strong linkages to what Dorzh called a "bygone nomadic civilization" and try to revitalize elements of that culture via the language and vice versa. This approach is exemplifed by efforts to reteach Buryat readers and viewers the terms for items in a yurt, for instance, or terms for parts of a horse's bridle and saddle. Material conditions have changed over the past century such that it is highly unlikely the speaker will even have access to a horse, but the speaker, it is hoped, might gain respect for cultural traditions and an interest in Buryats' past.

Other activists share the assumption that Buryat indexes a bygone era and spatiotemporal marginality but do not see that indexicality as inevitable. Rather than abandoning the language or investing their efforts exclusively in reintroducing older ways of speaking alongside traditional lifeways, they seek to actively remake Buryat into a language for the contemporary era. This goal underlies my friend's entreaty to "not give up" when we could not find a clear Buryat term for 'language shift.' Likewise it underlies all efforts to introduce neologisms and gain traction for them—whether through institutions, such as periodic efforts to establish a Buryat-language style board on the model of the Académie Française, or through more diffuse, noninstitutional means, such as by suggesting tobsholuurai draiver (keyboard driver) and other new terms on internet boards. Other ways of "updating" Buryat are more subtle and thoroughgoing than lexical changes. The linguists, teachers, and code-savvy activists working on electronic dictionaries, tobsholuurai draiveruud for Buryat's "extra" Cyrillic letters and Mongolian script, and Buryat subtitles for pirated Hollywood films seek to re-index an "ancient language" through popular digital media. They aim to destabilize Buryat's existing indexicality and realign it with what they see as progressive, cosmopolitan, and open-source—if not open-border—twenty-first-century values.

The potential for re-indexing is a common reason for language revitalization movements to enthusiastically embrace digital media for minority languages, from Hawaiian to Potawatomi (Buszard-Welcher [2001] 2013, 337–38; Warschauer 1998). Because digital media are so strongly associated with modernity and technological innovation, they enable an indexical realignment of linguistic varieties that are otherwise seen as archaic or obsolete, relegated to "spatially and temporally dislocated and distant positions, away from geographical centers and the temporal present" (Eisenlohr 2004, 32). And it is not only digital media that have been mobilized to perform such re-indexing. Irish-language journalists have worked to "enhance the contemporary status" of a language that is otherwise seen as outdated, expanding its domains of use through radio news (Cotter [2001] 2013, 308). In the 1990s, Donald R. Browne (1996) documented indigenous media production in a wide variety of "new" electronic formats, from television to radio to audio and video cassette recording, that allowed a self-projection of contemporaneity to both indigenous and nonindigenous audiences (see also Ginsburg 1995). Indeed, this function of digital media in the early twenty-first century is but the latest iteration of a long-standing pattern of capitalizing on the "newness" of innovative media technologies to spatiotemporally reposition particular languages, communities, and individuals (Bolter and Grusin 1999; Carey and Elton 2010; Gitelman 2006; Gitelman and Pingree 2003; Weidman 2010).

Yet these possibilities of renegotiating belonging and repositioning publics are not as straightforward as moving from past to future or from periphery to center. The Buryat case suggests that understanding the role of minority-language media in social and linguistic change requires a much more nuanced approach to the minority language publics they are meant to—and do—evoke, particularly in terms of scale and temporality.

First, we must be clear about the scale at which belonging is being reworked. Buryat activists who hope to indexically reposition the language by circulating neologisms in newspapers and internet boards seek to do so for the Buryat language as a *whole*, sensing that their marginality at the scale of the federation is hindering political sovereignty and economic security. What they have in mind, at this scale, is a clear, discrete Buryat, encapsulated in a strong standard literary language. Rarely do activists seek to indexically reposition a stigmatized *variety* of Buryat, for instance by publishing articles in one of the so-called nonliterary dialects or encouraging some sort of mixing with Russian, even though this would go some distance to lessening would-be speakers' performance anxiety and arguably improve language maintenance. In the rare instances in which journalists do attempt to publish dialectisms, they encounter disagreement and opposition. Dolgora, writing articles for a dwindling Buryat-speaking audience in Ust'-Orda, thought that she was working for the preservation and revitalization of Buryat by incorporating dialectisms that local people were more likely to understand. These efforts do, however, work at cross-purposes with ethnonational efforts to present a united Buryat identity, and her practice is not acceptable everywhere. When I described Dolgora's efforts to Rinchin, Petra, and Tsypelma, television and radio journalists in Ulan-Ude, Tsypelma sighed. "I wish she wouldn't do that," she said. Rinchin and Petra understood Dolgora's reasoning, they said, and seemed impressed by her efforts but did not agree that writing in dialect was the solution. "Should they speak 'Ust'-Orda' and only we speak 'real Buryat'?" queried Rinchin, rhetorically. "Then what kind of future is there for our countrymen in our western territories?" He held up his left hand, spreading his fingers wide. "We live separately, like fingers that do not know they belong to the same hand." Other district newspapers that have attempted to incorporate dialectisms that deviate from the literary standard have come under political fire, such as the Sélénge newspaper on the Russian-Mongolian border that was reportedly ordered to stop publishing in the local dialect, more intermediate between standard Buryat and standard (Khalkh) Mongolian, in favor of SLB. In both Ust'-Orda and Sélénge, dialectisms were interpreted as a threat to the unity of the Buryat language, though the threat became politically salient only in the case on the national border. There the language choices of journalists appear to have been seen as a threat, by extension, to the unity of the territorial (ethno)nation of Buryatia and to its relationship to the Russian Federation. At stake in these scalar questions are different notions of the minority language public and its proper relationship to Buryat political configurations. District journalists speak of meeting an existing public of dialect and semispeakers where they are, whereas republic journalists seek to shape a more homogenous, idealized public, which they worry about as the unstable underpinning of ethnonational community.

Second, in thinking about how minority media might reconfigure spatiotemporal relationships, we must work beyond binary views of time as either backwards or progressive, static or dynamic, backward-looking or forward-moving. Chronotopic ideologies linking radio broadcasts to rural steppe landscapes of the 1950s, or cellphone video to urbanized futures, are complex discursive constructions that can be dis- and rearticulated, within which "future" and "past," "modern" and "traditional" are categories of practice that should be studied and troubled, not taken up blithely as categories of analysis (similarly see Brubaker and Cooper 2000). This is particularly the case for analyzing language shift, obsolescence, and revitalization movements. What is the target of revitalization efforts? What was lost, and what is to be revitalized? Even the terminology suggests that there exists a static, mythic past in which there was a whole, complete language that could be reinvigorated. The assumption is part of a long literary and scholarly tradition of treating rural spaces as the source of authentic, untrammeled, folk essences of the past—what Gal (1989, 316) calls the "pastoral tradition" (see also Williams 1973). Most of the Buryat-language journalists and media makers populating the pages of this book embrace this pastoral tradition, looking to village babushki as sources and discussing their work in terms of *sokhranenie* (preservation) and *razvitie* (development or ontogeny).

They do so because these are the temporal metaphors and master narratives they have to work with. Since the 1990s, Russia's non-Russian populations have been in a difficult, if not impossible, position. Post-Soviet Russia's movement away from the model of a multinational state has dovetailed with broader economic and cultural trends toward interconnectedness, hypermobility, and flexible citizenship—often referred to with the shorthand "globalization"—that also seem to challenge the notion of traditional nations. In the Soviet period, however, policies explicitly encouraged the development of distinct national identities based on shared language, culture, and territory. Many post-Soviet states outside of Russia—such as Kazakhstan, Georgia, and Ukraine—are actively engaged in European Enlightenment-style, ethnic group-based nation building, focusing on strong, standardized national languages. Despite having inherited the same ideal of a nation-state unified by language, Buryat efforts at nation building in the post-Soviet era have been stymied in part by truncated standardization. It is easy for Zhirinovsky to claim that Buryats are not identifiable as such, just as it was easy for proponents of dissolving the Buryat okrugs to claim that autonomy for Ust'-Orda had not preserved the language—at least not in a way recognizable to purists. Disagreements over the use of nonstandard forms in district newspapers are reminders that the standard literary language, while idealized as strong and well-established, is in fact quite tenuous. In addition to a partially standardized language that cannot serve as a lingua franca, Buryat would-be nationalists have partially "nativized" media institutions, with legacies of state funding, and professionalization pathways through local universities. These are the historical legacies of the Soviet project and its particular version of modernity, within which native Siberian peoples would be hurried along through stages of socioeconomic, cultural, and linguistic development.

The artificiality that some Buryats now ascribe to the "advances" of the twentieth century bespeaks a different interpretation of time. Slowly, the Buryat landscape sheds reminders of its Soviet years. On the central newspaper office building, a new skin of shiny peach- and white-colored tiles now hides the fading blue paint so emblematic of Soviet institutional style. People both young and old renovate their apartments, preferring "Euro" style cabinetry and faux-wood flooring to Soviet styles. The reminders that remain—neighborhood statues of Soviet heroes, the world's largest Lenin head on the city square—are largely taken as kitsch by the residents of the city. Teenagers and pensioners, construction workers and professional historians alike talk about bathing, the introduction of Western medicine, and public education as positive developments of the Soviet period or of longer-term Russification. But they also describe unnatural ruptures; artificial breaks from nature, from Mongolia, and from the past; and linguistic and cultural loss. The twentieth century's modernization efforts are locally figured, not unreasonably, as the culprits of that loss.

To the extent that modernity was a Soviet project, it looms now as something to be worked against or beyond. Thus when a young programmer seeks to "update" the language by introducing neologisms, or when Larisa/Yanzhima adopts a new Buryat name to shed her past self, they are not exactly pursuing modernity. They want to have it both ways—modernity and *its antidote*. Reclaiming a sense of belonging in contemporary Russia has become a matter of reaching back to the pre-Soviet era, an almost mythic time in many people's minds, and suturing old songs, stories, and black-and-white photographs together with twenty-first-century cosmopolitanism. Commentators on YouTube re-index the language paradoxically with neologisms and expectations of linguistic purity. Temporal periods overlap and collapse into one another.

From a practical standpoint, the gaps, disjunctures, and mixed messages endemic to minority media present not only interesting analytical puzzles but also problems to be solved. An elderly woman in the rural Tunka region asked me many years ago, at the very beginning of my research in 2005, why her five-year-old granddaughter did not speak Buryat. She leaned heavily on a wooden fence, looking off into the blue-green mountains before turning her weathered face to me with a look of sadness. It was not an idle question. She felt more comfortable speaking Buryat herself and was frustrated that her granddaughter always replied to her in Russian. If we looked only at the immediately visible factors, the answer to this grandmother's pained—and very common—question would not be clear. Her granddaughter's school offered two hours per week of Buryat language, the library was stocked with Buryat children's books, and she spent summers with her Buryat-dominant relatives. In fact, she understood Buryat well. Why are there so many children and adults like this granddaughter, when there continues to be state support for minority-language education and media? Though limited in important ways, the fact that such institutions exist at all should, according to conventional wisdom, put Buryat on firmer footing than thousands of other lesser-known languages. Among many language revitalization activists in Russia and beyond, conventional wisdom has it that having minority-language media itself will be the magic answer to minority-language attrition. Provide media, the logic goes, and people will speak. Such media are believed to preserve a language by providing models of speech and by raising the status of the minority language and its speakers (e.g., Cormack 2007). By these criteria, Buryat should be a success story. And it is not.

This book has explained why, even in cases in which there appear to be substantive institutional support and high political stakes for speaking a minority language, the language continues to recede from most domains of use. In the preceding chapters, we have seen some of the more nuanced reasons for language shift and loss, and we can answer the grandmother's question—which is the first step to positing a solution. Her granddaughter does not speak Buryat because, in the urban, Russian-dominant spaces she primarily inhabits, it indexes rurality and backwardness. Because she has a Russian accent in Buryat and does not want a Buryat accent in Russian. Because she learns SLB in school but her family speaks the western Tunka dialect, and she isn't sure what's correct. Because her parents rarely turn the television or radio to Buryat-language programming. Because what's on is mainly news anyway. Because she doesn't understand the television anchor when he speaks quickly. Because she is ashamed both to speak Buryat and not to speak it, and because if she does open her mouth, she might draw her elders' ire anyway. Because Buryat-language media were not historically developed for the purpose of language maintenance and revitalization; that has only recently become a primary goal. Because minority-language media actually serve many different functions, including reproducing a minority cultural elite who might not always be interested in democratizing language use—or expanding membership in the community. Because institutional projects to improve the status of minority languages and publics have unintended and contradictory consequences. Because it is extraordinarily difficult for Buryats to speak Buryat in socially satisfying ways.

These observations suggest some ways of improving the use of media in language revitalization and social justice for linguistic minorities. While it might be difficult to achieve true ethnolinguistic egalitarianism via mass media, certainly minority-language media can further that end. Buryat-language media *do* work, after all, to raise the status of many speakers of the language (especially of the so-called literary dialects), and they effectively sustain a small Buryat cultural elite and minority language public in the face of overwhelming pressure to shift to Russian. It is common practice and arguably an ethical duty for scholars of language loss and revitalization efforts to offer practical recommendations and support when requested (Grenoble and Whaley 1998, 2006; Hill and May 2013; Nevins 2013). When people in Buryatia ask me how we might improve Buryat's situation, I usually offer two suggestions based on my research.

Certainly a first step would be producing *more* media in Buryat, as visibly as possible. Given perennially limited resources, however, I more specifically suggest covering a wider variety of media genres. Focusing on children and teens in addition to the adults who are currently being reached through news would help. One of the most consistent laments I heard from audiences was that there was not more children's programming in Buryat. When the Buryat-language version of the Soviet newspaper *Buriat-Mongol'skii komsomolets* disappeared, nothing for teenagers replaced it. More recently, adults fondly remembered a cartoon for very young children that the activists subtitling Russian cartoons were trying to re-create. Grassroots efforts like this, undertaken by media-savvy educators and sometimes journalists in their off-hours, suggest a particularly promising area of development, at the intersection of existing language institutions. Media institutions could better capitalize on the strong pedagogical backgrounds of Buryat-language journalists by further integrating their production with educational projects—something that is beginning to happen on an ad hoc basis anyway. Beyond targeting different audiences and recruiting a younger minority language public, widening the range of genres in which Buryat is used to more "hard news" stories in politics, economics, and world events could significantly help to re-index the language. This is a principle that applies to what are likely many cases of language shift in which the minority language has become restricted in media to "soft news," cultural and "traditional" material, human interest stories, and the arts.

The second suggestion that emerges from this research is likewise applicable in many contexts beyond Buryatia. Shame, as we have seen throughout this book, is a formidable force in Buryat-Russian language shift. Being more aware of how shame and reticence are produced would go a long way to ameliorating the negative emotions associated with speaking (or not speaking) Buryat. I often emphasize this to journalists in particular because they are among the Buryat speakers most likely to criticize people they take to be semispeakers—especially, as we have seen, if they are "not trying." I would go further, however, and suggest that if the main goal of journalists and other media producers is to inspire greater use of the language, they should be open to nonstandard forms. Hewing close to a literary standard is highly rational in Buryatia's historical context, but since the language has not been standardized sufficiently to function as a regional lingua franca and remains closer to a dialect group, prescriptivism at this point appears to be self-defeating.

Of course, there are many reasons besides language revitalization to chide a hesitant television interviewee or police language use on YouTube threads, and many other ways that media can be used to pursue or preclude belonging. It is in the gaps between these ideals and practices, standards and realities, that we see how people come to recognize and refigure the value of speaking—or not speaking—the language they call their own.

Notes

INTRODUCTION

1. All personal names of living persons in this book are pseudonyms, except where a person is acting in a public capacity or specifically requested I use their real name. I have replaced traditionally Buryat names with other Buryat names of the appropriate gender, and traditionally Russian names with other Russian names of the appropriate gender. To protect the anonymity of media personnel and interviewees, I do not provide the date of broadcast or publication for material that I describe the production of. I also refer to media personnel in the aggregate and generalize when possible.

2. For a nice discussion of the distinction between *rossiianin* and *russkii* and the trouble the translation "Russian" can cause in English, see Tishkov 1997, x.

3. The People's Khural (B. Aradai khural, R. *Narodnyi khural*) functions like a parliament or a Russian duma. In tsarist Russia, local Buryat-Mongolian politics were organized around smaller such bodies called "steppe dumas." The khural, however, can trace its roots back to twelfth- and thirteenth-century Mongol government, and the contemporary use of the term khural rather than *duma* is significant in signaling indigenous authority. The term is also used in Buddhist contexts in Buryatia and Mongolia to mean 'religious services'—that is, when a group of monks gathers to read texts and prayers.

4. See, for example, Balzer 1981, 1999; Bloch 2003; Cruikshank and Argounova 2000; Grant 1993, 1995; Halemba 2006; Humphrey 1994, 1999; King 2011; Slezkine 1996; Ssorin-Chaikov 2003; Vitebsky 2005.

5. Compiling current census data, Eberhard, Simons, and Fennig (2019) estimate a total speaker population of 326,500 across Mongolia, the Russian Federation, and the People's Republic of China (PRC). Even granting that many census respondents report knowledge based on ethnic affiliation rather than active competence, this estimate is probably accurate, as there are also many semispeakers and people with passive competence who do *not* report knowledge of Buryat on the Russian census.

6. Of these speakers, 206,430 reported that they were ethnic Buryats, 5,581 ethnic Russians, and 1,036 ethnic Tatars. In much smaller numbers, there were Armenians, Chuvash, Yakuts (Sakha), Tuvans, and others.

7. For additional definitions and a critical discussion thereof, see Woolard 1998a. Language ideologies may also include attitudes, affect, emotional connections, and aesthetic sensibilities (Wilce 2009, 115–16).

8. Cf. Rumsey 1990, who implies more homogeneity than I have found in Buryat media practices. Similarly, Asif Agha (1998) and Michael Silverstein (2003) have pointed out that stereotypes cannot be perfectly shared, irrespective of the size of a community. Indeed, the framework of language ideologies is often preferable to concepts like "stereotype" or "world view" specifically because it does *not* appear as totalizing, stable, or evenly shared throughout a social group; "ideology" rather suggests "representations that are contestable, socially positioned, and laden with political interest" (Hill and Mannheim 1992, 382).

9. Such individuals are not referred to as "Buryat speakers" in this book. I carefully worded my research questions and materials to distinguish between *rodnoi iazyk* and self-reported *znanie* and between passive and active knowledge. Recruitment materials

for the focus groups, for instance, did not require that participants be "native speakers"; I avoided words such as *rodnoi* and *nositel'* entirely and instead asked "*Vy ponimaete buriatskii iazyk?*" (Do you **understand** Buryat?), emphasizing passive rather than active knowledge to lessen the possibility that embarrassment and shame would prohibit people from taking part. All the participants reported some kind of ability to speak Buryat, though competence was, as we shall see, variable.

10. Engin Isin (2002) argues that by its very nature, citizenship requires hierarchies of personhood within a nation-state; see also Benhabib 2002.

11. Cultural sovereignty is similarly important in North American Indian politics, as an alternative to the doctrine of territorial sovereignty (Coffey and Tsosie 2001). See Anya Bernstein's (2013) perceptive discussion of how Buryat cultural sovereignty is furthered in struggles to define Buddhism.

12. Fieldwork periods were June–August 2005, February–May 2007, September 2008–September 2009, August 2011, and July–August 2012. In the era of digital connectivity, one never really leaves "the field," and I collected data between and beyond these periods, especially for chapter 7. Working with journalists also ensured that my mediatized presence in Buryatia continued well beyond the fieldwork for this book. In between fieldwork periods, I recorded a short radio program for BGTRK, and television and radio interviews I gave during fieldwork are still broadcast in Buryatia.

13. I traveled at different times to Ust'-Orda, Ol'khon (B. Oikhon), Baikal'sk, and Irkutsk (B. Ėrkhüü) in the west; to Aga and Chita (B. Shėtė) in the east; and to many of the districts of the Republic of Buryatia, including Akha (R. Okinskii raion), Tünkhėn (R. Tunkinskii raion), Khabaanskha (R. Kabanskii raion), Ėbilgė (R. Ivolginskii raion), Sėlėngė (R. Selenginskii raion), Tarbagatai (R. Tarbagataiskii raion), Khiaagta (R. Kiakhtinskii raion), Zagarai (R. Zaigraevskii raion), Pribaikal'sk (R. Pribaikal'skii raion, B. Baigal shadarai aimag), Bargazhan (R. Barguzinskii raion), Khėzhėngė (R. Kizhinginskii raion), Khori (R. Khorinskii raion), and Iaruuna (R. Eravninskii raion). A map of the districts appears in chapter 4.

14. Archives consulted included the State Archives of the Russian Federation (GARF) in Moscow, f. 6903; the National Archives of the Republic of Buryatia (NARB) in Ulan-Ude, ff. 1, 914, 930, 955, 3843, and newspaper collection; Archives of the Institute of Mongolian, Buddhist, and Tibetan Studies of the Buryat Scientific Center, Siberian Branch of the Russian Academy of Sciences (OPP IMBiT) in Ulan-Ude, Inv. No. 356, MI-557, and MI-723; and the Archives of the former Aga Buryat Autonomous Okrug, then in Aginskoe, now in Chita.

15. Both the newspaper Buriaad ünėn and the publishing house Buriaad Ünėn have operated under several titles, which have changed with the tides of Buryat-Russian politics. In January 1991, shortly after Buryatia claimed independence (to shortly later join the new Russian Federation), *Buriat-Mongol'skaia pravda* split into Buriaad ünėn (Buryat-language organ of the new government), *Buriatiia* (Russian-language organ of the new government), and *Pravda Buriatii* (Russian-language organ of the Communist Party). It most often appears in this book as Buriaad ünėn. Today Buriaad ünėn dates its founding to the first issue of Shėnė baidal.

16. Many of the interviews and conversations reported in this book took place over libations such as cognac, beer, or vodka, and this was a particularly significant element of my interactions with journalists. Some of my interlocutors did not drink, but among those who did, drinking to excess was not uncommon. I turned my voice recorder off and ceased taking notes in these instances.

17. Television channels systematically reviewed included Arig Us, BGTRK (Channel 1), BGTRK (Channel 24), NTV, and, when possible during briefer stays in Irkutsk and Aga, IGTRK and ChGTRK. On radio, I focused on BGTRK's prolific programming.

Federation-scale publications reviewed included *Argumenty i fakty*, *Izvestiia*, *Karavan*, *Moia semia* (My family), *Rossiiskaia gazeta*, and the Russian editions of international magazines like *Cosmopolitan* and *Vogue*. Pan-Buryat publications reviewed included the Buryat literary journal <u>Baigal</u> (Baikal); the newspaper <u>Tolon</u> (Ray of light); and <u>Ugai zam</u> (Way of the ancestors), a political-historical scholarly journal in Russian. Republic-scale publications reviewed included *Buriat-Mongol'skaia pravda* and <u>Buriaad ünën</u> in their various incarnations (1924–2011); the daily *Buriatiia* and the weekly *Buriatiia-7*; *MK v Buriatii* (*Moskovskii komsomolets* in Buryatia); *Molodëzh' Buriatii* (Youth of Buryatia); and the historical publications *Amur* (published in 1862 for the Irkutsk region); *Baikal* (1897, 1903, 1905–6, for the Baikal region); bulletins of trade and internal affairs for the young BMASSR (1921–27); *Kiakhtinskii listok* (The Kiakhta page, 1862, for the Baikal region); the Russian-language *Molodoi skotovod* and Buryat-language <u>Zaluu malshan</u> (The young herder, 1926, for the BMASSR); *Verkhneudinskii listok"* (The Verkhneudinsk page, 1905–6) and *Vestnik"* (The herald, 1913–14), for what is now Ulan-Ude and east Baikal; *Vostochnoe obozrenie* (The eastern review, 1902, 1905, for the Irkutsk region); *Vostochno-sibirskaia pravda* (The Eastern Siberian truth, 1951, for the Irkutsk region); *Zabaikal'skaia mysl'* (The Zabaikal idea, 1915, for Verkhneudinsk and eastern Baikal); *Zabaikal'skaia nov'* (The eastern Baikal news, 1917, for the Chita region); and a flurry of short-lived newspapers produced for the Baikal region during Siberia's tumultuous Civil War years: *Krasnoe Pribaikal'e* (Red Baikal 1920–21); *Krasnyi Buriat-Mongol* (Red Buryat-Mongol, 1922–23); *Nabat* (The signal, 1921); *Pribaikal'e* (The Baikal); the pro-Red *Pribaikal'skaia pravda* (The Baikal truth); the pro-White *Pribaikal'skaia zhizn'* (Baikal life); *Vestnik sovetov Pribaikal'ia* (Herald of the Baikal soviets, 1918); and the three newspapers *Dal'ne-vostochnaia pravda* (The Far Eastern truth), *Dal'ne-vostochnaia Respublika* (The Far Eastern Republic), and *Golos Buriat-Mongola* (Voice of the Buryat-Mongol), published in 1920–21 for the short-lived Far Eastern Republic. Okrug-scale publications reviewed included *Aginskaia pravda* (The Aga truth) for Aga and the Russian- and Buryat-language analogues for Ust'-Orda, *Panorama okruga* (Panorama of the okrug) and <u>Ust'-Ordyn ünën</u> (The Ust'-Orda truth). City-scale publications reviewed that are sometimes distributed beyond Ulan-Ude included *Inform polis*, *Nomer odin* (Number one), and *Ulan-Udè reklama* (Ulan-Ude advertisement). District-scale publications reviewed included <u>Akha</u>, *Barguzinskaia pravda* (The Barguzin truth), *Dolina Kizhingi* (The valley of Kizhinga), its Buryat-language analogue <u>Khëzhéngé</u>, <u>Iaruuna</u> in Russian- and Buryat-language versions, *Ogni Kurumkana* (Fires of Kurumkan), and Khori aimag's *Udinskaia nov'* (The Uda news). Current copies of most of these publications are kept in the periodical room of the National Library of the Republic of Buryatia; historical publications can be found there, scattered in IMBiT's archives, and in NARB's newspaper room. Additional texts consulted, such as nineteenth- and early twentieth-century primers, alphabet books, translations, and works of Buryat linguistics, are in the rare book rooms of the National Library of the Republic of Buryatia and Buryat State University.

18. In 2009, there were approximately 0.86 males to every female in general, and in the sixty-five and up age category, only 0.46 males to every female (Rosstat 2009).

1. NATIVE AUTONOMY IN A MULTINATIONAL STATE

1. I do not know which historical documents (if any) the storyteller was drawing on, but the importance of the story was in his own belief and telling, not in its historical verifiability.

2. This "alliance" appears to have resulted from Jochi's subjugation of Buryat tribes, but that fact is elided today. Instead, Chinggis Khan is widely revered as a unifier and statesman, as he is in Mongolia.

3. It is likely that earlier than this, there were economic and personal contacts between local Buryats and fur traders, fortune hunters, exiles, and escaped convicts from European Russia (Schorkowitz 2001a).

4. See Chimitdorzhiev 2001a, 2001b; Forsyth 1992; Montgomery 2005; Schorkowitz 2001b; Zateev 2002; the documents compiled in Rumiantsev and Okun' 1960; and references to the "Bratsk people" in Kivelson 2006, 167, 195–96.

5. The ad hoc process by which ethnographic information about Siberian peoples was incorporated into delineating the early USSR's territories is detailed in Hirsch 2005.

6. Compare Argounova-Low 2013 and Balzer and Vinokurova 1996 on how Sakha indigeneity has evolved over the late Soviet and post-Soviet periods. Kun-hui Ku (2005) describes a similar uptake of international paradigms for indigenous citizenship in Taiwan.

7. Linguistic reconstruction was done by Rassadin, a specialist on Tofalar and neighboring languages. The first schoolbooks printed in Soyot, authored by Rassadin, were introduced in July 2009 for the 2009–10 school year. In speeches and locally distributed publications that I observed in 2009, local officials explicitly linked their reintroduction of Soyot to maintaining mineral and land rights.

8. An excellent discussion of these criteria can be found in Donahoe et al. 2008. In 2007, the Russian Federation abstained from the United Nations vote to adopt the Declaration on the Rights of Indigenous Peoples (2007), though the federal government has since unveiled some initiatives to the UN's Permanent Forum on Indigenous Issues. Technically, indigenous peoples have protections under article 69 of the Russian Constitution.

9. Broadcasts in Ewenki at BGTRK began in 1994, after years of requests for Ewenki-language programming. This date is recorded in BGTRK's small in-house museum. During my research, BGTRK employed a single Ewenki-speaking woman to produce their weekly cultural program.

10. Buryats played a key role in revolutionary Mongolia and Inner Mongolia (Atwood 2002). In the 1990s, Buryats again took up governmental posts in Mongolia but had to conceal their origins to avoid discrimination (Bulag 1998).

11. Mongolia and China are not the only Asian foils for Buryatia. Anya Bernstein (2013, 58) argues that among Buryat Buddhists, Buryatia's relationship with Tibet is even more polarizing than its relationship with Mongolia.

12. In fact, there are Mongolic-origin terms for 'dough' and baking activities, and it is likely that by the twelfth to fourteenth centuries, Mongolic-speaking peoples had been exposed to bread and potatoes through multiple border regions of the Mongol Empire. This does not change the fact, however, that bread and potatoes are thought of as Russian cultural borrowings.

13. Caroline Humphrey (2015) argues that to see Buryat villages as remote is an external, urban dweller's perspective, but the fact that Tarbagataians (for example) themselves call part of their village "Siberia" suggests that they have also internalized it.

14. In imperial Russia, these lands were part of Irkutsk Guberniia until 1851, then divided at Lake Baikal between Irkutsk Guberniia and Zabaikal' Oblast (1851–1922). During the chaotic Civil War—which extended well into the 1920s in Siberia—there were several short-lived attempts at establishing an independent Buryat-Mongolian state (1917–20) or Buryat-Mongolian polities within the RSFSR and the Far Eastern Republic (1920–22). When the BMASSR was established in 1923, it united most of the lands concerned.

15. A map showing the pre- and post-1937 borders can be found in Graber 2016, 183.

16. The 2010 census placed Aginskoe's population at 14,808 and Ust'-Ordynskii's at 14,900 (Rosstat 2011). Over the years covered in this book, Aginskoe grew rapidly, from

11,717 in 2002 (Rosstat 2004), due to housing projects and general economic well-being. Aginskoe's success made some residents chafe at suggestions that the okrug would benefit from uniting with Chita Oblast.

17. In 1993, after the disintegration of the Soviet Union and initial redrawing of internal lines, there were eighty-nine federal subjects within the Russian Federation. Since March 2008, there have been eighty-three. Russia currently claims eighty-five, based on the annexation of Crimea in 2014, but those territories are disputed.

18. A detailed account of the mergers can be found in Graber and Long 2009.

19. Corn was also attempted in vast fields under Khrushchev, but it failed, and the attempt is still the brunt of local jokes today.

20. The problem itself was not new or surprising; Russia's demographic situation had been a topic of discussion for at least a decade, following sharp emigration in the early 1990s and a simultaneous dip in the birthrate. What was new was that by the mid-2000s, the country's political and economic situation had stabilized sufficiently that the federal government began investing state resources in fixing the problem.

21. Construction and extraction jobs such as mining and oil-related work were particularly hard hit.

22. American audiences would likewise understand this kind of performance in terms of what Andrew Shryock (2004, 309) calls the "heritage format," in which a person acquires fluency in an ethnic identity of personal "heritage" that is thought to make her more tolerant of diversity, in addition to her civic identity as American.

23. This makes Buryatia a provocative counterpoint to independent republics in post-Soviet Central Asia like Kazakhstan and Kyrgyzstan, which have embraced ethnic nationalism over a multicultural, civic nationalism (Wachtel 2013).

24. It is in recognition of this that I am not using the terms "Buryat-Mongolia" and "Buryat-Mongolian," although I think an excellent case could be made for their reintroduction.

25. "Siberian" is emerging as a separate autonym, as evidenced most forcefully by the number of people who wrote it into their 2010 census forms (Anisimova and Echevskaya 2018).

26. Usually enthusiasm for the Friendship of the Peoples does not extend to intermarriage between a Buryat man and a non-Buryat woman, because that is seen as diluting the male line. So, while obnoxious when said in front of my husband (!), such comments also showed a sincere desire to incorporate me into Buryat families.

27. The exact wording is: "The President of the Republic of Buryatia should control the state languages of the Republic of Buryatia" (*Prezident Respubliki Buriatiia dolzhen vladet' gosudarstvennymi iazykami Respubliki Buriatiia*) (article 70).

28. Potentially disrupting this are new ideas of Asian modernity. In Buryatia, young people have sometimes seen alternative modernities (and futures for themselves) in South Korea and Japan, but more relevant at present is the economic ascendancy of Mongolia, southeast Asia, and especially China. Nonetheless, the institutions into which Buryats have been educated and socialized are still predominantly Russian.

2. MEDIA AND THE MAKING OF A BURYAT PUBLIC

1. As Curran notes, Marx himself never fully articulated a theory of the capitalist versus socialist press. Marxist critiques of capitalist media and the role of media in post-socialist transition have taken a number of forms.

2. This newspaper, *Zhizn' na vostochnoi okraine* / Züün zügei baidal (Life on the eastern frontier, also sometimes cited as *Zhizn' vostoka*), is usually considered a Russian-Mongolian publication, but some prominent scholars consider it distinctively Buryat

(e.g., Kim and Baldanov 1994). Badmaev also founded a group that was purged in the 1930s with the arrest, imprisonment, or execution of some 6,267 suspected "pan-Mongolists" (Andreyev 2003; Baabar 1999, 375).

3. *Korenizatsiia* was developed in Buryatia after mid-1924, when Mattvei Amagaev declared, "In view of the fact that the period of the organizational construction of state apparatuses has finished, [we must] turn to the Buryatization [*oburiachivanie*] of our state apparatuses, and also to the introduction of the Buryat language into clerical work" (NARB, f. 1, op. 1, d. 433, protocol 24). Already in 1923, Amagaev had advocated Buryat and Mongolian language classes for clerical workers, including ethnic Russians (NARB, f. 1, op. 1, d. 245, protocol 13). It is difficult to judge from archival records how much clerical work was conducted in Buryat. Even in Buryat-dominant institutions like the Buryat-language newspapers, most official party documents were required to be written in—or translated into—Russian in order to be legible to higher authorities outside the republic.

4. For example, the editor of <u>Buriaad ünén</u>'s predecessor <u>Shene baidal</u> was a twenty-four-year-old Russian, Innokentii P. Malkov, who was fluent in Buryat and Mongolian (Montgomery 2005; Namzhilova 2001).

5. This historical transformation is detailed in Graber 2012.

6. "Respublika Buriatiia garantiruet vsem ee narodam pravo na sokhranenie rodnogo iazyka, sozdanie uslovii dlia ego izucheniia i razvitiia" (article 67).

7. Article 28 of the Republic of Buryatia's language law states that "broadcasts of republic radio and television will be realized in Buryat and Russian." Article 20 of the Russian Federation's 1991 language law allows for mass media in the subjects of the Russian Federation to be produced in any state language but does not guarantee any particular support or protections.

8. Among other provisions of the law that remain unfulfilled is the promise to offer study in classical Mongolian script. Additional legislation to fulfill the law and begin a multiyear initiative for language "preservation and development" (*sokhranenie i razvitie buriatskogo iazyka*) was enacted in August 2010.

9. The organization has established stations in Moscow, St. Petersburg, Khabarovsk, Ussuriysk, and Ulaanbaatar. They have had a small ministry in Ulan-Ude since at least 2006.

10. Benjamin Lee (1997, 321–46) makes a similar point, regarding the construction of a national American public ("we") via the circulation of the phrase "we, the people." See also Lee [2001] 2014.

11. Linguistic anthropologists often distinguish between a language community and a speech community, per Silverstein 1998. Within a language community, speakers share a denotational code; within a speech community, they might speak many different languages, dialects, and so on, but they share norms of use.

12. See several large-scale audience studies of readership in post-Soviet Buryatia (e.g., Badmaeva 2002, 2004; Choiropov 1998; Osinskii, Bazarov, and Budaeva 2002). Declining circulation rates do not necessarily mean declining relevance. Liudmila Badmaeva (2002) has argued that the importance of the press in Buryatia actually increased over the early post-Soviet period. Subscription and circulation rates decreased, she contends, in response to economic hardship and climbing costs.

13. Similarly, Susan Gal ([2001] 2014) documents the movement of language ideologies through networks of Hungarian elites. Gal also points to how such movement can be blocked: when popular Hungarian magazines published exotic photographs from scholarly expeditions to Russia, Siberia, and Mongolia in search of evidence for the Finno-Ugric connection, journalists disagreed with scholars' conclusions of linguistic

kinship. "Unpatriotic opinions" and politically threatening views can be excised (Gal [2001] 2014, 37).

14. Mediascope offers timely ratings at http://mediascope.net/services/media/media-audience/tv/national-and-regional/audience/.

15. Ulan-Ude does not often make the national (federation-level) news, but it does sometimes make the regional Siberian news on *VESTI-Sibir'*. In May 2009, for example, a story about serious forest fires around Ulan-Ude ran on *VESTI-Sibir'*. *VESTI-Sibir'* thus provides a way of incorporating far-flung territories that otherwise remain unknown to more "central" audiences.

16. By contrast, its Russian-language equivalent, *Pravda Buriatii*, split into two collectives, *Buriatiia* taking up the role of government newspaper and *Pravda Buriatii* remaining an organ of the Communist Party.

17. In the Republic of Buryatia, the most-watched republic-level programs during my research were the locally produced programs on Channel One (BGTRK) and the local channels Tivikom and Arig Us.

18. Note that the condition of awareness is necessary but not sufficient. One also needs linguistic competence sufficient to participate in the circulation of texts—though this can be minimal, as we will see.

19. Studies of minority-language media often point out the difficulties of determining what counts as a "minority language," as well as the related practical problem of determining who one's audience for minority-language print, broadcasts, blogs, etc., might be (e.g., Cormack 2007).

3. RUPTURE AND RECLAMATION

1. Feelings of language ownership may take more protective forms as well (e.g., Debenport 2015).

2. Rates of death by intoxication and trauma among native peoples of the Russian Arctic and Siberia were already higher than among the general population during the Soviet period (Pika 1993). D. D. Bogoyavlensky (1997, 65) has called the alcoholism and violence rampant in indigenous communities "traumatorgenic self-annihilating behavior," referring not only to the plight of individuals but also to the fate of "native peoples as a whole."

3. In modern Buryat and Khalkh Mongolian, gér refers to both this style of dwelling—a round felt yurt—and a house or home in general. Thus a Brezhnev-era apartment is as much a gér as a yurt is. I use "yurt" to specify the traditional type of dwelling.

4. Students of Marx may note the discrepancy between this and the conditions of late capitalism that Marx and Engels described as the grounds for inevitable revolution. Champions of socialist revolution in Russia, eager to apply Marx's theory to a largely agrarian and preindustrial context, described the agrarian peasantry as Russia's proletariat. The targets of collectivization were thus farms and, in the Baikal region and many other parts of Siberia, as well as Mongolia, herds of animals.

5. Dorzh's reference to the lack of a "verbal image" (*slovesnogo obraza netu*), in Russian, hints at his training and interest in literature, philology, and literary theory. He was typical of Buryat-language newspaper journalists in this respect.

6. In the 2010 census, 2,245 ethnic Buryats in Russia reported knowledge of Mongolian (Rosstat 2012–13).

7. This date is based on comments and personal oral histories from Aga Buryats who were born in the 1940s and 1950s. As a general rule, pastoral nomadism and the use of yurts ended in the 1930s with forced collectivization.

8. This was 353,113 out of the 445,175 respondents who identified their nationality as Buryat (Rosstat 2004).

9. This was 206,430 out of 461,389 respondents who identified their nationality as Buryat (Rosstat 2012–13, 11, 146).

10. The 81 percent represents 222,107 out of 272,910 respondents within the republic who identified their nationality as Buryat (Rosstat 2004).

11. Both the 2002 and 2010 censuses distinguished between active linguistic knowledge and *rodnoi iazyk*, but the 2010 questionnaire helpfully moved "native language" below knowledge. Census respondents were asked, "Do you know [*vladet'*, lit. control] the Russian language?" (Yes/No), and "What other languages do you know?" with three blank spaces to write in the names of additional languages and their corresponding codes. Below this was a separate blank in which to indicate "your native language" and its corresponding code. In this census, 122,882 respondents out of 286,839 (43 percent) self-identified Buryats reported knowledge of Buryat in the first category, while 234,022 respondents out of those same 286,839 (82 percent) reported Buryat as their "native language" (Rosstat 2012–13, 212, 290).

12. Other statistically significant nationalities include Tatars, Ukrainians, Soyots, and Ewenks (Rosstat 2012–13, 290).

13. NARB, f. 914, op. 1, d. 8, p. 141 (1962); f. 914, op. 1, d. 20, p. 44 (1973); f. 914, op. 1, d. 22, p. 6 (1974); f. 914, op. 1, d. 34, pp. 3, 67 (1980).

14. On the shrinking number of letters received by Ünėn, see NARB, f. 3843, d. 1, pp. 8–14 (1969); f. 3843, op. 1, d. 3, p. 22 (1971); f. 3843, op. 1, d. 5, p. 92 (1973); and f. 3843, op. 1, d. 17, p. 80 (1979). On the advancing age of Buryat-language newspaper journalists and their concern over finding new cadres, see NARB, f. 3843, op. 1, d. 17, p. 69 (1979).

15. This dissonance—between a dualist policy on one hand and suppressive, assimilationist policies on the other hand—suggests that language policy in the late Soviet period, at least in Buryatia, was fundamentally intended to quell nationalist sentiment.

16. Soviet Stage Romani was similarly institutionalized into a division of (meta)linguistic labor between codes, according to which it took on primarily nonreferential functions (Lemon 2000, 2002). These examples suggest that Russian in the Soviet period became a *hyper*-referential code vis-à-vis minoritized languages.

17. Reorganizing the federation to reduce its number of administrative regions had been discussed under Yeltsin in the 1990s (Balzer and Vinokurova 1996), but it became a priority and began in earnest only with Putin's first administration in 2000 (Sakwa 2008).

18. James Collins (1998, 260) likewise found that speakers of the Athabaskan language Tolowa were "interested in words not grammar." There are some notable exceptions, including people grammatically policing Ukrainian (Bilaniuk 2005) and Catalan (Woolard 2016).

19. A detailed analysis of this interaction appears in Graber 2017.

20. Similarly, Dipesh Chakrabarty (1999) describes how Bengali *adda*, "comforting" or "comfortable talk," evokes a particular form of Bengali modernity that has since slipped away. Soviet "anecdotes" (*anekdoty*) function this way in the post-Soviet period (Ries 1997).

21. Buryat buuza are generally smaller and leaner than their Mongolian counterparts, buuz. They are similar to Tibetan momo, Turkish and Central Asian manti, or Chinese jiaozi or filled baozi, but buuza are characterized by tight circular folds around the top opening. Buryat buuza chefs also tend to eschew pork, which they identify as cheap and Chinese. The origin of these various dumpling forms and contents can, as a topic of conversation and debate, incite great passion, one's position vis-à-vis their relative deliciousness indicating allegiance to one or another theory of Eurasian cultural history.

22. Many older residents of Buryatia have some knowledge of French or German as second languages learned in school or university.

23. In a study of Russian-language newspapers in Buryatia, Eleanor Peers (2009, 79) found evidence of the increasing importance of a "pan-Buryat identity with a spiritual significance." Media representations of Buryat culture often share this view of a transcendent dimension, either as a "generalized aesthetic creative force" or "a spiritual energy" (Peers 2009, 79).

4. A LITERARY STANDARD AND ITS DISCONTENTS

1. In Russophone scholarship, what I am calling "SLB" is generally referred to as the "literary Buryat language" (*literaturnyi buriatskii iazyk*), though there is considerable variation in what is taken to constitute *literaturnyi*; I add "Standard" to emphasize the role of institutions and standardization projects in fixing—or attempting to fix—the register as a discrete code.

2. They were native speakers in the sense that Masha reported speaking Buryat at home with her relatives and with some friends, and Ayuur reported having spoken "since childhood" (*s detstva*).

3. This is closer to Charles Ferguson's original 1959 (1972) formulation of diglossia to describe two varieties of the same language, as opposed to Joshua Fishman's (1967) reformulation to embrace multiple unrelated codes.

4. The "kitchen language" assessment thus shifts between the scales of code and register, such that both Buryat as a whole code and an informal, highly Russified *form* of Buryat may be called "kitchen language" (Graber 2017).

5. Some classic cases of diglossia have been disputed along similar lines. See, for example, Schiffman 1993 on a collapsed diglossic hierarchy between Swiss German and standard German, or Cochran 1997 on *tri*glossia in Greek.

6. I use the Russian term henceforth, as it encompasses a greater range of forms and phenomena than "conversational" or "colloquial."

7. Widely used in both Buryat and Russian bureaucratic language through the 1950s, the word aimag fell out of use sometime in the 1960s. In the post-Soviet period it has enjoyed a resurgence in popularity, as a small reclamation of Buryat administrative terminology.

8. O. G. Makarova (2005) presents a standard dialect division in her Buryat language textbook, published by the Ministry of Education and Science for use in state high schools and colleges. For other influential classifications of Buryat dialects, see Budaev 1978, 24; Buraev 1988, 21, 1996, 14; and Poppe 1933.

9. Barbra Meek (2010) describes a similar practice in the Yukon, where intergenerational language transmission is similarly focused on the relationship between grandparents and grandchildren.

10. If Vasilii's interpretation is correct, it presents a provocative contrast to situations in which rural women speaking a lower-status language choose urban husbands who control mainly or exclusively the prestige code (e.g., Gal 1978).

11. Similarly, see Lemon 2000, 106–7, 239.

12. Emphasis on the Mongolian origin of Buryat-Mongols and on the injustice of their political separation from Mongolia has been most pronounced in the voluminous scholarship of the prominent Buryat historian and Mongolist Shirab Bodievich Chimitdorzhiev, some of which is referenced herein (see especially 2001a, 2004). Chimitdorzhiev routinely uses the term "Buryat-Mongol." His books were popular among my research participants, including nonelites and monolingual Russian speakers.

13. Dialectology boomed throughout the Soviet Union in the 1960s–70s, with an emphasis on showing how varieties influenced one another in the ethnic and linguistic

intermixing discussed in the preceding chapter. With rapid industrialization and massive internal migration, there was a "salvage linguistics" aspect to this as well.

14. *Babushka* (plural *babushki*) literally means 'grandmother,' but it is frequently used in Russian to refer to elderly women more generally. These students usually spoke Buryat with one another and occasionally with me, but they were speaking Russian in this instance.

15. In other words, the interaction may be socially framed as being in one code, despite significant influence from a second code (Hill and Hill 1986; Urciuoli 1991).

16. This is an instance of the *sibirskii da* (Siberian yes) referenced in chapter 1.

17. Vowel lengthening is also a common way of nativizing Russian personal names into Buryat. Conversely, Buryat personal names can be pronounced *po-russki* (in Russian) by replacing Buryat vowel length with Russian stress. See Graber 2017 for additional examples of nativizing Russian through vowel lengthening in conversational Buryat.

18. For other examples of mixing of Buryat and Russian (and English) in teenagers' speech, see Aiusheev 2009.

19. Humphrey (1989) suggests that during the late Soviet period, when cynicism with Soviet rhetoric was high, Russian-origin forms might have been used in Buryat to index the speaker's social or ideological distance from what was being said.

20. Longer discussions of this text's position in Buryat cultural politics can be found in Graber 2012, 127 and Graber and Murray 2015.

21. In 1908, the Russian Geographical Society reported an official literacy rate (possibly in Russian, though it is unclear) among western Buryats of 5.2 percent and among eastern Buryats of 8.4 percent. Based on a spot check in eastern Buryat communities, however, it appeared that 14 percent of lay (i.e., nonmonastic) males were able to read and write fluently in classical Mongolian and a remarkable 10 percent in Tibetan (Iurtsovskii 1923; Turchaninov 1914). Later, Soviet linguists and historians downplayed the 1908 numbers, partly under pressure to exaggerate the gains in literacy achieved among native Siberians under Soviet rule. Both the 1897 and 1926 censuses were methodologically suspect, especially in remote provinces (Hirsch 2005). It has been suggested that many eastern Buryats hid their own literacy in Mongolian from officials, fearing political repression. It is also not clear in what languages literacy was tested or how (M. K. 1904; Montgomery 2005). A joke to this effect circulates among some contemporary Buryat scholars: "Of course the Buryats were considered 'illiterate'! They didn't speak **Russian!**"

22. On Buryatia's alphabet wars in this period, see Arai 2006 and Montgomery 2005.

23. The primary cultural groups considered in pan-Mongolic constructions have been the Khalkhs of Outer Mongolia, the Kalmyks of the Russian and Kyrgyz steppes, and the Buryats of Siberia. Tibetans, Tuvans, Altaians, and others are sometimes included. Pan-Mongolists have at times concerned themselves with Mongolic groups in Inner Mongolia; however, as with Tibetans, sustained cooperative efforts have been limited by Soviet, Russian, and Chinese politics, as well as by language barriers.

24. For a detailed account of this decision, as well as the extensive debates surrounding reforms to the Mongolian script and subsequent Latinization in the 1920s and 1930s, see Bazarova 2006.

25. This interpretation is supported by Rupen (1966, 46), who wrote against Soviet historiography to assert that the alphabet choices and standardization projects that took place in Kalmykia, Buryatia, and Tannu Tuva "fixed and even exaggerated linguistic differences among the various Mongolian groups" in an explicit attempt to thwart pan-Mongolism.

26. The dialect change was accompanied by a flurry of interest in establishing the "ethnogenesis" of the Buryats as mediated primarily through the Khori (e.g., Rumiantsev 1962; Viatkina 1956).

27. There are some notable exceptions to these views among workers in print media, particularly among newspaper journalists who write poetry or creative prose or otherwise have literary aspirations.

28. *Buriatskii iazyk kak gosudarstvennyi* (Buryat as a state language) is a set phrase describing both state-required courses in Buryat for non-native speakers (i.e., education in Buryat as an official language, as opposed to education in Buryat as a native or heritage language) and a college concentration that is required for future public school teachers of Buryat. In 2008–9, the world financial crisis and a sharp decline in the value of the Russian ruble prompted many native-speaking Buryat students to enroll at NGI in this otherwise low-status and low-paid major, seeking job security.

29. BNTs does not train undergraduates but has large, active programs granting "candidate" degrees (*kandidatskaia stepen'*) and doctoral degrees. Additionally, the faculty at BNTs guides students and teachers in many language-related disciplines across the Republic of Buryatia's degree-granting colleges and universities, including Buryat State University, the East Siberian State Academy of Culture and Arts (VSGAKI), and the East Siberian State Technological University (VSGTU).

30. Developing a "high," formal register of a creole through language standardization, for instance, may help destigmatize the language as a whole (Garrett 2000).

5. ANCHORS OF AUTHORITY

1. The development of news media in Buryatia has received careful attention from a number of historians and media sociologists. A complete history could be pieced together through the detailed studies of D. Ts. Namzhilova (2001; covering 1862–1937), Buianto Tsydenovich Dondokov (1960; covering 1918–37), and E. A. Kuchmurukova (2002; covering the 1930s–91). Less attention has been given specifically to the issue of Buryat-language media, with the notable exception of Elena Nikolaevna Grosheva's excellent history of Buryat-language book publishing (2008).

2. NARB, f. 930, op. 1, d. 5, p. 171.

3. NARB, f. 914, op. 1, d. 8, p. 58.

4. NARB, f. 914, op. 1, d. 39, p. 38.

5. This is a common negative interpretation of Soviet news media among post-Soviet Russian audiences (Mickiewicz 2008).

6. This does not mean that no Buryat is spoken in Russian-language news offices, or that it would not help one's career to know Buryat in addition to Russian. For example, *Buriatiia-7* is a weekly, government-run Russian-language counterpart to Buriaad ünén that runs financial, tax, and administrative news. Although it is a Russian-language publication, many of the editorial staff are Buryat-speaking members of the Buryat cultural elite.

7. The administrative need to speak Russian *well* does not appear to have been uniform, however. Handwritten Buryat notes and partial translations in Soviet-era archival materials indicate that editorial meetings of Buriaad ünén and the Buryat-language radio and television divisions were often held in Buryat, with notes translated into Russian after the fact by typists. Senior editors and writers noted in interviews in 2008–9 that writers with poor Russian skills (including themselves) were hired as recently as the 1960s.

8. The count of fifty includes journalists monolingual in Russian who worked in bilingual offices with Buryat departments, as well as bilingual Buryat-Russian journalists who produced most of their materials in Russian. Approximately thirty-five of the fifty were regularly producing primarily Buryat-language media. Among newspaper workers, I did not include the dozens of occasional contributors who are not on staff, although I interviewed some of them in other contexts and analyzed many of their published materials.

9. Philological education in Buryat has slowly moved from Irkutsk to Ulan-Ude. Prior to 1990, Buryat language education was available at Buryat State Pedagogical Institute in a joint department of history and philology. One of the great institutional coups for Buryatia's nationalist movement in the late 1980s to early 1990s was establishing separate departments of history and Buryat philology at the renamed Buryat State University in 1991–92. In 2002, the Department of Buryat Philology became NGI, a semi-independent center within the larger university.

10. The East Siberian State Academy of Culture and Arts has unique programs in traditional Buryat dance and music, which produce many revered Buryat culture workers for the republic and foster a community of Buryat cultural activists. VSGAKI is also a major source of news anchors, correspondents, and tech workers for local television companies; a number of VSGAKI graduates worked in Ulan-Ude's Russian-language radio and television broadcasting companies in 2008–9. Archival records show that theatrical and voice training have been common backgrounds among *Russian*-language journalists since at least the 1970s, but the same has not been true of Buryat-language journalists (NARB, f. 914).

11. Of the remaining eight, six were from southwestern mountain districts, including Akha, Tünkhėn, and Zakhaamin in the Republic of Buryatia. The other two were interesting regional outliers: one hailed from Kachuga in Irkutsk Oblast, home of what is usually considered an Ėkhiritskii or Ėkhirit-Bulagatskii dialect; the other hailed from Sėlėngė, home to a southern Mongol-Buryat dialect. A few additional Buryat-language journalists, not included in the demographic snapshot, work for their local district newspapers. Had they been included, the percentage of Buryat-language journalists hailing from the eastern steppe regions and southwestern mountain regions would have been even higher. It may seem odd that no one was from Khori District, namesake of the Khori dialect. Ironically, Khori District has been subject to extreme Russification, particularly the district capital of Khorinsk. Khorinsk is primarily Russian-speaking, and few Buryat culture workers in the republic hail from the district.

12. The majority of NGI students are native speakers of literary dialects as well.

13. In the 1940s–50s, this meant that there was a lot of drinking on the job, behind closed doors.

14. These numbers are estimates based on interviews and informal conversations, in which money (or the lack thereof) frequently came up.

15. This was especially an issue in the 1930s, when party leaders became paranoid about Buryat-language translations.

16. Journalists based in Aga, where it is possible to use Buryat in public life, have a different experience. They report higher use of Buryat at home and work, which is consonant with my observation.

17. It was never clear to me why, for these individuals, *ėkran* did not also count as an internationalism. Selective etymology is often practiced to justify a speaker's intuition that something is more Buryat, more Russian, or more foreign (Graber 2019).

18. Talbot Taylor describes a similar paradox in the work of the *Oxford English Dictionary*: it "simply reports the facts" of linguistic behavior and yet is "by far the most authoritative and influential normative influence on the behaviour of individual speakers and writers of English" (1990, 22).

6. PERFORMANCE ANXIETY

1. See also Labov 1972, 117, 133.

2. By the same token, jokes about "pidgin" Buryat are only told privately (Graber 2017).

3. Hip-hop is popular among young Buryats, partly for this reason. (Buryat-language pop music, however, is rarely hip-hop—that is believed to be the province of Khalkh Mongols, due to what many people describe as Khalkh Mongolian's "harsh sounds" and what they view as a grittier existence south of the border.) A sense of shared marginalization may be the basis for a new kind of cultural politics in Buryatia, which would draw on Buryats' peripheral status in Russian society and, perhaps, the fact that they are in a position structurally similar to that of other native Siberians. Stuart Hall ([1988] 1996) and Ben Rampton (1995) suggest an alternative kind of ethnicity that might be based around such shared marginalization, rather than around essentialist notions of nation or race. To date, however, such alternatives have not found much traction in Buryatia.

4. See Dorian 1977, 2014 for notable exceptions, but with reference to "complete" and "incomplete" knowledge. Blommaert (2010) analyzes semispeakers in terms of the "truncated repertoires" discussed in chapter 4 but not in the context of language shift.

5. Dates of filming and broadcast are withheld because the broadcast material is linked to off-camera observations. For further discussion of the news story described here and language use in the topical genre of science and medicine, see Graber 2019.

6. There was some disagreement among BGTRK's videographers regarding the ethics and legality of filming patients. In some other cases, patients were filmed.

7. This transcript includes a real name because it is not linked to any private information.

8. In line 4, for instance, she uses the Tünkhèn (R. Tunkinskii) dialectal form zhorgoon for 'six,' instead of SLB zurgaan. Similarly, in lines 1 and 9, she uses the first-person plural pronoun manii (our) instead of SLB manai.

9. Using the days of the week in Russian in lines 5–6 might also be considered a full codeswitch. But the days of the week are well-established borrowings from Russian, and very few Buryat speakers are aware of other possibilities for naming the days of a seven-day week—which include both a cosmologically derived Tibetan- and Mongolian-origin Buddhist system and an ordinal numbering system.

10. Otdeleni is a modern but well-established borrowing into Buryat and appears in Buryat dictionaries.

11. November 16, 1959 (NARB, f. 914, op. 1, d. 5, p. 99).

12. NARB, f. 914, op. 1, d. 8, p. 141.

13. March 4, 1980 (NARB, f. 914, op. 1, d. 34, p. 3).

14. NARB, f. 914, op. 1, d. 34, p. 67.

15. May 30, 1973 (NARB, f. 914, op. 1, d. 20, p. 44).

7. EMERGENT MINORITY PUBLICS

1. Histories of reading practices demonstrate how culturally and historically specific this image of newspaper consumption is (e.g., Fischer 2003).

2. These are statements that deserve our attention as reminders that nation-states still very much matter. They are not, however, statements backed by threat of force.

Works Cited

ARCHIVES

NARB. National Archives of the Republic of Buryatia, Ulan-Ude, Russian Federation. Fonds 914, 930, and 3843.

OPP IMBiT. Inv. No. MI-557. Archives of the Institute of Mongolian, Buddhist, and Tibetan Studies of the Buryat Scientific Center, Siberian Branch of the Russian Academy of Sciences, Ulan-Ude, Russian Federation.

LEGISLATION

Konstitutsiia Rossiiskoi Federatsii, 1993.

O iazykakh narodov Rossiiskoi Federatsii. Zakon RF ot 25 oktiabria 1991 g. No. 1807-I.

O iazykakh narodov Respubliki Buriatiia. Zakon Respubliki Buriatiia ot 10 iiunia 1992 g. No. 221-XII.

Ob utverzhdenii Gosudarstvennoi programmy Respubliki Buriatiia "Sokhranenie i razvitie buriatskogo iazyka" na 2011–2014 gody ot 2 avgusta 2010 g. No. 312, 2010.

Respublika Buriatiia Konstitutsiia, 1996.

PUBLISHED WORKS

Abaeva, L. L., and N. L. Zhukovskaia. 2004. *Buriaty*. Moscow: Nauka.

Abu-Lughod, Lila. 2004. *Dramas of Nationhood: The Politics of Television in Egypt.* Chicago: University of Chicago Press.

Agha, Asif. 1998. "Stereotypes and Registers of Honorific Language." *Language in Society* 27:151–94.

——. 2011. "Meet Mediatization." *Language & Communication* 31(3):163–70.

Ahearn, Laura. 2001. *Invitations to Love: Literacy, Love Letters, and Social Change in Nepal.* Ann Arbor: University of Michigan Press.

Aikhenvald, Alexandra Y. 2001. "Language Awareness and Correct Speech among the Tariana of Northwest Amazonia." *Anthropological Linguistics* 43(4):411–30.

——. 2003. "Teaching Tariana, an Endangered Language from Northwest Amazonia." *International Journal of the Sociology of Language* 161:125–39.

——. 2013. "Shifting Attitudes in North-West Amazonia." *International Journal of the Sociology of Language* 222:195–216.

Aiusheev, Bator Bal'zhinimaevich 2009. "Studencheskii sleng v usloviiakh dvuiazychiia (na primere vuzov g. Ulan-Udė)." In *Buriatskii iazyk v polikul'turnom prostranstve (sotsiolingvoistoricheskoe issledovanie)*, by Galina Aleksandrovna Dyrkheeva, Nadezhda Bairovna Darzhaeva, Tsytsygma Tsydendorzhievna Bal'zhinimaeva, et al., 130–59. Ulan-Ude: BNTs SO RAN.

Amagaev, N., and Alamzhi-Mėrgėn. 1910. *Novyi mongolo-buriatskii alfavit*. St. Petersburg: Imperial Academy of Sciences.

Amogolonova, Darima Dashievna. 2008. *Sovremennaia buriatskaia ėtnosfera: Diskursy, paradigmy, sotsiokul'turnye praktiki*. Ulan-Ude: IMBiT SO RAN.

Anderson, Benedict. 1991. *Imagined Communities: Reflections on the Origin and Spread of Nationalism*. New York: Verso.

Anisimova, Alla, and Olga Echevskaya. 2018. "Siberian Regional Identity: Self-Perception, Solidarity, or Political Claim?" In *Russia's Regional Identities: The Power of the Provinces*, edited by Edith W. Clowes, Gisela Erbslöh, and Ani Kokobobo, 189–205. New York: Routledge.

Andreyev, Alexandre. 2003. *Soviet Russia and Tibet: The Debacle of Secret Diplomacy, 1918–1930s*. Leiden: Brill.

Arai, Yukiyasu. 2006. "Integration and Separation of 'Language': Language Policies of Mongolian Peoples in the USSR and Mongolia, 1920–1940." In *Slavic Eurasian Studies*, vol. 10: *Reconstruction and Interaction of Slavic Eurasia and Its Neighboring Worlds*, 309–34. Slavic Research Center (Hokkaido University, Sapporo).

Arel, Dominique. 2001. "Fixing Ethnicity in Identity Documents: The Rise and Fall of Passport Nationality in Russia." NCEEER Working Paper.

Argounova-Low, Tatiana. 2013. *The Politics of Nationalism in the Republic of Sakha (Northeastern Siberia), 1900–2000: Ethnic Conflicts under the Soviet Regime*. Lewiston, NY: Edwin Mellen.

Ar-Sergi, Viacheslav. 2007. "'A vy i ne sprashivali . . .': Moi zasechki udmurtskim toporom." *Druzhba narodov*, no. 10.

Atwood, Christopher Pratt. 2002. *Young Mongols and Vigilantes in Inner Mongolia's Interregnum Decades, 1911–1931*. Vol. 2. Leiden: Brill.

Avineri, Netta. 2019. "The Heritage Narratives of Yiddish Metalinguistic Community Members: Processes of Distancing and Closeness." In *Storytelling as Narrative Practice: Ethnographic Approaches to the Tales We Tell*. Studies in Pragmatics, vol. 19, edited by Elizabeth A. Falconi and Kathryn E. Graber, 90–135. Leiden: Brill.

Baabar, Bat-Erdeniin. 1999. *Twentieth Century Mongolia*. Edited by Christopher Kaplonski. Translated by D. Sühjargalmaa, S. Burenbayar, H. Hulan, and N. Tuya. Cambridge: White Horse Press.

Babuev, S. D. 2001. "Buriaad khèlèeè khügzhöökhè tukhai." *Buriaad Ünèn*, December 6.

———. 2006. "O dal'neishikh perspektivakh razvitiia buriatskogo iazyka." In *Istoriia razvitiia buriatskogo iazyka*, edited by V. I. Rassadin and D. D. Dondokova, 131–34. Ulan-Ude: BNTs SO RAN.

Badmaeva, Liudmila Vladimirovna. 2002. "SMI i auditoriia: Problemy privlekatel'nosti." In *Obshchestvennoe mnenie zhitelei Buriatii na rubezhe vekov: Materialy seminara*, edited by B. Bazarov and I. Osinskii, 134–58. Ulan-Ude: VSGTU.

———. 2004. "Regional'nye SMI i auditoriia: Osobennosti funktsionirovaniia v period transformatsii rossiiskogo obshchestva (na materialakh Respubliki Buriatiia)." Candidate's diss., East Siberian State Technological University (Ulan-Ude).

Bakhtin, M. M. (1934–35) 1981. *The Dialogic Imagination: Four Essays*. Edited by Michael Holquist, translated by Caryl Emerson and Michael Holquist. Austin: University of Texas Press.

Baldano, M. N. 2003. "Arkhivnye materialy o poezdke khori-buriat k Tsariu Petru I." In *Narody Buriatii v sostave Rossii: Ot protivostoianiia k soglasiiu (300 let ukazu Petra I)*, part 4, edited by V. M. Alekseeva et al., 68–75. Ulan-Ude: Respublikanskaia tipografiia.

Balzer, Marjorie Mandelstam. 1981. "Rituals of Gender Identity: Markers of Siberian Khanty Ethnicity, Status, and Belief." *American Anthropologist* 83(4):850–67.

———. 1999. *The Tenacity of Ethnicity: A Siberian Saga in Global Perspective*. Princeton, NJ: Princeton University Press.

Balzer, Marjorie Mandelstam, and Uliana Alekseevna Vinokurova. 1996. "Nationalism, Interethnic Relations and Federalism: The Case of the Sakha Republic (Yakutia)." *Europe-Asia Studies* 48(1):101–20.

Bawden, Charles R. 1985. *Shamans, Lamas, and Evangelicals: The English Missionaries in Siberia*. London: Routledge & Kegan Paul.

Bazarova, V. V. 2006. *Latinizatsiia buriat-mongol'skoi pis'mennosti v 1920–1930 gg.* Ulan-Ude: FGOU VPO VSGAKI.

Bazheeva, T. P. 2002. *Sotsial'nyi i iazykovoi aspekty formirovaniia rannego (detskogo) buriatsko-russkogo i russko-buriatskogo dvuiazychiia.* Ulan-Ude: BNTs SO RAN.

Bell, Allan. 1991. *The Language of News Media*. Cambridge, MA: Blackwell.

Bell, Allan, and Peter Garrett, eds. 1998. *Approaches to Media Discourse.* Malden, MA: Blackwell.

Benhabib, Seyla. 2002. "Transformations of Citizenship: The Case of Contemporary Europe." *Government and Opposition* 37(4):439–65.

Bernal, Victoria. 2005. "Eritrea On-Line: Diaspora, Cyberspace, and the Public Sphere." *American Ethnologist* 32(4):660–75.

Bernstein, Anya. 2013. *Religious Bodies Politic: Rituals of Sovereignty in Buryat Buddhism.* Chicago: University of Chicago Press.

Bertagaev, T. A. 1961. *K issledovaniiu leksiki mongol'skikh iazykov: Opyt sravnitel'no-statisticheskogo issledovaniia leksiki buriatskikh govorov.* Ulan-Ude: AN SSSR.

Bilaniuk, Laada. 2004. "A Typology of Surzhyk: Mixed Ukrainian-Russian Language." *International Journal of Bilingualism* 8(4):409–25.

——. 2005. *Contested Tongues: Language Politics and Cultural Correction in Ukraine.* Ithaca, NY: Cornell University Press.

Bird, S. Elizabeth, ed. 2010a. *The Anthropology of News and Journalism.* Bloomington: Indiana University Press.

——. 2010b. "Introduction: The Anthropology of News and Journalism: Why Now?" In *The Anthropology of News and Journalism*, edited by S. Elizabeth Bird, 1–18. Bloomington: Indiana University Press.

Bloch, Alexia. 2003. *Red Ties and Residential Schools: Indigenous Siberians in a Post-Soviet State*. Philadelphia: University of Pennsylvania Press.

Blommaert, Jan. 2010. *The Sociolinguistics of Globalization.* Cambridge: Cambridge University Press.

Bogoyavlensky, Dmitri D. 1997. "Native Peoples of Kamchatka: Epidemiological Transition and Violent Death." Translated by Michael Volshonsky. *Arctic Anthropology* 34(1):57–67.

Bolter, Jay David, and Richard Grusin. 1999. *Remediation: Understanding New Media.* Cambridge, MA: MIT Press.

Bonner, Donna M. 1982. "Garifuna Children's Language Shame: Ethnic Stereotypes, National Affiliation, and Transnational Immigration as Factors in Language Choice in Southern Belize." *Language in Society* 30:81–96.

Bourdieu, Pierre. (1982) 1991. *Language and Symbolic Power.* Translated by Gino Raymond and Matthew Adamson. Cambridge, MA: Harvard University Press.

Boyer, Dominic. 2000. "On the Sedimentation and Accreditation of Social Knowledges of Difference: Mass Media, Journalism, and the Reproduction of East/West Alterities in Unified Germany." *Cultural Anthropology* 15(4):459–91.

——. 2001. "The Impact and Embodiment of Western Expertise in the Restructuring of the East German Media after 1990." *Anthropology of East Europe Review* 19(1):77–84.

——. 2005. *Spirit and System: Media, Intellectuals, and the Dialectic in Modern German Culture.* Chicago: University of Chicago Press.

Boym, Svetlana. 2001. *The Future of Nostalgia*. New York: Basic Books.
Browne, Donald R. 1996. *Electronic Media and Indigenous Peoples: A Voice of Our Own?* Ames: Iowa State University Press.
Brubaker, Rogers, and Frederick Cooper. 2000. "Beyond 'Identity.'" *Theory and Society* 29(1):1–47.
Budaev, Ts. B. 1978. *Leksika buriatskikh dialektov v sravnitel'no-istoricheskom osveshchenii*. Novosibirsk: Nauka.
———. 1992. *Buriatskie dialekty: Opyt diakhronicheskogo issledovaniia*. Novosibirsk: Nauka.
Bulag, Uradyn Erden. 1998. *Nationalism and Hybridity in Mongolia*. New York: Oxford University Press.
Buraev, I. D. 1988. "Osnovnye ėtapy issledovaniia buriatskikh dialektov i ikh klassifikatsiia." In *Razvitie i vzaimodeistvie dialektov Pribaikal'ia*, edited by L. D. Shagdarov, 3–26. Ulan-Ude: Buryat Institute of Social Sciences.
———. 1996. "Problemy klassifikatsii buriatskikh dialektov." In *Problemy buriatskoi dialektologii*, edited by V. I. Rassadin, L. D. Shagdarov, and T. P. Bazheeva, 3–16. Ulan-Ude: BNTs SO RAN.
Burstat. 2010. *Chislennost' postoiannogo naseleniia po munitsipal'nym obrazovaniiam respubliki po sostoianiu na 1 ianvaria (1991–2010)*. Moscow: GKS Rosstat.
buryadxelen.org. 2006. *Toli*. (Part of an electronic textbook.) Ulan-Ude: Ministry of Education and Science, Republic of Buryatia.
Buszard-Welcher, Laura. (2001) 2013. "Can the Web Help Save My Language?" In *The Green Book of Language Revitalization in Practice*, edited by Leanne Hinton and Ken Hale, 331–45. Leiden: Brill.
Buyandelger, Manduhai. 2013. *Tragic Spirits: Shamanism, Memory, and Gender in Contemporary Mongolia*. Chicago: University of Chicago Press.
Cameron, Deborah. 2005. *Verbal Hygiene*. New York: Routledge.
Carey, John, and Martin C. J. Elton. 2010. *When Media Are New: Understanding the Dynamics of New Media Adoption and Use*. Ann Arbor: University of Michigan Press.
Carr, E. Summerson, and Michael Lempert. 2016. "Introduction: Pragmatics of Scale." In *Scale: Discourse and Dimensions of Social Life*, edited by E. Summerson Carr and Michael Lempert, 1–21. Oakland: University of California Press.
Carvalho, Anabela. 2008. "Media(ted) Discourse and Society: Rethinking the Framework of Critical Discourse Analysis." *Journalism Studies* 9(2):161–77.
Catenaccio, Paola, Colleen Cotter, Mark De Smedt, et al. 2011. "Towards a Linguistics of News Production." *Journal of Pragmatics* 43(7):1843–52.
Cattelino, Jessica R. 2010. "The Double Bind of American Indian Need-Based Sovereignty." *Cultural Anthropology* 25(2):235–62.
Cavanaugh, Jillian R. 2006. "Little Women and Vital Champions: Gendered Language Shift in a Northern Italian Town." *Journal of Linguistic Anthropology* 16(2):194–210.
Chakars, Melissa. 2014. *The Socialist Way of Life in Siberia: Transformation in Buryatia*. New York: Central European University Press.
Chakrabarty, Dipesh. 1999. "Adda, Calcutta: Dwelling in Modernity." *Public Culture* 11(1):109–45.
Chimitdorzhiev, Sh. B. 2001a. "Panmongolizm i ego opponenty na raznykh ėtapakh istorii." In *Buriatiia: Problemy regional'noi istorii i istoricheskogo obrazovaniia (1–2)*, edited by T. E. Sanzhieva and A. D. Tsybiktarov, 3–8. Ulan-Ude: Buryat State University.

———. 2001b. *Khozhdenie Khori-Buriat k Sagaan Khanu (Belomu tsariu): Ocherki po istorii khori-buriat. Srednevekov'e i novoe vremia.* Ulan-Ude: Buriatskoe knizhnoe izdatel'stvo.

———. 2004. *Kto my—Buriat-Mongoly?* 2nd ed. Ulan-Ude: Buriatskoe knizhnoe izdatel'stvo (Kongress buriatskogo naroda).

Choiropov, Ts. Ts. 1998. *Obshchestvennye peremeny Buriatii v usloviiakh transformatsii rossiiskogo obshchestva.* Ulan-Ude: VSGTU.

Clowes, Edith W. 2016. "Centrifugal Forces? Russia's Regional Identities and Initiatives." *REGION: Regional Studies of Russia, Eastern Europe, and Central Asia* 5(2):117–25.

Cochran, Effie Papatzikou. 1997. "An Instance of Triglossia? Codeswitching as Evidence for the Present State of Greece's 'Language Question.'" *International Journal of the Sociology of Language* 126(1):33–62.

Cody, Francis. 2013. *The Light of Knowledge: Literacy Activism and the Politics of Writing in South India.* Ithaca, NY: Cornell University Press.

Coffey, Wallace, and Rebecca A. Tsosie. 2001. "Rethinking the Tribal Sovereignty Doctrine: Cultural Sovereignty and the Collective Future of Indian Nations." *Stanford Law and Policy Review* 12(2):191–221.

Coleman, Gabriella. 2010. "Ethnographic Approaches to Digital Media." *Annual Review of Anthropology* 39:487–505.

Collins, James. 1998. "Our Ideologies and Theirs." In *Language Ideologies: Practice and Theory*, edited by Bambi B. Schieffelin, Kathryn A. Woolard, and Paul V. Kroskrity, 256–70. New York: Oxford University Press.

Comrie, Bernard. 1996. "Script Reform in and after the Soviet Union." In *The World's Writing Systems*, edited by Peter T. Daniels and William Bright, 781–84. New York: Oxford University Press.

Cormack, Mike. 1998. "Minority Language Media in Western Europe: Preliminary Considerations." *European Journal of Communication* 13(1):33–52.

———. 2007. "Introduction: Studying Minority Language Media." In *Minority Language Media: Concepts, Critiques and Case Studies*, edited by Mike Cormack and Niamh Hourigan, 1–16. Clevedon: Multilingual Matters.

Cormack, Mike, and Niamh Hourigan, eds. 2007. *Minority Language Media: Concepts, Critiques and Case Studies.* Clevedon: Multilingual Matters.

Cotter, Colleen. 2010. *News Talk: Investigating the Language of Journalism.* Cambridge: Cambridge University Press.

———. 2011. "Diversity Awareness and the Role of Language in Cultural Representations in News Stories." *Journal of Pragmatics* 43(7):1890–99.

———. (2001) 2013. "Continuity and Vitality: Expanding Domains through Irish-Language Radio." In *The Green Book of Language Revitalization in Practice*, edited by Leanne Hinton and Ken Hale, 301–11. Leiden: Brill.

Craig, Colette Grinevald. 1997. "Language Contact and Language Degeneration." In *The Handbook of Sociolinguistics*, edited by Florian Coulmas, 257–70. Oxford: Blackwell.

Cruikshank, Julie, and Tatiana Argounova. 2000. "Reinscribing Meaning: Memory and Indigenous Identity in the Sakha Republic (Yakutia)." *Arctic Anthropology* 37(1):96–119.

Curran, James. 1991. "Rethinking the Media as a Public Sphere." In *Communication and Citizenship: Journalism and the Public Sphere*, edited by Peter Dahlgren and Colin Sparks, 27–56. London: Routledge.

Dagbaev, Ėrdėm D. 1995. *Pressa i natsional'no-politicheskii protsess regiona.* Ulan-Ude: BNTs SO RAN.

——. 1999. *Sredstva massovoi informatsii i vlast'*. Ulan-Ude: Buryat State University.

——. 2004. *Sredstva massovoi informatsii: Dinamicheskie modeli politicheskoi kommunikatsii*. Ulan-Ude: Buryat State University.

Dareeva, O. A. 2007. *Sotsiokul'turnyi podkhod k obucheniiu buriatskomu iazyku kak vtoromu*. Ulan-Ude: Buryat State University.

Deacon, David, Natalie Fenton, and Alan Bryman. 1999. "From Inception to Reception: The Natural History of a News Item." *Media, Culture & Society* 21(1):5–31.

Debenport, Erin. 2015. *Fixing the Books: Secrecy, Literacy, and Perfectibility in Indigenous New Mexico*. Santa Fe: School for Advanced Research Press.

Demoskop Weekly. 2009. Selected data from the First Census of the Russian Empire, 1897. Naselenie i obshchestvo, Institute of Demography. Basic data by region available at http://demoscope.ru/weekly/ssp/rus_lan_97.php?reg=0.

Dinwoodie, David. 1998. "Authorizing Voices: Going Public in an Indigenous Language." *Cultural Anthropology* 13:193–223.

Donahoe, Brian, Joachim Otto Habeck, Agnieszka Halemba, and István Sántha. 2008. "Size and Place in the Construction of Indigeneity in the Russian Federation." *Current Anthropology* 49(6):993–1020.

Dondokov, Buianto Tsydenovich. 1960. *Vozniknovenie i razvitie partiino-sovetskoi pechati v Buriatii (1918–1937)*. Ulan-Ude: Buriatskoe knizhnoe izdatel'stvo.

Dorian, Nancy C. 1973. "Grammatical Change in a Dying Dialect." *Language* 49:413–38.

——. 1977. "The Problem of the Semi-Speaker in Language Death." *International Journal of the Sociology of Language* 12:23–32.

——. 1989a. "Introduction." In *Investigating Obsolescence: Studies in Language Contraction and Death*, edited by Nancy C. Dorian, 1–10. Cambridge: Cambridge University Press.

——, ed. 1989b. *Investigating Obsolescence: Studies in Language Contraction and Death*. Cambridge: Cambridge University Press.

——. 2014. *Small-Language Fates and Prospects: Lessons of Persistence and Change from Endangered Languages: Collected Essays*. Leiden: Brill.

Dorzhiev, D. D. 1994. *Staroburiatskii iazyk*. Ulan-Ude: Buryat State Pedagogical Institute.

Dugarova-Montgomery, Yeshen-Khorlo, and Robert Montgomery. 1999. "The Buriat Alphabet of Agvan Dorzhiev." In *Mongolia in the Twentieth Century: Landlocked Cosmopolitan*, edited by Stephen Kotkin and Bruce A. Elleman, 79–97. Armonk, NY: M. E. Sharpe.

Dyrkheeva, G. A. 2002. *Buriatskii iazyk v usloviiakh dvuiazychiia: Problemy funktsionirovaniia i perspektivy razvitiia*. Ulan-Ude: BNTs SO RAN.

——. 2003. *Iazykovaia situatsiia i iazykovoe zakonodatel'stvo v Respublike Buriatiia*. Moscow: Russian University of the Friendship of the Peoples.

Dyrkheeva, Galina Aleksandrovna, Nadezhda Bairovna Darzhaeva, Tsytsygma Tsydendorzhievna Bal'zhinimaeva, et al. 2009. *Buriatskii iazyk v polikul'turnom prostranstve (sotsiolingvoistoricheskoe issledovanie)*. Ulan-Ude: BNTs SO RAN.

Eagleton, Terry. 1991. *Ideology*. London: Verso.

Eberhard, David M., Gary F. Simons, and Charles D. Fennig, eds. 2019. *Ethnologue: Languages of the World*. 22nd ed. Dallas, TX: SIL International.

Eisenlohr, Patrick. 2004. "Language Revitalization and New Technologies: Cultures of Electronic Mediation and the Refiguring of Communities." *Annual Review of Anthropology* 33:21–45.

Eriksen, T. H. 2007. "Nationalism and the Internet." *Nations and Nationalism* 13(1):1–17.

Errington, Joseph. 1998. "Indonesian('s) Development: On the State of a Language of State." In *Language Ideologies: Practice and Theory*, edited by Bambi B. Schieffelin, Kathryn A. Woolard, and Paul V. Kroskrity, 271–84. New York: Oxford University Press.

——. 2003. "Getting Language Rights: The Rhetorics of Language Endangerment and Loss." *American Anthropologist* 105(4):723–32.

——. 2008. *Linguistics in a Colonial World: A Story of Language, Meaning, and Power.* Malden, MA: Blackwell.

Fairclough, Norman. 1989. *Language and Power.* New York: Longman.

——. 1995. *Media Discourse.* London: Edward Arnold.

Ferguson, Charles A. (1959) 1972. "Diglossia." In *Language and Social Context*, edited by Pier P. Giglioli, 232–51. Harmondsworth: Penguin Books.

Ferguson, Jenanne. 2019. *Words Like Birds: Sakha Language Discourses and Practices in the City.* Lincoln, NE: University of Nebraska Press.

Fikes, Kesha, and Alaina Lemon. 2002. "African Presence in Former Soviet Spaces." *Annual Review of Anthropology* 31:497–524.

Fischer, Steven Roger. 2003. *A History of Reading.* London: Reaktion Books.

Fisher, Daniel. 2016. *The Voice and Its Doubles: Music and Media in Northern Australia.* Durham, NC: Duke University Press.

Fishman, Joshua. 1967. "Bilingualism with and without Diglossia; Diglossia with and without Bilingualism." *Journal of Social Issues* 23(2):29–38.

Forsyth, James. 1992. *A History of the Peoples of Siberia: Russia's North Asian Colony, 1581–1990.* Cambridge: Cambridge University Press.

French, Brigittine. 2003. "The Politics of Mayan Linguistics in Guatemala: Native Speakers, Expert Analysis, and the Nation." *Pragmatics* 13(4):483–98.

Gal, Susan. 1978. "Peasant Men Can't Get Wives: Language Change and Sex Roles in a Bilingual Community." *Language in Society* 7:1–16.

——. 1988. "The Political Economy of Code Choice." In *Codeswitching: Anthropological and Sociolinguistic Perspectives*, edited by Monica Heller, 245–64. Berlin: Mouton de Gruyter.

——. 1989. "Lexical Innovation and Loss: Restricted Hungarian." In *Investigating Obsolescence: Studies in Language Contraction and Death*, edited by Nancy C. Dorian, 313–31. Cambridge: Cambridge University Press.

——. 2005. "Language Ideologies Compared: Metaphors of Public/Private." *Journal of Linguistic Anthropology* 15:23–37.

——. (2001) 2014. "Linguistic Theories and National Images in Nineteenth-Century Hungary." In *Languages and Publics: The Making of Authority*, edited by Susan Gal and Kathryn A. Woolard, 30–45. New York: Routledge.

Gal, Susan, and Gail Kligman. 2000. *The Politics of Gender after Socialism: A Comparative-Historical Essay.* Princeton, NJ: Princeton University Press.

Gal, Susan, and Kathryn A. Woolard. (2001) 2014. "Constructing Languages and Publics: Authority and Representation." In *Languages and Publics: The Making of Authority*, edited by Susan Gal and Kathryn A. Woolard, 1–12. New York: Routledge.

Gans, Herbert J. (1979) 2004. *Deciding What's News: A Study of CBS Evening News, NBC Nightly News, Newsweek, and Time.* Evanston, IL: Northwestern University Press.

Garnham, Nicholas. 1992. "The Media and the Public Sphere." In *Habermas and the Public Sphere*, edited by Craig Calhoun, 359–76. Cambridge, MA: MIT Press.

Garrett, Paul. 2000. "'High' Kwéyòl: The Emergence of a Formal Creole Register in St. Lucia." In *Language Change and Language Contact in Pidgins and Creoles*, edited by John McWhorter, 63–101. Philadelphia: John Benjamins.

Geraci, Robert P. 2001. *Window on the East: National and Imperial Identities in Late Tsarist Russia.* Ithaca, NY: Cornell University Press.

Ginsburg, Faye. 1995. "Production Values: Indigenous Media and the Rhetoric of Self-Determination." In *Rhetorics of Self-Making,* edited by Debbora Battaglia, 121–38. Berkeley: University of California Press.

Gitelman, Lisa. 2006. *Always Already New: Media, History, and the Data of Culture.* Cambridge, MA: MIT Press.

Gitelman, Lisa, and Geoffrey B. Pingree, eds. 2003. *New Media, 1740–1915.* Cambridge, MA: MIT Press.

Goffman, Erving. 1959. *The Presentation of Self in Everyday Life.* New York: Anchor.

——. 1981. *Forms of Talk.* Philadelphia: University of Pennsylvania Press.

Golding, Peter, and Phillip Elliott. 1979. *Making the News.* Harlow: Longman.

Golub, Alex. 2007. "From Agency to Agents: Forging Landowner Identities in Porgera." In *Customary Land Tenure and Registration in Australia and Papua New Guinea: Anthropological Perspectives,* edited by James Weiner and Katie Glaskin, 73–96. Canberra: Australian National University Press.

Gorenburg, Dmitry. 1999. "Identity Change in Bashkortostan: Tatars into Bashkirs and Back." *Ethnic and Racial Studies* 22(3):556–82.

Gorham, Michael S. 2003. *Speaking in Soviet Tongues: Language Culture and the Politics of Voice in Revolutionary Russia.* DeKalb: Northern Illinois University Press.

Gorham, Michael S., Ingunn Lunde, and Martin Paulsen, eds. 2014. *Digital Russia: The Language, Culture and Politics of New Media Communication.* London: Routledge.

Graber, Kathryn E. 2012. "Public Information: The Shifting Roles of Minority-Language News Media in the Buryat Territories of Russia." *Language & Communication* 32(2):124–36.

——. 2013. "What They Said (She Said) I Said: Attribution and Expertise in Digital Circulation." *Culture, Theory and Critique* 54(3):285–300.

——. 2016. "The All-Buriat 'Ray of Light': Independence and Identity in Native-Language Media." *REGION: Regional Studies of Russia, Eastern Europe, and Central Asia* 5(2):175–200.

——. 2017. "The Kitchen, the Cat, and the Table: Domestic Affairs of a Siberian Language." *Journal of Linguistic Anthropology* 27(2):151–70.

——. 2019. "'Syphilis Is Syphilis!': Purity and Genre in a Buryat-Russian News Story." In *Storytelling as Narrative Practice: Ethnographic Approaches to the Tales We Tell.* Studies in Pragmatics, vol. 19, edited by Elizabeth A. Falconi and Kathryn E. Graber, 226–52. Leiden: Brill.

Graber, Kathryn, and Joseph Long. 2009. "The Dissolution of the Buryat Autonomous Okrugs in Siberia: Notes from the Field." *Inner Asia* 11(1):147–55.

Graber, Kathryn E., and Jesse D. Murray. 2015. "The Local History of an Imperial Category: Language and Religion in Russia's Eastern Borderlands, 1860s–1930s." *Slavic Review* 74(1):127–52.

Grant, Bruce. 1993. "Siberia Hot and Cold: Reconstructing the Image of Siberian Indigenous Peoples." In *Between Heaven and Hell: The Myth of Siberia in Russian Culture,* edited by Galya Diment and Yuri Slezkine, 227–53. New York: St. Martin's Press.

——. 1995. *In the Soviet House of Culture: A Century of Perestroikas.* Princeton, NJ: Princeton University Press.

Grenoble, Lenore A., and Lindsay J. Whaley, eds. 1998. *Endangered Languages: Language Loss and Community Response.* Cambridge: Cambridge University Press.

———. 2006. *Saving Languages: An Introduction to Language Revitalization*. New York: Cambridge University Press.

Grillo, Ralph. 1989. *Dominant Languages: Language and Hierarchy in Britain and France*. Cambridge: Cambridge University Press.

Grinevald, Colette. 2005. "Why the Tiger Language and Not Rama Cay Creole? Language Revitalization Made Harder." *Language Documentation and Description* 3:196–224.

Grosheva, E. N. 2008. *Knigoizdanie na buriatskom iazyke (XIX–nachalo XXI vv.)*. Ulan-Ude: Respublikanskaia tipografiia.

Gumperz, John J. 1982. *Discourse Strategies*. Cambridge: Cambridge University Press.

Gürsel, Zeynep Devrim. 2010. "*U.S. Newsworld*: The Rule of Text and Everyday Practices of Editing the World." In *The Anthropology of News and Journalism*, edited by S. Elizabeth Bird, 35–53. Bloomington: Indiana University Press.

Habermas, Jürgen. (1962) 1989. *The Structural Transformation of the Public Sphere: An Inquiry into a Category of Bourgeois Society*. Translated by Thomas Burger. Cambridge, MA: MIT Press.

Halemba, Agnieszka. 2006. *The Telengits of Southern Siberia: Landscape, Religion, and Knowledge in Motion*. London: Routledge.

Hall, Stuart. (1988) 1996. "New Ethnicities." In *Stuart Hall: Critical Dialogues in Cultural Studies*, edited by David Morley and Kuan-Hsing, 441–49. New York: Routledge.

Hannerz, Ulf. 2002. "Among the Foreign Correspondents: Reflections on Anthropological Styles and Audiences." *Ethnos* 67(1):57–74.

———. 2004. *Foreign News: Exploring the World of Foreign Correspondents*. Chicago: University of Chicago Press.

Harnel, Rainer Enrique. 1997. "Language Conflict and Language Shift: A Sociolinguistic Framework for Linguistic Human Rights." *International Journal of the Sociology of Language* 127:105–34.

Hasty, Jennifer. 2005. *The Press and Political Culture in Ghana*. Bloomington: Indiana University Press.

Heller, Monica. 2007. *Linguistic Minorities and Modernity: A Sociolinguistic Ethnography*. 2nd ed. New York: Continuum International.

Hill, Jane H. 2001. "Dimensions of Attrition in Language Death." In *On Biocultural Diversity: Linking Language, Knowledge, and the Environment*, edited by Luisa Maffi, 175–89. Washington, DC: Smithsonian Institution Press.

Hill, Jane H., and Kenneth C. Hill. 1980. "Mixed Grammar, Purist Grammar, and Language Attitudes in Modern Nahuatl." *Language in Society* 9:321–48.

———. 1986. *Speaking Mexicano: Dynamics of Syncretic Language in Central Mexico*. Tucson: University of Arizona Press.

Hill, Jane H., and Bruce Mannheim. 1992. "Language and Worldview." *Annual Review of Anthropology* 21:381–406.

Hill, Richard, and Stephen May. 2013. "Non-Indigenous Researchers in Indigenous Language Education: Ethical Implications." *International Journal of the Sociology of Language* 219:47–65.

Hirsch, Francine. 2005. *Empire of Nations: Ethnographic Knowledge and the Making of the Soviet Union*. Ithaca, NY: Cornell University Press.

Hornberger, Nancy H., and Kendall A. King. 1998. "Authenticity and Unification in Quechua Language Planning." *Language, Culture, and Curriculum* 11(3):390–410.

Humphrey, Caroline. 1989. "Janus-Faced Signs: The Political Language of a Soviet Minority before *Glasnost'*." *Sociological Review* 36:145–75.

———. 1994. "Shamanic Practices and the State in Northern Asia: Views from the Center and Periphery." In *Shamanism, History, and the State*, edited by Nicholas Thomas and Caroline Humphrey, 191–225. Ann Arbor: University of Michigan Press.

———. 1999. *Marx Went Away—But Karl Stayed Behind*. Updated ed. of *Karl Marx Collective: Economy, Society and Religion in a Siberian Collective Farm*. Ann Arbor: University of Michigan Press.

———. 2015. "'Remote' Areas and Minoritized Spatial Orders at the Russia–Mongolia Border." *Études mongoles & sibériennes centrasiatiques & tibétaines* 46.

Humphrey, Caroline, and David Sneath. 1999. *The End of Nomadism? Society, State, and the Environment in Inner Asia*. Durham, NC: Duke University Press.

Irvine, Judith T. 1989. "When Talk Isn't Cheap: Language and Political Economy." *American Ethnologist* 16(2):248–67.

Irvine, Judith, and Susan Gal. 2000. "Language Ideology and Linguistic Differentiation." In *Regimes of Language: Ideologies, Polities, and Identities*, edited by Paul V. Kroskrity, 35–83. Santa Fe: School for Advanced Research Press.

Isin, Engin F. 2002. *Being Political: Genealogies of Citizenship*. Minneapolis: University of Minnesota Press.

Iurtsovskii, N. S. 1923. "Ocherki po istorii prosveshcheniia v Sibiri." In *Obshchii khod razvitiia shkol'nogo dela v Sibiri, 1703–1917 gg.*, Vol. 1. Novonikolaevsk: Sibirskoe oblastnoe gosudarstvennoe izdatel'stvo.

Jaffe, Alexandra. 1999. *Ideologies in Action: Language Politics on Corsica*. New York: Mouton de Gruyter.

Johnson, Sally. 2005. *Spelling Trouble? Language, Ideology and the Reform of German Orthography*. Clevedon: Multilingual Matters.

Jerryson, Michael K., and Mark Juergensmeyer, eds. 2010. *Buddhist Warfare*. New York: Oxford University Press.

Kara, György. 1996. "Aramaic Scripts for Altaic Languages." In *The World's Writing Systems*, edited by Peter T. Daniels and William Bright, 536–58. New York: Oxford University Press.

———. 2005. *Books of the Mongolian Nomads*. Translated by John Richard Krueger. Bloomington: Research Institute for Inner Asian Studies.

Karim, Karim H., ed. 2003. *The Media of Diaspora*. London: Routledge.

Kendzior, Sarah. 2011. "Digital Distrust: Uzbek Cynicism and Solidarity in the Internet Age." *American Ethnologist* 38(3):559–75.

Khamaganov, Evgenii. 2007. "V 2008 godu na karte Rossii poiavitsia Zabaikal'skii krai." *Inform polis*, March 14.

Khamutaev, V. A. 2005. *Buriatskoe natsional'noe dvizhenie, 1980–2000-e gg*. Ulan-Ude: BNTs SO RAN.

Khilkhanova, Erjen, and Dorji Khilkhanov. 2003. "The Changing Dynamics of Language and Ethnic Identity Link by Russian Minorities: The Buryat Case Study." *Journal of Eurasian Research* 2(1):26–30, 39.

Khilkhanova, Èrzhen Vladimirovna. 2007. *Faktory kollektivnogo vybora iazyka i ètnokul'turnaia identichnost' u sovremennykh Buriat (diskurs-analiticheskii podkhod)*. Ulan-Ude: FGOU VPO VSGAKI.

———. 2009. "Faktory iazykovogo sdviga i sokhraneniia minoritarnykh iazykov: Diskursnyi i sotsiolingvisticheskii analiz (na materiale iazykovoi situatsii v ètnicheskoi Buriatii)." Doctoral diss., VSGAKI (Ulan-Ude and Barnaul).

Kim, N., and S. Baldanov. 1994. "Buriaad khélén dééré garahan türüüshyn gazeté." *Buriaad Ünén*, October 11.

King, Alexander D. 2006. "The Siberian Studies Manifesto." *Sibirica* 5(1):v–xv.

———. 2011. *Living with Koryak Traditions: Playing with Culture in Siberia*. Lincoln: University of Nebraska Press.

Kittler, Friedrich A. 1999. *Gramophone, Film, Typewriter*. Translated by Geoffrey Winthrop-Young and Michael Wutz. Stanford, CA: Stanford University Press.

Kivelson, Valerie. 2006. *Cartographies of Tsardom: The Land and Its Meanings in Seventeenth-Century Russia*. Ithaca, NY: Cornell University Press.

Klumbytė, Neringa. 2010. "The Soviet Sausage Renaissance." *American Anthropologist* 112(1):22–37.

Kroskrity, Paul V. 1998. "Arizona Tewa Speech as a Manifestation of a Dominant Language Ideology." In *Language Ideologies: Practice and Theory*, edited by Bambi B. Schieffelin, Kathryn A. Woolard, and Paul V. Kroskrity, 103–22. New York: Oxford University Press.

Ku, Kun-hui. 2005. "Rights to Recognition: Minority/Indigenous Politics in the Emerging Taiwanese Nationalism." *Social Analysis* 49(2):99–121.

Kuchmurukova, E. A. 2002. *Istoriia knigoizdaniia Buriatii (vtoraia polovina 1930-kh– 1991 gg.)*. Ulan-Ude: VSGAKI.

Kulick, Don. 1992. *Language Shift and Cultural Reproduction: Socialization, Self, and Syncretism in a Papua New Guinean Village*. Cambridge: Cambridge University Press.

———. 1998. "Anger, Gender, Language Shift, and the Politics of Revelation in a Papua New Guinean Village." In *Language Ideologies: Practice and Theory*, edited by Bambi B. Schieffelin, Kathryn A. Woolard, and Paul V. Kroskrity, 87–102. New York: Oxford University Press.

Kunreuther, Laura. 2014. *Voicing Subjects: Public Intimacy and Mediation in Kathmandu*. Berkeley: University of California Press.

Kuzar, Ron. 2001. *Hebrew and Zionism: A Discourse Analytic Cultural Study*. New York: Mouton de Gruyter.

Labov, William. 1966. *The Social Stratification of English in New York City*. Washington, DC: Center for Applied Linguistics.

———. 1972. *Sociolinguistic Patterns*. Philadelphia: University of Pennsylvania Press.

Lampland, Martha. 1995. *The Object of Labor: Commodification in Socialist Hungary*. Chicago: University of Chicago Press.

Larkin, Brian. 2008. *Signal and Noise: Media, Infrastructure, and Urban Culture in Nigeria*. Durham, NC: Duke University Press.

Larson, Jonathan L. 2013. *Critical Thinking in Slovakia after Socialism*. Rochester, NY: University of Rochester Press.

Lave, Jean, and Etienne Wenger. 1991. *Situated Learning: Legitimate Peripheral Participation*. Cambridge: Cambridge University Press.

Lee, Benjamin. 1997. *Talking Heads: Language, Metalanguage, and the Semiotics of Subjectivity*. Durham, NC: Duke University Press.

———. (2001) 2014. "Circulating the People." In *Languages and Publics: The Making of Authority*, edited by Susan Gal and Kathryn A. Woolard, 164–81. New York: Routledge.

LeMaster, Barbara. 2006. "Language Contraction, Revitalization, and Irish Women." *Journal of Linguistic Anthropology* 16(2):211–28.

Lemon, Alaina. 2000. *Between Two Fires: Gypsy Performance and Romani Memory from Pushkin to Postsocialism*. Durham, NC: Duke University Press.

———. 2002. "'Form' and 'Function' in Soviet Stage Romani: Modeling Metapragmatics through Performance Institutions." *Language in Society* 31:29–64.

———. 2003. "Talking Transit and Spectating Transition: The Moscow Metro." In *Altering States: Ethnographies of Transition in Eastern Europe and the Former Soviet Union*, edited by Daphne Berdahl, Matti Bunzl, and Martha Lampland, 14–39. Ann Arbor: University of Michigan Press.

Leonard, Wesley. 2008. "When Is an 'Extinct' Language Not Extinct?: Miami, a Formerly Sleeping Language." In *Sustaining Linguistic Diversity: Endangered and Minority Languages and Language Varieties*, edited by Kendall A. King, Natalie Schilling-Estes, Jia Jackie Lou, Lyn Fogle, and Barbara Soukup, 23–33. Washington, DC: Georgetown University Press.

M. K. 1904. "Iz istorii prosveshcheniia sibirskikh inorodtsev." *Vestnik Evropy*, no. 4:281–89.

Makarova, O. G. 2005. *Buriatskii iazyk: Intensivnyi kurs po razvitiiu navykov ustnoi rechi*. Ulan-Ude: Bėlig (Ministry of Education and Science of the Republic of Buryatia).

Mandel, Ruth. 2002. "A Marshall Plan of the Mind: The Political Economy of a Kazakh Soap Opera." In *Media Worlds: Anthropology on New Terrain*, edited by Faye D. Ginsburg, Lila Abu-Lughod, and Brian Larkin, 211–28. Berkeley: University of California Press.

Martin, Terry. 2001. *The Affirmative Action Empire: Nations and Nationalism in the Soviet Union, 1923–1939*. Ithaca, NY: Cornell University Press.

McLendon, Sally. 1978. "How Languages Die: A Social History of Unstable Bilingualism among the Eastern Pomo." In *American Indian and Indo-European Studies*, edited by Margaret Langdon, Shirley Silver, and Kathryn Klar, 137–50. The Hague: Mouton.

Meek, Barbra A. 2007. "Respecting the Language of Elders: Ideological Shift and Linguistic Discontinuity in a Northern Athapascan Community." *Journal of Linguistic Anthropology* 17(1):23–43.

——. 2010. *We Are Our Language: An Ethnography of Language Revitalization in a Northern Athabaskan Community*. Tucson: University of Arizona Press.

Mickiewicz, Ellen (Propper). 2008. *Television, Power, and the Public in Russia*. Cambridge: Cambridge University Press.

Milroy, James. 2000. "Historical Description and the Ideology of the Standard Language." In *The Development of Standard English, 1300–1800*, edited by Laura Wright, 11–28. Cambridge: Cambridge University Press.

——. 2001. "Language Ideologies and the Consequences of Standardization." *Journal of Sociolinguistics* 5:530–55.

Mitypov, V. G. 2003. "Tainaia chast' khorinskoi missii." In *Narody Buriatii v sostave Rossii: ot protivostoianiia k soglasiiu (300 let ukazu Petra I)*, part 4, edited by V. M. Alekseeva et al., 31–38. Ulan-Ude: Respublikanskaia tipografiia.

Montgomery, Robert W. 2005. *Late Tsarist and Early Soviet Nationality and Cultural Policy: The Buryats and Their Language*. Lewiston, NY: Edwin Mellen.

Moore, Robert E. 2006. "Disappearing, Inc.: Glimpsing the Sublime in the Politics of Access to Endangered Languages." *Language & Communication* 26(3–4):201–380.

Muehlebach, Andrea M. 2001. "Making Place at the United Nations: An Anthropological Inquiry into the United Nations Working Group on Indigenous Populations." *Cultural Anthropology* 16(3):415–35.

Muehlmann, Shaylih. 2008. "'Spread Your Ass Cheeks': And Other Things That Should Not Be Said in Indigenous Languages." *American Ethnologist* 35(1):34–48.

——. 2012. "Von Humboldt's Parrot and the Countdown of Last Speakers in the Colorado Delta." *Language & Communication* 32(2):162–68.

Murray, Jesse D. 2012. "Building Empire among the Buryats: Conversion Encounters in Russia's Baikal Region, 1860s–1917." PhD diss., University of Illinois, Urbana-Champaign.

Muzaev, Timur. 1999. *Ėtnicheskii separatizm v Rossii*. Moscow: Panorama.

Myers-Scotton, Carol. 1997. "Code-Switching." In *The Handbook of Sociolinguistics*, edited by Florian Coulmas, 217–37. Oxford: Blackwell.

Nadasdy, Paul. 2002. "'Property' and Aboriginal Land Claims in the Canadian Subarctic: Some Theoretical Considerations." *American Anthropologist* 104(1):247–61.

Namzhilova, D. Ts. 2001. *Periodicheskaia pechat' Buriatii: Istoriia stanovleniia i razvitiia (vtoraia polovina XIX veka–1937 g.)*. Ulan-Ude: VSGAKI.

Nettle, Daniel, and Suzanne Romaine. 2000. *Vanishing Voices: The Extinction of the World's Languages*. Oxford: Oxford University Press.

Nevins, M. Eleanor. 2013. *Lessons from Fort Apache: Beyond Language Endangerment and Maintenance*. Malden, MA: Wiley-Blackwell.

Niezen, Ronald. 2000. "Recognizing Indigenism: Canadian Unity and the International Movement of Indigenous Peoples." *Comparative Studies in Society and History* 41(1):119–48.

Ong, Aihwa. 2000. "Graduated Sovereignty in South-East Asia." *Theory, Culture and Society* 17(4):55–75.

Osinskii, I. I., B. V. Bazarov, and Ts. B. Budaeva, eds. 2002. *Obshchestvennoe mnenie zhitelei Buriatii na rubezhe vekov*. (Sbornik dokladov i soobshchenii regional'nogo seminara.) Ulan-Ude: VSGTU.

Owens, Thompson W., and Paul M. Baker. 1984. "Linguistic Insecurity in Winnipeg: Validation of a Canadian Index of Linguistic Insecurity." *Language in Society* 13(3):337–50.

Panagakos, A. N., and Horst, H. A. 2006. "Return to Cyberia: Technology and the Social Worlds of Transnational Migrants." *Global Networks* 6(2):109–24.

Parham, A. A. 2004. "Diaspora, Community, and Communication: Internet Use in Transnational Haiti." *Global Networks* 4(2):199–217.

Pedelty, Mark. 1995. *War Stories: The Culture of Foreign Correspondents*. New York: Routledge.

Peers, Eleanor. 2009. "Representations of the Buryat in Political and Popular Newspaper Discourse: The Sanctification of Buryat Culture." *Inner Asia* 11:65–81.

Peery, Char. 2012. "New Deal Navajo Linguistics: Language Ideology and Political Transformation." *Language & Communication* 32(2):114–23.

Perrin, Daniel. 2003. "Progression Analysis (PA): Investigating Writing Strategies at the Workplace." *Journal of Pragmatics* 35(6):907–21.

Peterson, Mark Allen. 2001. "Getting to the Story: Unwriteable Discourse and Interpretive Practice in American Journalism." *Anthropological Quarterly* 74(4):201–11.

———. 2003. *Anthropology and Mass Communication*. New York: Berghahn.

Petrova, E. 2006. "Vybor sdelan: Oblast' i okrug progolosovali za ob"edinenie." *Vostochno-sibirskaia pravda*, April 18.

Philo, Greg. 2007. "Can Discourse Analysis Successfully Explain the Content of Media and Journalistic Practice?" *Journalism Studies* 8(2):175–96.

Pika, Alexander. 1993. "The Spatial-Temporal Dynamic of Violent Death among the Native Peoples of Northern Russia." Translated by Eugenia W. Davis, edited by Igor I. Krupnik. *Arctic Anthropology* 30(2):61–76.

Poppe, Nicholas (Nikolai). 1933. *Buriat-mongol'skoe iazykoznanie*. Leningrad: AN SSSR.

Povinelli, Elizabeth A. 1998. "The State of Shame: Australian Multiculturalism and the Crisis of Indigenous Citizenship." *Critical Inquiry* 24(2):575–610.

———. 2002. *The Cunning of Recognition: Indigenous Alterities and the Making of Australian Multiculturalism*. Durham, NC: Duke University Press.

Pustai, Janos. 2005. "O polozhenii finno-ugrov v Rossii." Plenary report at the Fourth
    International Congress of the Finno-Ugric Peoples, Tallinn, Estonia, 2004.
    Pravozashchitnik 43:5–15.
Queen, Robin. 2001. "Bilingual Intonation Patterns: Evidence of Language
    Change from Turkish-German Bilingual Children." *Language in Society*
    30(1):55–80.
Quijada, Justine Buck. 2019. *Buddhists, Shamans, and Soviets: Rituals of History in
    Post-Soviet Buryatia*. New York: Oxford University Press.
Quijada, Justine B., Kathryn E. Graber, and Eric Stephen. 2015. "Finding 'Their Own':
    Revitalizing Buryat Culture through Shamanic Practices in Ulan-Ude." *Problems
    of Post-Communism* 62(5):258–72.
Radziminovich, N. A., N. A. Gileva, V. I. Melnikova, and M. G. Ochkovskaya. 2012.
    "Seismicity of the Baikal Rift System from Regional Network Observations."
    Journal of Asian Earth Sciences 62:146–61.
Ramaswamy, Sumathi. 1997. *Passions of the Tongue: Language Devotion in Tamil India,
    1891–1970*. Berkeley: University of California Press.
Rampton, Ben. 1995. *Crossing: Language and Ethnicity among Adolescents*. New York:
    Longman.
Rausing, Sigrid. 2004. *History, Memory, and Identity in Post-Soviet Estonia: The End of
    a Collective Farm*. Oxford: Oxford University Press.
Rickford, John R., and John McWhorter. 1997. "Language Contact and Language
    Generation: Pidgins and Creoles." In *The Handbook of Sociolinguistics*, edited by
    Florian Coulmas, 238–56. Oxford: Blackwell.
Ries, Nancy. 1997. *Russian Talk: Culture and Conversation during Perestroika*. Ithaca,
    NY: Cornell University Press.
Riggins, Stephen Harold, ed. 1992. *Ethnic Minority Media: An International Perspective*.
    London: Sage.
Rivkin-Fish, Michele. 2010. "Pronatalism, Gender Politics, and the Renewal of Family
    Support in Russia: Towards a Feminist Anthropology of 'Maternity Capital.'"
    Slavic Review 69(3):701–24.
Rosstat (Federal'naia sluzhba gosudarstvennoi statistiki). 2004. *Vserossiiskaia perepis'
    naseleniia 2002 goda*. http://www.perepis2002.ru/index.html?id=11.
———. 2009. *Demograficheskii ezhegodnik Rossii—2009 g*. http://www.gks.ru/bgd/regl/
    B09_16/IssWWW.exe/Stg/01-03.htm.
———. 2011. *Chislennost' gorodskogo i sel'skogo naseleniia Rossiiskoi Federatsii*. http://
    www.perepis-2010.ru/message-rosstat.php.
———. 2012–13. *Itogi Vserossiiskoi perepisi naseleniia 2010 goda*. Tom 4, *Natsional'nyi
    sostav i vladenie iazykami, grazhdanstvo*. http://www.gks.ru/free_doc/new_site/
    perepis2010/croc/perepis_itogi1612.htm.
Roudakova, Natalia. 2017. *Losing Pravda: Ethics and the Press in Post-Truth Russia*.
    Cambridge: Cambridge University Press.
Rumiantsev, G. N. 1962. *Proiskhozhdenie khorinskikh buriat*. Edited by E. M. Zalkind.
    Ulan-Ude: Buriatskoe knizhnoe izdatel'stvo.
Rumiantsev, G. N., and S. B. Okun', eds. 1960. *Sbornik materialov po istorii Buriatii:
    XVII vek*. Ulan-Ude: Buryat Institute of Social Sciences.
Rumsey, Alan. 1990. "Wording, Meaning, and Linguistic Ideology." *American
    Anthropologist* 92:346–61.
Rupen, Robert. 1964. *Mongols of the Twentieth Century*. 2 vols. Bloomington: Indiana
    University Uralic and Altaic Series.
———. 1966. *The Mongolian People's Republic*. Edited by Jan F. Triska. Stanford, CA:
    Hoover Institution on War, Revolution, and Peace.

Sagan, Natasha. 2016. "Vladimir Zhirinovskii: 'Buriat pridumali bol'sheviki.'" *Inform polis*, March 16.

Sakwa, Richard. 2008. *Russian Politics and Society*. 4th ed. Abingdon: Routledge.

Schiffman, Harold F. 1993. "The Balance of Power in Multiglossic Languages: Implications for Language Shift." *International Journal of the Sociology of Language* 103:115–48.

Schlesinger, Philip. 1987. *Putting "Reality" Together*. 2nd ed. London: Methuen.

Schmid, Monika S. 2011. *Language Attrition*. Cambridge: Cambridge University Press.

Schorkowitz, Dittmar. 2001a. "The Orthodox Church, Lamaism, and Shamanism." In *Of Religion and Empire: Missions, Conversions, and Tolerance in Tsarist Russia*, edited by Robert P. Geraci and Michael Khodarkovsky, 201–28. Ithaca, NY: Cornell University Press.

———. 2001b. "Staat und Nationalitäten in Rußland: Der Integrationsprozeß der Burjaten und Kalmücken, 1822–1925." *Quellen und Studien zur Geschichte des östlichen Europa* 61. Stuttgart: Franz Steiner.

Schrøder, Kim Christian. 2007. "Media Discourse Analysis: Researching Cultural Meanings from Inception to Reception." *Textual Cultures: Text, Contexts, Interpretation* 2(2):77–99.

Shagdarov, L. D. 1967. *Stanovlenie edinikh norm buriatskogo literaturnogo iazyka v sovetskuiu epokhu*. Ulan-Ude: BION AN SSSR.

———. 1974. *Funktsional'no-stilisticheskaia differentsiatsiia buriatskogo literaturnogo iazyka*. Ulan-Ude: Buriatskoe knizhnoe izdatel'stvo.

———. 1993. "Formirovanie i razvitie natsional'nogo iazyka u buriat." In *Issledovaniia po istorii mongol'skikh iazykov: Sbornik statei*, edited by Valentin Ivanovich Rassadin, Ėleonora Ivanovna Biuraeva, and G. A. Dyrkheeva, 17–36. Ulan-Ude: BNTs SO RAN.

Shevchenko, Olga. 2009. *Crisis and the Everyday in Postsocialist Moscow*. Bloomington: Indiana University Press.

Shryock, Andrew. 2004. "In the Double Remoteness of Arab Detroit: Reflections on Ethnography, Culture Work, and the Intimate Disciplines of Americanization." In *Off Stage/On Display: Intimacy and Ethnography in the Age of Public Culture*, edited by Andrew Shryock, 131–54. Stanford, CA: Stanford University Press.

Silverstein, Michael. 1981. "The Limits of Awareness." *Texas Working Papers in Sociolinguistics*, no. 84. Austin, TX: Southwest Educational Development Laboratory.

———. 1998. "Contemporary Transformations of Local Linguistic Communities." *Annual Review of Anthropology* 27:401–26.

———. 2000. "Whorfianism and the Linguistic Imagination of Nationality." In *Regimes of Language: Ideologies, Polities, and Identities*, edited by Paul V. Kroskrity, 85–138. Santa Fe, NM: School for Advanced Research Press.

———. 2003. "Indexical Order and the Dialectics of Sociolinguistic Life." *Language & Communication* 23:193–230.

———. 2010. "Society, Polity, and Language Community: An Enlightenment Trinity in Anthropological Perspective." *Journal of Language and Politics* 9(3):339–63.

Slezkine, Yuri. 1994. *Arctic Mirrors: Russia and the Small Peoples of the North*. Ithaca, NY: Cornell University Press.

———. 1996. "The USSR as a Communal Apartment, or How a Socialist State Promoted Ethnic Particularism." In *Becoming National*, edited by Geoff Eley and Ronald Grigor Suny, 203–38. New York: Oxford University Press.

Slezkine, Yuri, and Galya Diment. 1993. "Introduction." In *Between Heaven and Hell: The Myth of Siberia in Russian Culture*, edited by Galya Diment and Yuri Slezkine, 1–14. New York: St. Martin's Press.

Smith, Michael G. 1998. *Language and Power in the Creation of the USSR, 1917–1953*. New York: Mouton de Gruyter.

Spitulnik, Debra. 1996. "The Social Circulation of Media Discourse and the Mediation of Communities." *Journal of Linguistic Anthropology* 6(2):161–87.

——. 1998. "Mediating Unity and Diversity: The Production of Language Ideologies in Zambian Broadcasting." In *Language Ideologies: Practice and Theory*, edited by Bambi B. Schieffelin, Kathryn A. Woolard, and Paul V. Kroskrity, 163–88. New York: Oxford University Press.

Splichal, Slavko. 1994. *Media beyond Socialism: Theory and Practice in East-Central Europe*. Boulder, CO: Westview.

Ssorin-Chaikov, Nikolai. 2003. *A Social Life of the State in Subarctic Siberia*. Stanford, CA: Stanford University Press.

Ståhlberg, Per. 2013. *Writing Society through Media: Ethnography of a Hindi Daily*. Jaipur: Rawat Publications.

Suny, Ronald Grigor. 1993. *The Revenge of the Past: Nationalism, Revolution, and the Collapse of the Soviet Union*. Stanford, CA: Stanford University Press.

——. 1998. *The Soviet Experiment: Russia, the USSR, and the Successor States*. Oxford: Oxford University Press.

Suslak, Daniel F. 2003. "The Story of ö: Orthography and Cultural Politics in the Mixe Highlands." *Pragmatics* 13(4):551–63.

Swinehart, Karl F. 2012. "Metadiscursive Regime and Register Formation on Aymara Radio." *Language & Communication* 32(2):102–13.

Taylor, Talbot J. 1990. "Which Is To Be Master? The Institutionalization of Authority in the Science of Language." In *Ideologies of Language*, edited by John E. Joseph and Talbot J. Taylor, 9–26. New York: Routledge.

Thomason, Sarah G. 2001. *Language Contact: An Introduction*. Washington, DC: Georgetown University Press.

Thomason, Sarah Grey, and Terrence Kaufman. 1988. *Language Contact, Creolization, and Genetic Linguistics*. Berkeley: University of California Press.

Tishkov, Valery. 1997. *Ethnicity, Nationalism, and Conflict in and after the Soviet Union: The Mind Aflame*. London: Sage.

Troinitskii, N. A., ed. 1905. *Pervaia Vseobshchaia perepis' naseleniia Rossiiskoi Imperii 1897 g.* St. Petersburg: Tsentral'nyi statisticheskii komitet, Ministerstvo vnutrennikh del.

Trudgill, Peter. 1972. "Sex, Covert Prestige, and Linguistic Change in the Urban British English of Norwich." *Language in Society* 1(2):179–95.

Tsing, Anna Lowenhaupt. 1993. *In the Realm of the Diamond Queen: Marginality in an Out-of-the-Way Place*. Princeton, NJ: Princeton University Press.

Tsitsipis, Lukas. 1998. *A Linguistic Anthropology of Praxis and Language Shift: Arvanítika (Albanian) and Greek in Contact*. Oxford: Oxford University Press.

Tsydendambaev, Tsybikzhap Boboevich. 1972. *Buriatskie istoricheskie khroniki i rodoslovnye*. Ulan-Ude: Buriatskoe knizhnoe izdatel'stvo.

Tuchman, Gaye. 1978. *Making News: A Study in the Construction of Reality*. New York: Free Press.

Turchaninov, N. V. 1914. "Shkol'noe delo za Uralom." In *Aziatskaia Rossiia*, Vol. I, edited by G. V. Glinka, 243–69. St. Petersburg: Pereselencheskoe upravlenie glavnago upravleniia zemleustroistva i zemledeliia.

Ulturgasheva, Olga. 2012. *Narrating the Future in Siberia: Childhood, Adolescence, and Autobiography among the Eveny*. New York: Berghahn Books.

United Nations. 2007. Declaration on the Rights of Indigenous Peoples. http://www.un.org/esa/socdev/unpfii/documents/DRIPS_en.pdf.

Urciuoli, Bonnie. 1991. "The Political Topography of Spanish and English." *American Ethnologist* 18(2):295–310.

——. 1996. *Exposing Prejudice: Puerto Rican Experiences of Language, Race, and Class.* Boulder, CO: Westview.

Urla, Jacqueline. 1993. "Cultural Politics in an Age of Statistics: Numbers, Nations, and the Making of Basque Identity." *American Ethnologist* 20(4):818–43.

——. 2012. *Reclaiming Basque: Language, Nation, and Cultural Activism.* Las Vegas: University of Nevada Press.

Van Hout, Tom, and Felicitas Macgilchrist. 2010. "Framing the News: An Ethnographic View of Business Newswriting." *Text & Talk* 30(2):169–91.

Viatkina, K. V. 1956. "Buriaty." In *Narody Sibiri: Ètnograficheskie ocherki*, edited by M. G. Levin and L. P. Potapov, 217–66. Moscow: AN SSSR (Institute of Ethnography).

Vitebsky, Piers. 2005. *The Reindeer People: Living with Animals and Spirits in Siberia.* Boston: Houghton Mifflin.

Vostok Teleinform. 2009. "V Buriatii proidet miting pamiati Baira Sambueva, pogibshego v Moskve." October 20. https://vtinform.com/news/149/44334/?sphrase_id=968659.

Wachtel, Andrew. 2013. "Kyrgyzstan between Democracy and Ethnic Intolerance." *Nationalities Papers* 41(6):971–86.

Warner, Michael. 2002. *Publics and Counterpublics.* New York: Zone Books.

Warschauer, Mark. 1998. "Technology and Indigenous Language Revitalization: Analyzing the Experience of Hawai'i." *Canadian Modern Language Review/La Revue canadienne des langues vivantes* 55(1):139–59.

Weaver, Hilary N. 2001. "Indigenous Identity: What Is It, and Who Really Has It?" *American Indian Quarterly* 25(2):240–55.

Weidman, Amanda. 2010. "Sound and the City: Mimicry and Media in South India." *Journal of Linguistic Anthropology* 20(2):294–313.

Wertheim, Suzanne. 2003. "Language Ideologies and the 'Purification' of Post-Soviet Tatar." *Ab Imperio*, no. 1: 347–69.

——. 2009. "Who's Using Who? The Fieldworker as Documenter and Tool of Language Revitalization." *Language & Communication* 29(3):271–85.

Whitaker, M. P. 2004. "Tamilnet.com: Some Reflections on Popular Anthropology, Nationalism, and the Internet." *Anthropological Quarterly* 77(3):469–98.

Wilce, James M. 2009. *Language and Emotion.* Cambridge: Cambridge University Press.

Williams, Raymond. 1973. *The Country and the City.* New York: Oxford University Press.

Wolfe, Thomas C. 2005. *Governing Soviet Journalism: The Press and the Socialist Person after Stalin.* Bloomington: Indiana University Press.

Woolard, Kathryn A. 1995. "Changing Forms of Codeswitching in Catalan Comedy." *Catalan Review* 9(2):223–52.

——. 1998a. "Introduction: Language Ideology as a Field of Inquiry." In *Language Ideologies: Practice and Theory*, edited by Bambi B. Schieffelin, Kathryn A. Woolard, and Paul V. Kroskrity, 3–50. New York: Oxford University Press.

——. 1998b. "Simultaneity and Bivalency as Strategies in Bilingualism." *Journal of Linguistic Anthropology* 8(1):3–29.

——. 2016. *Singular and Plural: Ideologies of Linguistic Authority in 21st Century Catalonia.* New York: Oxford University Press.

Woolard, Kathryn, Aida Ribot Bencomo, and Josep Soler Carbonell. 2013. "What's So Funny Now? The Strength of Weak Pronouns in Catalonia." *Journal of Linguistic Anthropology* 23(3):127–41.

Woolhiser, Curt. 2001. "Language Ideology and Language Conflict in Post-Soviet Belarus." In *Language, Ethnicity and the State*, Vol. 2, edited by Camille O'Reilly, 91–122. Hampshire, NY: Palgrave.

Yurchak, Alexei. 2006. *Everything Was Forever, until It Was No More: The Last Soviet Generation*. Princeton, NJ: Princeton University Press.

Zateev, V. I. 2002. *Russkie v Buriatii: Istoriia i sovremennost'*. Ulan-Ude: Buryat State University.

Zdravomyslova, Elena. 1996. "Kafe Saigon kak obshchestvennoe mesto." In *Materials of the International Seminar "Civil Society in the European North."* St. Petersburg: Centre for Independent Social Research.

Zhimbiev, Ts. A., and Sh. B. Chimitdorzhiev. 2000. *Poezdka delegatsii khori-buriat k Petru Pervomu v 1702–1703 gg.* Ulan-Ude: Buriaad Ünėn.

Index

Page numbers in *italics* refer to illustrations. The letter *t* following a page number denotes a table.